Praise for ***American Archaeology***

"Burrillo will change what you thought you knew about archaeology, transforming what began as a science focused on division into a communal project of understanding and healing."

—RILEY BLACK, *The Shortest History of the Dinosaurs*

"*American Archaeology* is a fascinating and entertaining conversation about the science of the human past."

—DR. KENNETH L. FEDER, *Native America*

"A delightful, boots-on-the-ground romp that overturns archaeology's staid image, using the discipline as a mirror on America's colonial past. Burrillo exposes the cultural theft and harm to Indigenous peoples and shows how reckoning with our past offers a brighter future."

—ANNETTE MCGIVNEY, *Pure Land*

"Burrillo's observations are acerbic and erudite, as well as funny and big-hearted."

—BETSY GAINES QUAMMEN, *True West*

"Who knew archaeology could be this fun? Burrillo's expert treatise on the state of archaeology today is as knowledgeable as it is entertaining to read. In an America where history itself is under attack, Burrillo provides personal profiles of the colorful people working to keep archaeological truth alive."

—SCOTT GRAHAM, *Death Valley Duel*

"Buckle in for a page-turning foray into how archaeology became a science, how and why archaeologists create knowledge in response to social and political trends, and the ways that knowledge gets used, abused, amplified, and silenced."

—JOHN R. WELCH, *Archaeology Southwest*

"A simultaneously joyous and maddening journey. For anyone who might think that archeology is static or dry, this book will disabuse you of that."

—DAVID EVERITT, Back of Beyond Books

"Burrillo uncovers the truth and humanity embedded in the field of archaeology with humor and respect. Though the book is an account of the history of archaeology, it clearly documents crucial details of this moment that will someday become part of the archaeological record."

—MORGAN SJOGREN, *Path of Light*

"Accessible, genuine, and impassioned, Burrillo gives us a sweeping history of archaeology from its earliest days to its most recent conundrums, as archaeology sheds its colonial past and reinvents itself."

—STEPHEN H. LEKSON, Curator of Archaeology, Jubilado,
University of Colorado Museum of Natural History

"He's done it again! Burrillo has weaved a fascinating and highly readable history of American archaeology, with tidbits I was unaware of. Once I got started, I found it nearly impossible to put this book down. Readers are in for a real treat!"

—PAUL F. REED, *Archaeology Southwest*

"*American Archaeology* is captivating and important work. Burrillo excavates the origins and progression of American archaeology with scholarly expertise and a deft literary touch."

—OSHA GRAY DAVIDSON, *Clean Break*

Praise for **R. E. Burrillo**

"Burrillo makes a commanding debut in a consistently fascinating distillation of the unrivaled mosaic nature of the land's history."

—*THE UTAH REVIEW*

"Solid history and archaeology combined with an understated call to preserve Bears Ears—all of it, not just a sliver."

—*KIRKUS REVIEWS*

Playful, fierce, reverent . . . an epic story of endurance that reaches back into prehistory and casts a line into the future with the hope that all people can come to know and love this sacred land, and work together to preserve it."

—*FOREWORD REVIEWS*

"Burrillo describes the area's physical geography and cultural history as well as its meaning and value to those who have been shaped and impacted by the land. For Burrillo, this includes a heartfelt identification with the area's healing power and force of place. This splendidly crafted book will appeal to regional specialists and general readers."

—*LIBRARY JOURNAL*

"Burrillo conjures empathy for ethnography, transforms soil strata into living stories. Fierce yet playful, admonishing and ambitious, *Behind the Bears Ears* is as vast and consuming as the landscape itself."

—AMY IRVINE, *Air Mail* and *Desert Cabal*

"Mixing fighting words and wonder, Burrillo extends the boundaries of 'backwoods' to back yards, city riots, and the depth of the Grand Canyon. He reminds us to be vexed, amused, and serious about the mark we put on the world."

—CRAIG CHILDS, *The Wild Dark*

"Burrillo is an archaeologist who writes nothing like an archaeologist—not stuffy and technical but conversational and enquiring. Drawing from his explorations and fieldwork of the region's plateaus and canyons, his love and hope for Bears Ears binds these pages with honest glue."

—GREG CHILD, *Over the Edge*

An engagingly personal, well-informed, wide-ranging account of Bears Ears and its archaeology, its ongoing importance to Native peoples, and its future."

—STEPHEN H. LEKSON, *A Study of Southwestern Archaeology*

"*Behind the Bears Ears* conveys a deep respect for the place and the people who have lived closest to it. A fine primer for newcomers to the region and an entertaining refresher course for those already embedded in the landscape."

—SCOTT THYBONY, *The Disappearances*

"An entertaining wander through some serious topics—whiteness and racism, land use and abuse,and how our pasts shape and follow us. Burrillo is part philosopher, part activist as he explores numerous rabbit trails, but he shines most brightly when he returns to his beloved path of archaeology and Indigenous people, providing original insight, irony, and wit."

—JULIA CORBETT, *Out of the Woods*

"An eclectic constellation of essays inspired by the author's deep love of place, *The Backwoods of Everywhere* leads us into fascinating landscapes while compelling us to reassess both their exploitation and their preservation. By turns bracing and meditative, Burrillo's compelling narrative voice illuminates how adventures far afield can inspire us to a vital reimagination of our concept of home."

—MICHAEL P. BRANCH, *On the Trail of the Jackalope*

AMERICAN ARCHAEOLOGY

AMERICAN ARCHAEOLOGY

LIVING HISTORY STOLEN PAST

R.E. Burrillo

TORREY HOUSE PRESS

Salt Lake City • Torrey

First Torrey House Press Edition, April 2026

Published by Torrey House Press
Salt Lake City, Utah
www.torreyhouse.org

International Standard Book Number: 979-8-89092-032-4
E-book ISBN: 979-8-89092-033-1
Library of Congress Control Number: 2025932626

Cover design by Kathleen Metcalf
Interior design by Eryon Shondíín Greenburg
Distributed to the trade by Consortium Book Sales and Distribution

Torrey House Press offices in Salt Lake City sit on the homelands of Ute, Goshute, Shoshone, and Paiute nations. Offices in Torrey are on the homelands of Southern Paiute, Ute, and Navajo nations.

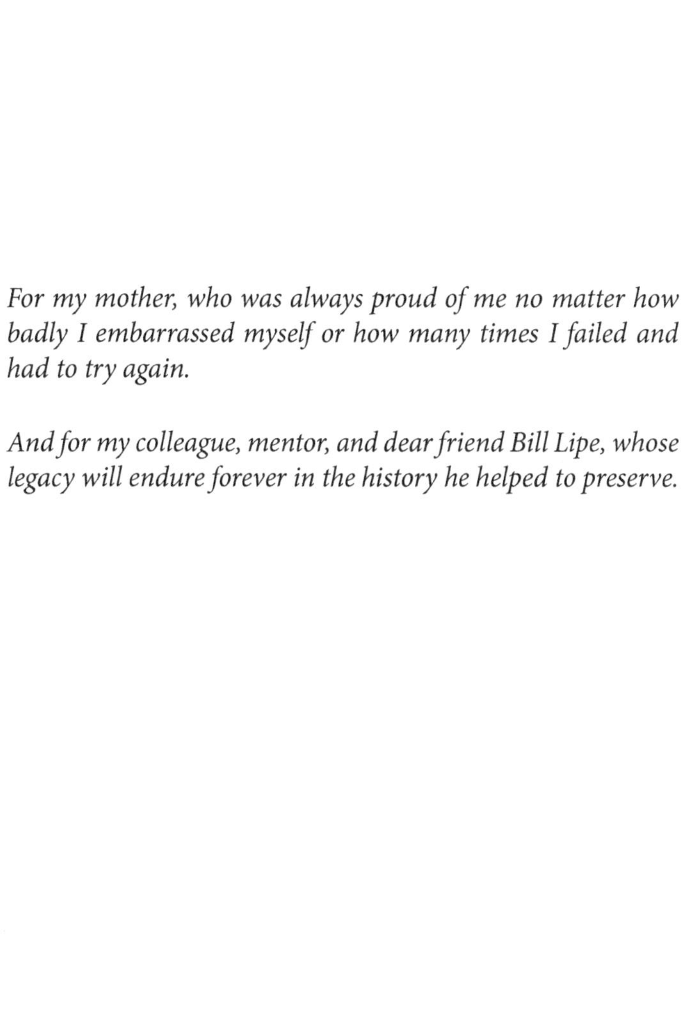

For my mother, who was always proud of me no matter how badly I embarrassed myself or how many times I failed and had to try again.

And for my colleague, mentor, and dear friend Bill Lipe, whose legacy will endure forever in the history he helped to preserve.

CONTENTS

INTRODUCTION

Drinks were involved. Drinks are usually involved in this sort of thing.

I was having a few with a Flagstaff-area social organizer and Indigenous/Mestiza activist whom I'd met through a few mutual friends. They were interested in examining how, why, and to what extent I articulated with activist spheres as an archaeologist—or, as my companion put it, as a colonizer.

My companion was especially intrigued by the fact that I'm a white dude with no obvious flaws or quirks beyond going bald in my early twenties, traditionally masculine in most respects (scratchy voice, angular jawline, beard, etc.), part of the "outdoorsy" community, and an avowed scientist. And yet I wasn't going around giving talks and raising awareness about saving wilderness, at least not as a primary focus. I was going around giving talks and raising awareness about Indigenous peoples and their connections to the land, particularly in southeastern Utah. This was surprising to my new friend, and I was frankly surprised at how surprising it was.

Indigenous peoples are those whose history is most firmly rooted in local environments, and they tend to bear the marks of this in both their bodies and their cultures. Relative latecomers to the Americas like my family and most of our neighbors, for example, don't bear the marks of our local environment in the same way—except in the literal sense of occasional cuts, bruises, and sunburns. Nor is our culture as firmly rooted in the land as those of Indigenous peoples. Jefferson and his ilk may have envisioned a country of farmers, but they definitely meant that in the sense of European-style farms, complete with perilous monocropping and someone else doing all the labor.

So, to me it seems self-evident that caring about the natural world also means caring about the people most closely associated with it, the ones who know it best, whose cultures were shaped by it and whose cultures helped shape it in return. That last part is often a real sticking point for those environmentalists who make the mistake of thinking there's such a thing as wilderness untouched and unshaped by humanity to some extent. There's not.

Most of the privileged class in the United States thinks of "wilderness" as "untrammeled by man," as the Wilderness Act of 1964 states it—or "untouched by the hand of man," in the words of the bill's congressional sponsor Hubert Humphrey. Wilderness is where you go when the rest of the world is too people-y, and you just need to get away from it all. And the reason you can get away from all the people in America's unparalleled wilderness areas is because all the people were kicked out of them.

Hale and hearty Anglos are therefore free to don overpriced apparel and go spend the weekend in a lush forest or a winding canyon where families hunted and foraged for generations before the Subarus and Jeeps arrived. Most of these outdoorspeople don't often think of Indigenous people when they think of the great out-of-doors—and to be fair to them, why would they? American culture and politics have worked hand-in-hand for several entire centuries to wipe Indigenous presence from the landscape, in terms of both cultural erasure and literal mass murder.

Most modern critics of the American environmental movement point to this speech, made by Theodore Roosevelt at the dedication of Grand Canyon National Park, as emblematic of the problem:

> Leave it as it is. You cannot improve on it. The ages have been at work on it, and man can only mar it. What you can do is to keep it for your children, your children's children, and for all who come after you, as the one great sight which every American should see.

Except "as it is" includes scores of generations of people having considerably more than zero effect on the place.

This flavor of philosophy is how someone can point to a place like the Grand Canyon and proclaim that it has, in effect, no human history. The ages have been at work on it in peace, and human beings with all their carelessness and destructiveness only just arrived. I guess the great abundance of ancient pictographs, petroglyphs, storage structures, wall alignments, roasting pits, figurines, projectile points, and so on doesn't count.

Because of this, the average college kid or bartender or investment banker with a free weekend and a fancy fleece can spend whole days in the American woods without having much thought for the folks that lived there first and longest. Why would they? The people who sold them the hiking attire, the gasoline, the food, the map, and the backcountry permit usually look just like they do.

Nor would it be out of place for our hypothetical hiker to donate money, share memes for awareness, join volunteer projects, or harass lawmakers to preserve wilderness without having much thought for the folks whose cultures are—at least to a point—all but inseparable from it. Again, why would they? The country's august forebears made certain they wouldn't encounter any of these folks on their weekend excursions.

It's annoying, but it's not really their fault, the same as it's not the average citizen's fault if they aren't up to snuff on how much slave labor went into the creation of their favorite chocolate bar. Our sociopolitical system discourages looking into how things came to be the way they are. You are not supposed to flip the gorgeous tapestry of our worldview over and see the snarled chaos that makes up the backside.

◆ ◆ ◆

As an archaeologist, I'm deeply curious about how things came to be the way they are—the seemingly haphazard pattern of threads and knots on the backside of the tapestry that makes the front side look all orderly and neat. I find it fascinating to explore the possible reasons we became bipedal, developed an omnivorous rather than specialist diet, and figured out agriculture. I find it no less fascinating to examine the construction of the modern world happening in real time, the naked political agendas and absurd cultural myths that still explain a depressing amount of it, and the nature and implications of just how consciously detached we are from the very systems of which we're all a part.

At a recent public event intended to teach fourth graders about history and grazing on public lands, I noted a local ranch hand explaining how it's important to have cows because they give us things like hamburgers. Which . . . okay, sure. I could throw stones but it's not the most egregious propaganda I've ever heard. In any case, he was interrupted by a precocious lad who started yelling, "Don't kill the cows! You have to murder the cows to make hamburgers! Don't murder the animals!" He kept yelling this all through the ranch hand's talk, despite repeated reprimands.

At the end of his talk, the ranch hand passed out salted beef sticks as a treat to all the little kiddies who sat and listened to his pro-grazing spiel. The don't-murder-the-animals kid was the only one of the whole group to ask for seconds.

Because salted beef sticks aren't animals—they're food. And the Grand Canyon was untouched by humans until the 1800s.

◆ ◆ ◆

Archaeology is a popular subject in the United States. And that's a bit of a problem.

Dictionaries generally provide two definitions for the word popular: something that is liked, admired, or enjoyed by a large group of people and/or within a given group of them; or something that is intended or suited to the taste, understanding, or means of the general public rather than specialists. The first refers to something that has become liked by lots of folks, while the second refers to something that is designed specifically to be liked by as many folks as possible. In the consumerist culture of the United States, the two functions are often synergistic, with something first becoming popular on its own and then subsequent things being built or modified to jump on that bandwagon.

Both definitions speak to the fact that popularity is a function of scale, as well as to the fact that popularity is a function of population. Something that is very popular—or that is designed to be very popular—within a given population very likely won't be popular within a different one. Think American versus European football, both of which are intensely popular in their respective realms but are about as different from each other as American and European archaeology—and they are indeed different in a handful of ways.

Despite germinating in the exact same historical soil, American and European archaeology have grown in fascinatingly divergent directions. Reasons for this split are also deeply rooted in American culture and its unique approach to all things mysterious and "other." But the biggest split between them is that European archaeology focuses on European material history, while American archaeology focuses on Indigenous—or, to put that another way, pre-American—material history.

This is also why the "football" metaphor is such a useful one. The roots of European football are embedded in ancient China, Greece, and Rome, where groups of people were maneuvering balls around a field with their feet for centuries. By contrast, the American version as we know it today was greatly influenced by Native American sports and players—including the overhead spiral and forward pass, both of which are now considered bedrock parts of the game but didn't really exist before Jim Thorpe and the rest of the Carlisle Indians introduced them in the early 1900s. The game has become immensely popular since then, for better or for worse, in a manner not entirely dissimilar to how archaeology has.

Why this is a problem for the sciences in general is because whenever something jumps the gap from specialists to generalists there's an accompanying jettison of propriety. Which is a fancy way of saying that when a concept or theory becomes popular with people who haven't spent months, years, or decades studying it, the version that becomes popular is often very stripped-down and devoid of important details, nuances, or applications.

Why this is a problem for archaeology in particular is because archaeology is a humanistic discipline. It is humans investigating humans, proximately in terms of rocks and whatnot but ultimately in terms of social behavior. And when the investigation of human social behavior becomes, itself, a form of human social behavior, the whole thing verges on a fatuous exercise in bias. The versions that become popular only do so because they appeal to what the target population already likes or believes, and the versions that are designed to be popular are then skewed toward those same tropes. The result is sort of autocatalytic awfulness.

For this and a whole host of other reasons, there is a great need in this country for more—and better—public scholarship, in all domains of technical research but especially in archaeology. Climate change, terrestrial extinction, oceanic ecological collapse, overgrazing, microplastics, zoonotic infections, and a whole host of other ills best understood by specialists but of real concern to generalists need their pop translators as well, but those topics aren't hip the way that archaeology is. Nobody sits down to watch a show about a rugged adventurer strapping on a fedora and heading out to explore shrinking ice caps. Although now that I mention it . . .

People do tune in to programming that shows such characters exploring the depths of human history, however, and this content can have significant impacts. because the human present is the living embodiment of the human past. Our history is what produced us, and it's us who need to face up to the consequences of our actions. That's a lot harder to do when that history is bent, buggered, and bastardized in pursuit of ratings and ad revenue.

As mainstream sensibilities in the modern world continue to lurch between increasingly disparate themes of progressive utopianism and authoritative totalitarianism, nuance is in danger of extinction right alongside rhinos and polar bears. Snarky pop intellectual Tim Minchin described our current sociopolitical discourse as being "like two tennis players trying to win a match by hitting beautifully executed shots from either end of separate tennis courts."

One could just as easily port this metaphor over to the realm of archaeology. Academics wave their arms and caterwaul over whether a paper has enough citations or if a study took enough variability into account. At the same time, big-budget entertainment venues and a slew of online influencers jostle for attention by presenting the most unexpected and outrageous "discoveries" to one-up their competitors. The only time these two subgroups interact with each other is when a member of the former group gets enraged and goes after someone in the latter group, usually in the form of a pedantic takedown published in some obscure technical journal where most people will never see it anyway. Otherwise, they're worlds apart.

On the subject of obscure technical journals most people will never see anyway: that, too, is a major problem in archaeology and the bulk of modern science research in general. Science didn't become a national concern until after World War II, when governments like those of the United States realized scientific research can be useful for things like, say, designing bombs. Prior to that, science was mostly done by wealthy hobbyists. The rise of state-funded science was quickly followed by the rise of technical scientific journals, with German-based Pergamon Press—owned and operated by Robert Maxwell, father of Ghislaine—leading the charge.

It's largely a big scam that should be getting a lot more attention. To borrow from a 2011 piece written by Stephen Buranyi for *The Guardian*:

> Scientists create work under their own direction fund ed largely by governments—and give it to publishers for free; the publisher pays scientific editors who judge whether the work is worth publishing and check its grammar, but the bulk of the editorial burden—checking the scientific validity and evaluating the experiments, a process known as peer review—is done by working scientists on a volunteer basis. The publishers then sell the product back to government-funded institutional and university libraries, to be read by scientists—who, in a collective sense, created the product in the first place.

To unpack that a little, taxpayers foot the bill for most of the major scientific research being conducted these days via grants to institutions from entities like the National Science Foundation, the results of which are published with no cost to the publisher for the material or its review, and then the publisher sells the resulting publication to those same institutions at exorbitant costs—also picked up by the taxpayer. It's a remarkably effective grift if you don't happen to be one of those taxpayers.

For this very reason, some of the most lauded scientists I've known—including Kristen Hawkes, a member of the National Academy of Sciences and originator of the Grandmothering Hypothesis of human behavioral evolution—refuse to be members of professional societies who direct these publications. If your intention is to expand and enrich our knowledge of the wondrous drama that is the natural world and our place within it, actively participating in what is functionally subsidized theft in order to get it published shouldn't sit well with you. And it certainly doesn't with me.

The current war on intellectualism has ammunition like this at their disposal. The scientific research itself is often very important and effective, especially when it comes to medical research, but the public pays for it twice and never really gets to see the result—except in a roundabout way like taking a better pill or hearing more songbirds than they did last year. What's missing for them is effective messaging, a narrative telling the public all about the research they're indirectly funding and its overall importance, so they know they're part of something that is actually worthwhile.

What's missing, in other words, is the story.

◆ ◆ ◆

This is . . . well, not *the* story of American archaeology. More like *a* story of American archaeology.

At its simplest, archaeology is the process of reconstructing the past. It's most often used to reconstruct past events so we can explore the why and how of the way things played out as they did, while other times it's used to reconstruct past behaviors to try to understand the overall human condition a little better, and still other times it's simply a means to show off literal things from the past as a point of interest or pride.

At its most complex, archaeology is a loosely defined term that refers to anyone saying anything about the past based on any—or, in some cases, no—amount of evidence. A dedicated researcher painstakingly counting pollen grains and a TV personality screaming nonsense about extraterrestrial landing pads are both considered "archaeologists" in about the same way that Walter Cronkite and Tucker Carlson are both considered "journalists."

And therein lies the problem. Unlike with lawyers or medical doctors, where you must pass codified qualifications to legally call yourself one, the ambiguity of disciplines like archaeology makes it just as easy to call yourself one as it is to call yourself a journalist. You are one if you say you are. This precipitates a lot of misconceptions, misunderstandings, and outright malevolence.

Back in 1976, the Society of Professional Archaeologists was formed with the intent of raking up the leaves by vetting and enforcing professional standards, not entirely unlike a legal bar association. But the effort stalled and eventually devolved into the Register of Professional Archaeologists—which is, in form and function, more like an archaeological version of the Elks Club. No follow-up efforts ever really got off the ground.

Archaeology, like the natural philosophy that long preceded it, is a practice motivated primarily by wonder, and wonder can lead people down all sorts of paths. What's often missing on those paths are informed, reliable, trustworthy guides. Guides who aren't motivated primarily by greed or ego. Guides who know the history, the science, and the culture of archaeological inquiry but aren't incapable of speaking to the public about those things without driving that public into gibbering bewilderment through overabundance of jargon. Guides who understand that what most people really want isn't a pile of facts and figures. What most people want is a story.

The path taken by many modern archaeologists led them from pedestrian infatuation with really old stuff to a focus on management, conservation, and preservation of this incredible land, its rich history, and the people most intimately intertwined with both. That strikes me as a solid basis for a pretty cool story.

CHAPTER 1

ANCIENTS AND ANTIQUARIANS

There are precious few things that count as genuine universals among human beings. Apart from all of us being mammals, all of us needing food and water, all of us needing to sleep at some point, and all of us being mortal, there aren't a whole lot of personal attributes we actually share in common. Not really.

This is why so much of what is generously called scientific psychology suffers from what's been dubbed the WEIRD bias—an acronym for Western, educated, industrialized, rich, and democratic. These are most of the people who can afford to go to college in the first place, as well as the people most likely to visit a psychiatrist or take part in a psychological study. Trying to glean species-wide behavioral universals from that is like trying to understand the behavior of all canines by studying the habits of toy poodles.

However, on the list of things that are close to human universals is curiosity about the past. There appears to be some version of this practice in every known human culture or society, whether it's in the form of history documentation or simply recapitulation of traditions established by one's ancestors. People in ancient Mexico venerated the cultures of more-ancient Mexico, people in ancient Egypt venerated the cultures of more-ancient Egypt—two examples to which I'll return—and people throughout Eurasia did it with cave paintings, and then scrolls, and then books, and so on. The past is what resulted in the present, after all. It's hard to understand the Now without understanding the Then that preceded it.

Examining history in the absence of written records or long-established traditions is where things get tricky. Mythology, lies, and wild-ass guesswork will only take one so far down that path, and are furthermore subject to subversion by other people's mythology, lies, and wild-ass guesswork. The formal practice of archaeology congealed out of that miasma as an earnest attempt to avoid it altogether.

The archaeological record was probably best summarized in a 2005 article in *World Archaeology* as "the joint product of what ancient people made, did, and dropped and of the natural processes of deposition and decay." Archaeology is the formal study of that record.

It manifests in the United States as a branch or subfield of the distinctly Western science of anthropology. Anthropology in turn is broadly defined as the systematic study of humanity through comparative analyses to understand our evolutionary origins, our various societies and cultures, and whatever it is that makes *Homo sapiens* so unique and different from the rest of the animal kingdom. It is both eloquent and grandiose—and could be picked apart like a cow in a piranha tank if one was so inclined.

Back in Europe, meanwhile—from whence American archaeology spawned—it's more often regarded as a branch of history rather than anthropology. The reasons for this disparity, as well as its repercussions, form a load-bearing strut in the story to come.

To put it frankly, American archaeology wouldn't have passed the IRS's Nondiscrimination Testing or the Motion Picture Academy's Inclusion Standards until very recently—and even today, from all that I can gather, much of it wouldn't pass #MeToo scrutiny. It's a complicated science-adjacent field comprising great people, terrible people, great ideas, terrible ideas, and more misconceptions than actual conceptions, especially among the general public. It is variously regarded by Americans* as a fun pastime, a method of colonialism, a way of salvaging the past, a way of plundering the past, a method of inquiry rooted in serious science, a bunch of hogwash propped up by pseudoscience, a tool for conservation, a tool for exploitation, a way of securing a steady job in the outdoors, and a way of wasting

* The ones who know what archaeology even is, at any rate. It has *almost* nothing to do with dinosaurs.

piles of money on pointless academic rigamarole all at the same time, and *none of these perspectives are wrong.*

◆ ◆ ◆

The actual process of archaeology is the construction of history by investigation of the past through analysis of physical stuff that's been left behind. We do this by looking at that stuff and reconstructing the scene or behavior that made it come about.

You come home to find a houseplant smashed on the floor. You collect data on related variables, like the paw prints on the dusty windowsill and the conspicuous absence of your cat, and you determine that the cat did it while you were at work and is now hiding from you. That doesn't tell you why the cat did it, necessarily, but you've probably got a few theories in that direction as well.

Archaeologists are basically detectives in that sense—at least during the data-gathering and analysis portions of what we do. We assemble clues, carefully analyze them, apply critical thinking to the results of our analyses, and then confidently hypothesize that Colonel Mustard did it in a rock shelter with a sharpened stick approximately four thousand years ago. Again, this doesn't tell us why he did it, and charging forth into that kind of speculation carries its own special troubles. But that's essentially how archaeologists use inference and science to reconstruct historical events or behaviors when we can't just read written testimony or listen to well-established oral histories about it.

As a useful heuristic for understanding this process in terms of behavioral reconstruction, consider the Standard Service Agreements (SSAs) for any modern big-tech gadgetry. The reason those things tend to be a million words long is because new caveats are added every time the company gets sued over some imbecilic thing someone did with their product. The initial release of something like a smartphone might include a one-page SSA about how you shouldn't use it as a paperweight, while the second version includes a two-page SSA that now contains a missive against using it as a hammer. Then the third version includes a three-page SSA that absolves the company from liability if you use the product as a cudgel in armed combat. And so on.

This is why some researchers refer to such contracts as "social artifacts." Contracts bear the markings of broad social contexts, reflecting both the economic and cultural environments in which they emerge. And, like all artifacts, they are themselves capable of affecting those environments in turn, usually by giving culturally specific instructions about how to interpret them and anything related to them. If a box of toothpicks includes specific instructions for use along with a warning about sticking them in your eye, for example, you can read that as a literal directive as well as interpret it as a reflection of the culture in which the product was manufactured.

This is also what drove Wonko the Sane to condemn all of humanity to a mental institution in Douglas Adams' classic book *So Long, and Thanks for all the Fish.**

Given the year this book is hitting shelves, it could be argued that an even better heuristic is that of large language models, or what we euphemistically call "artificial intelligence" (it's not). These things work by scraping the world's collective dataset in order to spot trends in images and text that allow it to make predictive results based on detailed prompts. They steal data, in other words, and then analyze those data for patterns in order to provide ostensibly satisfying results when presented with a request by the sort of people who would prefer not to deal with other people.

That is indeed—sadly, regrettably, and not a little infuriatingly—a spot-on analogy for the way archaeology has traditionally been conducted in the United States. White people stealing data from non-white people, applying a bunch of math and theory and behavioral models to it, and then proudly proclaiming they've solved another mystery about human beings without ever having to engage with any of them along the way.

---

* As far as I know, no popular author has been invoked more often than Adams by archaeologists trying to be funny or clever in their research—including a 2012 article by James O'Connell and Jim Allen that appeared in a prestigious journal under the title "The Restaurant at The End Of The Universe: Modelling the Colonization of Sahul." We never miss a chance to honor our heroes.

It's not like that, anymore. Or at least it's less like that—and getting lesser by the day. More and more we are in the business of recreating and preserving history rather than stealing it. The history of our evolving relationship with history is the driving undercurrent of the story to come.

◆ ◆ ◆

Meanwhile, the history of science in general is a relatively modern discipline. As such, in a hilariously meta fashion considering archaeologists' obsession with chronologies, it often makes the same mistake a lot of the formal sciences did in their own infancies: reducing a chaotic yarn snarl of various ideas, approaches, methods, and theories into nice, ordered schema delineating graduated periods or phases. It's like sorting through an SSAs that extends across hundreds of years.

In the case of American archaeology, these are typically the Speculative, Descriptive, and finally Explanatory periods. When I studied archaeology in graduate school at the University of Utah in the early 2010s, they presented this very model with—not surprisingly—their own approach as the pinnacle beneath which the other periods or phases were pathetically compiled. All institutions do this.

Of course, anytime someone proposes a straightforward model you'll find a bucket of crabs ready to drag it back into chaos. The history of American archaeology is no different. Back in 1942, Yale psychology and archaeology professor Clark Wissler got the ball rolling by proposing an initial or Pioneer Period (1492–1800), a period of increasing cross-cultural and bio-anatomical analysis that I'll call the Comparative Period (1800–1860), then a Museum Period (1860–1900), and finally, an Academic Period (1900–whenever) when museums like the Smithsonian gradually gave their institutional supremacy over to universities. He wrote this long before the very notion of for-profit heritage management firms had emerged.

After that came Willam Duncan Strong's 1952 seriation of Pioneer-Speculative (1492–1847), Pioneer-Scientific (1847–1916), Developed-Scientific (1916–recent years), and Systematic-Anthropological (whenever–whenever) phases. Then in 1965, we got Belmont and Williams' Birth (1745–1820), Pioneer (1820–1893), Professional (1893–1930), and Modern (1930–present) chronology. Then Gordon R. Willey's 1968 version: Pioneer (whenever–1850), Descriptive (1850–1920), Descriptive-Historic (1920–1950), and Comparative-Historic (1950–present) periods.

Res ipsa loquitur. It's a mess.

Based on all this, a simplistic and accurate chronology of the development of American archaeology probably isn't possible. In a 1966 paper on the use of behavioral models in population biology, Richard Levins argued that no single model can be maximally realistic, precise, and general at the same time because these properties trade-off against one another. Because of this, in any given behavioral model, you can maximize up to two of these properties, but never all three of them. You can sacrifice generality for the sake of realism and precision, like doing a study on a specific butterfly species in a specific place that doesn't apply to other butterflies. You can sacrifice precision for the sake of realism and generality, like doing a study on butterflies at an aggregate level to determine trends that do not necessarily apply to any one member of the population (casinos and insurance companies operate on this sort of model). Or you can sacrifice realism for the sake of precision and generality, which in lay terms means ignoring as many variables as possible to create a model that applies to as many circumstances as possible, like when meteorologists use broad predictive strategies that don't consider all those pesky butterflies causing typhoons.

This is a handy way to contemplate history reconstruction. Is it precise? Then it will probably only appeal to a narrow group of specialists—the classic academic dilemma. Is it general? Then you're probably glossing over a ton of stuff. Is it realistic? Then it will probably be a billion pages long.

◆ ◆ ◆

To reiterate, all human groups appear to be interested in their own past. Many social scientists even believe that knowledge of sociocultural origins is fundamental for the development of individual and social identity—although this could be read as social scientists trying to justify their own jobs so, you know, take that for what it is.

A useful case study for the earliest form of what eventually became archaeology is that of Khaemweset. He was born around 1285 BC* as the fourth son of Egyptian pharaoh Rameses II, otherwise known as Rameses the Great, but Khaemweset himself was not destined to rule. By the time he was born, much of Egypt's material history could already be called "ancient," with many of the Old Kingdom structures—like the Great Sphinx and Pyramids of Giza—being partially buried and generally in a state of ruinous decay.

Khaemweset attained the station of High Priest of Ptah at Memphis by the age of thirty-two, which included duties like caring for the deity's statue and temple, officiating state funerals, and overseeing daily rituals. He also had access to the finest temple libraries in the region at that time, and he seemed to have become a voracious devourer of history texts. This also inspired him to go out and investigate the temples and other monumental structures throughout northern Egypt. The prince decided this situation simply wouldn't do and dedicated himself to restoring those ancient structures and informing the populace of their historical importance.

His efforts began in Saqqara, where Prince Khaemweset found a vast necropolis or "city of the dead" where many of the monuments were badly dilapidated. He and an unnamed team of workers then set about restoring as many of them as they could, including the Pyramid of Unas on which he added an inscription commemorating the restoration. He also enlarged the Serapeum or burial site of the mummified Apis bulls, literal sacred cows that were interpreted as reincarnations of the son of Old Kingdom goddess Hathor, whose initial role was that of being sacrificed and reborn as part of the her worship rites.

* Another note about terminology: BC stands for Before Christ and AD stands for Anno Domini or "Year of Our Lord." A lot of people find this offensive, for frankly understandable reasons, and have proposed alternatives like BCE/CE or Before the Common Era/Common Era as more respectful terminology.This fails to actually address the problem, because the dates are exactly the same—it just whitewashes it.

Khaemweset was so enamored of the Serapeum, and of the work he did to restore and expand it, that he was later buried in its catacombs at the end of his life—supposedly. Much later, in AD 1851, the site was excavated by French archaeologist François Auguste Ferdinand Mariette who found the impressive sarcophagi of more than sixty animals, as well as the virtually untouched tomb of the prince. But the full story is a little murky. While working at the site, Mariette encountered an enormous rock that could only be removed with explosives, something archaeologists are rather more hesitant to do these days.

Inside the chamber was an intact coffin containing the mummified remains of a man, according to Mariette, along with several funerary items—including a gold mask over the man's face and amulets that gave his name as Prince Khaemweset, son of Rameses II and builder of the Serapeum. All these things have since been lost, and a few modern Egyptologists like Aidan Dodson claim that it was more likely the remains of a sacrificed Apis bull made into a human form to resemble the prince as a way of honoring him.

I like to think that I'd know the difference between a human body and a chimera of cow parts made to look like a human body, but Dodson insists that it's not that straightforward. According to him, the mummy "proved to be a mass of fragrant resin containing a quantity of disordered bone" rather than a cadaver wrapped in fabric like the one that harassed Abbott and Costello. This is how the Apis bulls were often interred, their bones mixed with fragrant resin rather than remaining articulated. There's also no evidence that any of the others were then molded Play-Doh style into human forms.

Khaemweset accomplished much in his life, documenting and restoring numerous monuments throughout the region and placing new inscriptions on them that told future generations who'd built them, why they were built, and that he restored them. In this last regard he was a bit of a showboat, and some critics think he did it all not out of a sense of pride or honor for history so much as to be the ultimate Instagram influencer of his day. The inscription on the restored tomb of Fourth Dynasty king Shepsekaf at Saqqara, for example, reads like this:

> His Majesty [Rameses II] instructed the High Priest of Ptah and Setem, Khaemweset, to inscribe the cartouche of king Shepsekaf, since his name could not be found on the face of his pyramid, inasmuch as the Setem Khaemweset loved to restore the monuments of the kings, making firm again what had fallen into ruin.

He also devoted some energies to restoring misplaced statues, and again he couldn't help but draw extra attention to himself and his father for his efforts. So, it's probably safe to say that critics of Khaemweset are right for accusing him of the earliest recorded form of engaging in public displays of conservation just for the upvotes.

No matter—the result is the same. His efforts to restore the Great Pyramids and other monuments at Giza alone were remarkable and are a big part of why they remain such popular attractions to this day, although it is worth noting that the Sphinx was at least partially dug out of the sand by Tuthmosis IV about a hundred years before. But it was primarily Khaemweset's work that preserved what are without a doubt the most famous archaeological sites in Egypt to this day.

◆ ◆ ◆

Apart from monument restorers like Khaemweset, the first people to call themselves "archaeologists" were only interested in historical times, in the sense that history is usually defined as "old written stuff" and everything that came before is considered prehistory.

That's still largely the case in official American archaeological standards, with the Historic Period in the Southwest having therefore commenced at the end of the Mexican American War in the mid-1800s when the US Government started creating written records about the area. Mexicans and earlier Spanish colonists created their own written records about the area, of course—to say nothing of the rich traditions of Indigenous petroglyphs (carved into stone) and pictographs (painted onto stone) going back many thousands of years. But I guess those don't count as "writing."

To borrow a phrase from the great Terry Pratchett, when one

of his main characters was trying to describe democracy to another one, it came down to "everyone had a vote—apart from the women, children, slaves, idiots, and people who weren't really our kind of people." History works rather the same way—as, increasingly, does modern American democracy. You have history only if the ruling class says you have history. If not, then you've simply got a past.

There is, in fact, a big difference between having history and having a past. The past is a done thing, complete and over and never to be changed. History, meanwhile, is an ongoing inquiry, subject to discussion and revision and reinterpretation as circumstances change or new elements come to light, and it has a definite impact on the present.

The past is your partner having put the car keys in the freezer. History is the complex and fascinating narrative explaining why in holy hell they would do that.

Denying people history is therefore a great way of challenging and undermining their humanity. All living things have a past, after all. Ask any fossil. But history is itself a living thing, composed and maintained as a product of uniquely human consciousness. And if you don't have history, then presumably you aren't fully human.

Back in olden-days Europe, there was a handy cut-off for this: everything that came before all the official written history was covered by the Bible, which included a lot of very hasty world-building, some unfortunate misunderstandings about an apple, lots of wandering around, and a great big flood that acted as a reset button. Nobody but Noah's nuclear family and a tightly cramped coterie of extremely well-behaved animals survived that flood, so the history of the human world obviously began the next sunny day after landfall. Asking questions about what happened before then was liable to earn derisive laughter or a visit by the clergy.

Because of this, according to archaeology historian Bruce G. Trigger, the earliest European archaeologists "ignored at least 95 percent of human history extending from the earliest known hominids who existed some four million years ago to the non-literate peoples who lived in many parts of the world until recent times." Their forebears were the antiquarians, a loosely defined title that refers not to a professional group or social movement so much as a sociocultural trend that flourished during the Middle Ages. It was a hobby, in other words, and would remain so—for the most part—until almost the dawn of the twentieth century.

◆ ◆ ◆

In the Americas, following Columbus's initial voyages and the resulting crush of colonists flocking to what they called the New World to explore and exploit it, this hobby of contemplating a past propped up by confident biblical underpinnings got shaken. Badly.

The Americas included a whole bunch of animals and human beings that were partly or entirely unlike anything Europeans had yet encountered. The collision between this and what the Old World colonists believed in the sixteenth century threatened to upend not only their conceptions of theology and philosophy, but also their conception of history. For the first couple centuries of European occupation, the narratives and myths commonplace in European culture failed entirely to account for the Americas and their rich diversity of people and animals with histories totally divorced from the Old World. Even the mighty civilizations of the Aztecs and the Incas lacked printed money, bound books, metal tools, gunpowder, and other such hallmarks of Civilization with a capital C as the colonists saw it.

Because of all this, early European and Euro-American authors writing about the Americas and its people began looking for explanations in what I will generously call creative ways. Relying on written accounts to study history just wasn't going to cut it in the Americas because there weren't any (this was long before the Mayan stelae were deciphered), approximately 90 percent of Indigenous peoples were wiped out by colonialism so it's not like colonists could just ask them about their history, and racism toward Indigenous people precluded taking their answers at face value anyway.

Instead, the alleged "savage condition" or "state of nature" of Indigenous peoples in the Americas—along with the concept of "nature" preceding "history" in the organization of social life—was explored through naturalistic philosophy. Indigenous history wasn't understood to be human history, in other words, but natural history.

This exploration of Indigenous peoples through the lens of natural history set a bit of a precedent. Ever since the "discovery" of the so-called New World, Europeans puzzled over who the extant inhabitants were and from whence they came—a trend that passed to Americans when they manifested a bit later. Moreover, given the brutality of the Colonial Period, concomitant investigations into these questions were ideological rather than objective and shot through with a desperate search for justifications for that brutality.

During the sixteenth and seventeenth centuries, various scholars openly speculated that Native Americans were the descendants of Iberians, Carthaginians, Israelites (this one would stick around), Canaanites, or Tartars. Some even suspected they were refugees from the sunken city of Atlantis, a word that becomes annoying right quick when examining the history of archaeology.

The hypothesis that gradually came to the fore was one first proposed by a Franciscan friar in the 1500s, oddly enough—the one that said they'd come from Siberia. This was based primarily on nothing more than observed physical characteristics, although it would come to be bolstered by the discovery that Diné peoples of the Southwest and Athabaskan peoples of the far north share a distinctive language family. It would wind up being bolstered even more when genetics came to the fore in studies of population biology.

These migration stories were not the only type of theory kicking around at the time, however. Many evolutionists, including John Locke, became convinced that Indigenous peoples here and elsewhere represented humanity that was somehow frozen in an earlier state. "Thus in the beginning, all the world was America, and more so than that is now," he famously said in his *Second Treatise of Government* in 1689. He went on to explain how America offers "a pattern of the first ages in Asia and Europe," and in doing so set the stage for subsequent generations of researchers treating Indigenous peoples as living fossils they could study to understand the deep past of humanity *in toto*. They were still doing this when I was in grad school.

It was largely—if not entirely—because of Locke's philosophy and resulting treatises that both colonization and capitalism came to take their respective shapes. There's still a primordial waste out there, richly covered in natural resources that the local inhabitants aren't bothering to exploit. If they won't exploit them then damnit somebody has to.

According to this worldview, the Americas were the perfect place to plunder riches and dispose of England's surplus population (poor people, etc.) because the American continents were considered an inexhaustible land of richness populated entirely by what were essentially considered proto-humans. Later thinkers would add all sorts of details to this picture, from religious assumptions that Indigenous peoples' "degeneracy" was a sign of displeasure from God (this, too, would stick around) to scientific assumptions that climatic factors prevented Native Americans from attaining the lofty technological heights of Eurasia. This would help set the stage for American archaeology in an unfortunate way.

◆ ◆ ◆

Upon their arrival on the eastern seaboard of North America, the English colonists of what they creatively dubbed New England generally held the Indigenous residents in ill regard. Notorious disciplinarian and Puritan* clergy leader Cotton Mather described Native Americans as "ruines of Mankind." It was an attitude both dismissive and productive in its scope because it meant the Native peoples' customs needn't be treated with anything like basic respect—especially when they conflicted with the colonists' needs.

Graverobbing, for example, was rampant in the early New England colonies. The colonists noted how Indigenous customs

* Puritan and Pilgrim get conflated a lot, and for good reason, but they are technically separate entities. The Pilgrims were religious separatists who first absconded to the Netherlands to escape persecution, and then boarded the Mayflower—and another ship called the Speedwell that was almost immediately sabotaged by its own crew—to seek better fortunes in the New World in 1620. The Puritans, who were non-separatist fundamentalists, came a decade later and in much greater number. Within a few decades the Puritans were firmly in charge.

included burying a great deal of useful stuff with their dead—weapons, skins, wampum or beaded belts used for trade, that sort of thing—and concluded that these were "rotting in the ground for no reason" and sought to "liberate" them. This appears in writings from as early as 1610, only three years after the first English colonists arrived and ten years before the Pilgrims did, so they clearly wasted no time drawing this conclusion.

This, naturally enough, led to some tension. When the colonists looted the grave of a Massachusett chief's mother of "two great Beares skinnes sowed together at full length," for example, they very nearly paid for the loot with their lives. Massachusett warriors considered it "impious, and inhumane, to deface the monuments of the dead," according to a 1643 study on Native customs and language by British minister Roger Williams. The minister himself was expelled from the Massachusetts Bay colony in 1635 for questioning the Puritan leadership and thereafter spent his life in the colony of Rhode Island, where he maintained generally friendly relations with the local Narragansett peoples. This might explain why the Puritan leaders didn't like him very much.

The attitude of the Puritans toward the Indigenous peoples of the Americas was further fueled by religious hatred. Because the Native locals were perceived as fundamentally barbaric and less than fully human, digging up and desecrating their graves was also a way of stamping out their heathen religion. The Puritans weren't there to save souls the way the Spanish were way down south. They were more about persecution and saving souls in the afterlife than saving anyone who was still breathing—a point to which they returned in the Massachusett colony toward the end of the 1600s when fourteen women and six men from their own ranks were killed after being accused of practicing witchcraft. Many more were imprisoned and tortured. I can only imagine how the Indigenous onlookers felt about these pious invaders with a superiority complex mutilating their own community members for such heinous transgressions as looking vaguely suspicious when someone else's chickens started disappearing.

That said, and in the interest of fairness, slaughter of one's own community members is a rare but fairly ubiquitous thing to which groups are occasionally pushed throughout human history. One of the reasons the Spanish were so appalled upon reaching Tenochtitlan was the shock at seeing the Aztecs committing mass human sacrifices to their deities—which I take to mean they totally forgot about the Spanish Inquisition doing pretty much the same thing at that exact same time back in Europe. Then there's the starvation policies of the British Empire and Stalinist Russia, the purges of the Khmer Rouge in Cambodia and the Glorious Revolution in China, and the death camps where the Nazis sent millions of German citizens.

The details change but the shape of the act does not: lots of members of a given community being killed because the rest of them were convinced it was of greater benefit to them. Nowadays it's often because they're labeled as criminals or, I don't know, "gang members." Back in colonial New England, that reason was witchcraft.

The aforementioned Cotton Mather had a lot to do with those witch trials, by the way. He even wrote a book called *The Wonders of the Invisible World: Observations As well Historical as Theological, upon the Nature, the Number, and the Operations of the Devils* in 1693 in which he argued that witches were tools of Satan sent to "overturn this poor plantation, the Puritan colony." His father, a man named Increase Mather—the Puritans could get really creative with names, including a man whose parents christened him If-Christ-Had-Not-Died-For-Thee-Thou-Hadst-Been-Damned Barbon (son of Praise-God Barbon) who opted instead to go by Nicholas for reasons I can't imagine—published his own book about witchcraft in 1684 called *Remarkable Providence* that got the whole Witch Trial ball rolling. He published another one in 1692 called *Cases of Conscience Concerning Evil Spirits* in which he also defended the trials.

Attitudes like those of the Puritans weren't exactly conducive to archaeological inquiry, given as they were to the contention that Indigenous peoples and their customs were heathen idolatry at best and literal Satanic possession at worst. And yes, the pious New Englanders practiced plenty of violence toward the Natives before they turned their torches on their own people, despite what Thanksgiving myths have to say about the matter.

This tradition never really died out in Euro-American culture.

There is often a chorus of "looks like Satan to me" whenever Christian Americans and their geologically recent European ancestors encounter any type of art, ritual, or pageantry they've never seen before. It happened when Cortez encountered the Aztecs. It happened when the Puritans encountered Indigenous peoples of the eastern seaboard. It happened when suburbanites encountered their own kids playing Dungeons and Dragons in the 1980s. And it happened in response to the Olympic opening ceremonies while this book was being edited. It's a practice as American as, well, Thanksgiving.

Granted, not all the Thanksgiving-y tales we tell are tall ones. The colonists did indeed survive their first several winters thanks to help from the Wampanoag Tribe, although historians mostly think this is because the Wampanoag didn't yet perceive them as a threat—more like a small group of weird travelers who appeared one day and would probably be gone before too long. But the longer they stayed, and the larger their colonies grew, the more the Indigenous groups got nervous. It didn't take long for those nerves to break.

Take the occurrence at Mystic River during the Pequot War of 1637. Fearing that the Pequots were seeking alliance with the nearby Narragansetts to drive the Pilgrims of Plymouth and the Puritans of Massachusetts into the sea, the colonists banded together with the Narragansetts as allies against their Narragansett enemies. According to the Plymouth colony governor, William Bradford, armed soldiers surrounded the Pequot village and set it on fire, destroying their homes and killing many of them in the process—including shooting down any survivors who fled the flames. Bradford believed the soldiers killed four hundred people.

John Winthrop, the governor of what became Massachusetts (named for the Massachusett Tribe but with an "s" at the end to indicate that it's their territory—or used to be, anyway), estimated that the number of those murdered during the war or captured and enslaved totaled about seven hundred. "It was a fearful sight to see them thus frying in the fire and the streams of blood quenching the same," Bradford wrote of that terrible night, but the deaths were a "sweet sacrifice," a phrase from Leviticus, for which the colonists "gave the praise thereof to God."

Just under forty years later, they visited the same courtesy on the Narragansett themselves, killing almost a hundred of them in a single night by setting fire to their encampment in what is remembered now as the Great Swamp Massacre. By then a Wampanoag headman named Metacomet had rallied several Indigenous groups to stymie the colonists' advance. His rebellion stretched across pretty much all of what we still call New England. The fire came after a series of conflicts that saw many dead on both sides, and Metacomet himself was found, decapitated, and quartered as a warning to others in 1676. Massachusetts colonists sold the rest of the captured Natives into slavery in the West Indies. The famous trials of witches commenced in that same colony a little over a decade later.

Persecutors being persecuted is one of those satisfying little eddies that occasionally form in the river of history, where the people with knives out and vengeance in their hearts suddenly find knives and vengeance on their own doorsteps. So it was with the Puritans accusing each other of witchcraft and burning each other alive shortly after doing so to the very groups who'd helped the Pilgrims survive when they first landed. Much can be learned from watching people rage against being treated the same way they, or people like them, have treated others.

This, too, is a tradition that has yet to die out in mainstream American culture. It's how we get people like Justin Giles, a member of the Oathkeeper gang who marched out to defend Mormon constitutional cultist Cliven Bundy from having to pay $1.34 per month per cow/calf pair in grazing fees, claiming the federal government is "literally treating western United States citizens, ranchers, rural folks like . . . the modern-day Indians. We're being driven off our lands. We're being forced into reservations known as cities." Our lands being, in this case, territory that was settled by the Bundy clan after the feds forced the Paiute Tribe off them in 1875.

Bundy would go on to unsettle all but his most ardent defenders with a series of public talks where he outright asserted that Black people would be better off as slaves than on federal welfare, like all of them apparently are. (He said this during the Obama administration, by the way.) In a not wildly dissimilar manner, the Puritans would go into steep decline and ultimate obscurity starting about the time of the witch trials, partly because of the Glorious Revolution back in England and partly because religious New Englanders began splintering into various factions that weren't as eager to barbecue one another.

But all those traditions remain, in one form or another, because cultures rarely go completely extinct. This is a yet another theme that pops up again and again in this book.

* * *

Interest in material history only gradually started to grow in the minds of American colonists thereafter but didn't really ramp up until the Revolutionary period. Much of it was focused on early academic interest in the origins of the Native Americans and how, exactly, they fit into the "history" presented in biblical teachings that altogether failed to mention their existence. It was part and parcel of the grander scheme to explore and explain all the wondrous and vexing mysteries of the New World.

Because of such interests, many of the first Western explorers not only explored what they considered unknown lands, but also brought back objects for early naturalists to study. Those collectors were also operating on a thesis that lumped Indigenous people in with plants and animals and rocks but decidedly not with humanity, and these factors together explain why so much American archaeology is currently housed in Museums of Natural History.

That's not an inherently bad thing, by the way. Or it wouldn't be if it was applied universally. Humans are part of nature, after all, whether we accept that fact or not. The problem is that a lot of people quite often don't, and that's especially true when the ruling class (that is: the ones who build museums) predominantly think of themselves as God's special creation.

The proto archaeologists who hauled objects back for paying naturalists to scrutinize were not professionally trained, and their methods of collection varied considerably. They were often jack-of-all-trades types with training in geology, biology, hydrology, and—

most importantly—basic survival skills. Some were sent out on government-sponsored expeditions, but most of them were looking for exotic plants, animals, and cultural gewgaws both ancient and contemporary so they could pass them along to wealthy naturalists for a fee.

This was the "exploratory" period in archaeological history, and it involved no small amount of graverobbing, while asking broad questions about how all that material history fit together to create a picture of history just wasn't a priority. That part was covered by the Bible. Fieldwork in those days was predicated mostly on finding something novel that no other European explorer had found before and then getting safely back to the colony without dying in some equally novel fashion.

◆ ◆ ◆

The first North American antiquities to receive more than a passing glance by Europeans were the pictographs and petroglyphs found throughout the continent. Stone artifacts often turned up here and there as well, but weren't given much thought, and nobody was yet commenting on ancient architecture because they hadn't stumbled into any of it yet.

During their 1673 exploration of the upper Mississippi River, for example, Jacques Marquette and Louis Jolliet reported seeing "two painted monsters" on a high rockface somewhere between the Missouri and Illinois River confluences. Marquette made a drawing of the things that was subsequently lost, but his description was precise enough to identify them as underwater panthers, which are a fairly common and important mythical being for many Indigenous groups in the Northeastern Woodlands or Great Lakes region—particularly among the Anishinaabe peoples, who call them Mishipeshu and consider them the most powerful of all underworld beings. They were said to live in the deepest parts of lakes and rivers, especially the Great Lakes, where they liked to cause severe storms when they didn't feel placated enough. Someone should have told Gordon Lightfoot about this.

Arguably, the first earnest—if not actually professional—archaeological investigations in the United States were conducted under the direction of Thomas Jefferson. The prevailing thought at the time was that Native Americans must not have been in the Americas for very long prior to European arrival, because the world itself was only about six thousand years old at that point. In that time, Europeans had devised such clever things as books, cannons, and flushing toilets, and since history only ever follows one trajectory it must mean that these Indigenous fellows have a very young culture indeed.

Jefferson was heavily influenced by the ideas and thinkers of the European Enlightenment, when Western thinkers in general were moving in the direction of placing a premium on empirical data, scientific methods of investigation, rational inquiry in general, and other radical notions like representative governments. But they were also the progenitors of less-savory intellectual bugbears like race science. This wasn't lost on Jefferson either.

In 1784, or thereabouts—nobody is totally sure of the date—he directed the excavation of what is now called Jefferson's Mound near the Rivanna River, one of about thirteen such mounds known at the time. He found the remains of humans of all stages of life and estimated that there could be as many as a thousand people buried there. To Jefferson's credit, most historians don't believe he collected any of these remains after he was finished.

This one project set the tone for much of what was to come in the *practice* of American archaeology, if not its perceptions or principles. Archaeology was excavation—period. Fieldwork consisted of digging in order to answer questions, or digging in order to find treasures, or digging in order to remove and preserve underground archaeology in places slated to become parking lots.

It's only since about the middle of the 1900s that archaeological survey, or the walking back-and-forth of areas to see and record what's there without necessarily hacking into it, started nudging excavation aside as the dominant form of archaeological inquiry. It's only in the last few decades that excavation *in toto* has evolved in the minds of most American archaeologists as a last resort for preservation rather than a first resort for satisfying one's curiosity. This is among the biggest misunderstandings about modern archaeology that endure in the public collective consciousness.

Oddly enough, the 1784-ish excavation was provoked not by Jefferson's own curiosity but by a questionnaire sent late in the American Revolution by François de Barbé-Marbois of the French delegation to each state in the newly formed nation. It asked for information about each state's resources, history, and "aborigines." Part of the questionnaire asked about "Indian monuments," and here's where the baseline colonialist attitude toward Native Americans came oozing out of Jefferson. From his *Notes on the State of Virginia*:

> I know of no such thing existing as an Indian monument: for I would not honour with that name arrow points, stone hatchets, stone pipes and half-shapen images. Of labour on the large scale I think there is no remain as respectable as would be a common ditch for the draining of lands; unless it be the Barrows of which many are to be found all over this country.

He went on to lay out competing ideas about the mounds' origin and function, and decided to dig into one to see if he could satisfy his curiosity. One of those competing ideas was the Lost Race theory that was unfortunately wildly popular then and, even more unfortunately, still rather popular today.

The thinking, inspired primarily by a man named Josiah Priest, was that the impressive mounds of the Mississippi Valley and surrounding environs could be traced back to some lost race of humans that had once inhabited North America and since gone extinct. Whomever these chaps were, early archaeologists identified them as anything from the predecessors of the Aztecs (this has its own weird consequences in the Southwest later on), to the Vikings, to biblical figures who got so lost they managed to wander all the way across the Pacific.

That last point would later be incorporated into Mormon mythology. Later still, we'd end up with Erich von Däniken and

Ancient Aliens—the former of which is a pseudoarchaeologist who began publishing in the 1960s and the latter of which is a pseudoarchaeological show that began its run in 2009. Both are alive and well to this day, much to my chagrin, and both continue to spew fetid bullshit about how pre-literate non-European people were patently incapable of doing anything beyond whacking each other with sticks without extraterrestrial assistance. They spout anything but the simple and obvious conclusion that Indigenous history in the Americas and elsewhere is really complex, ranging from small bands of hunter-gatherers to state-level societies with monumental architecture and impressively precise calendars.

What's a little ironic about Jefferson's story, though, is that his *Notes* also included one of the earliest contradictions to this notion. Quoted in its original wording, he notes that about thirty years before his excavation a group of local Native peoples "went through the woods directly to [the mound], without any instructions or enquiry, and having staid about it some time, with expressions which were construed to be those of sorrow, they returned to the high road, which they had left about a dozen miles to pay this visit, and pursued their journey."

They were there to visit and pay respects to the graves of their ancestors. Obviously.

◆ ◆ ◆

As all this was taking place, curious developments occurring to the south of North America would also take a big role in shaping what was to come.

While the intensely religious Spanish initially sought to raze all things culturally Indigenous—or just generally non-Christian—from the surface of the planet starting in early 1500s, the 1700s saw them increasingly interested in filling their museums with impressive treasures from their conquered territories in a game of one-upmanship with the British. The Brits were by then busily stuffing their hold with items from places like Egypt, since their colonies on the east coast of North America remained stubbornly bereft of eye-catching obelisks and mummies. But the Spanish did control a region in the Americas rich with things like obelisks and mummies, and despite nearly two centuries of trying to destroy it all they hadn't quite succeeded. As a result, archaeology conducted solely for the purpose of collecting items for museum display pre-dated archaeology for the purpose of nationalism in Mesoamerica. The reverse would be true in the United States.

Seismic changes and reorganization of the Spanish state marked the transition into the eighteenth century, chiefly ignited by the War of Spanish Succession in 1701–1715 and modeled in many ways on the centralization and homogenization practiced by the French. This included "promotion of culture" in a way that sort of presaged the full expression of what we would later come to call nationalism, and was accompanied by the creation of the Royal Library in 1716 and several academies devoted to History (in 1738) and Fine Arts (in 1752).

The purpose of these institutions was to establish a patriotic culture centered on language, history, and the arts—again, setting the foundation for what would evolve into the concept of nationalism in the following century. King Charles III even enacted some rather harsh measures to tighten controls on all things Spanish and proud: he issued a ban on exporting any paintings by "well-known deceased masters" in 1779, and later ordered that any antiquities discovered in the kingdom should be communicated to the Academy of History.

The operative part of that sentence is *discovered in the kingdom*. This was during a time when there was a sharp divide between what European scholars and elites considered their own, civilized history and the "natural history" of the less-civilized peoples native to their colonies. The cultivation of natural sciences was another concern during this period, albeit an adjacent one that more closely aligned with desires for "more efficient and centralized administration of the colonial empire," according to José María Lanzarote Guiral—likely because the empire was in a lot of trouble by then.

Natural and "ethnographic" samples were collected in the Royal Botanical Garden starting in 1755 and the Cabinet of Natural History starting in 1771, and in 1781 Charles III ordered that they be combined in what is today still called the Museo del Prado—although it never actually hosted those collections. It took a series of false starts and a bit of nationalistic panic over the process of losing their American territories to independence before the Museo Arqueológico Nacional finally opened in 1867 by a Royal Decree of Isabella II.

By the time the Cabinet of Natural History was established in Spain, the British Museum in London was already eighteen years old and had been open to the public for twelve of them. Seeing their colonial rivals get the jump on them like that undoubtedly had a catalyzing effect on Charles III. The Spanish oversaw the greatest empire in the history of the world from roughly 1492 to the early 1700s, but by the mid-1700s, the British Empire was of at least comparable size and strength.

In times of stress, leaders often turn to pounding the drums of patriotism. The more despotic and desperate those leaders are, the harder they pound those drums. To that end, Charles III began sending orders to the Spanish colonies in the Americas to stop wrecking and get to looting. The ancient Mayan city of Palenque, located in the Mexican State of Chiapas, is easily the best example of this. The site is smaller than more famous Mayan city-state complexes like Chichén Itzá or Tulum, but its architecture and sculptures are among the finest and best-preserved among all Mayan sites. It was gradually built and occupied between about 226 BC and AD 799 before being depopulated and left to the tender mercies of the jungle during the early Post-Classic Period. There was a lot of this in the Southern Lowlands at the time, leading a lot of early Western scholars to postulate a "collapse" of Mayan culture—as they are wont to do—although in reality it was a combination of some city-state dwellers shifting power toward the north and others giving up on the whole city-state thing altogether in favor of returning to simpler ways of life.

Palenque was first reported to the Spanish by local farmers in the nearby village of Santo Domingo de Palenque sometime in the mid- or late 1700s, although official records don't appear until 1773, when Ramón de Ordóñez y Aguilar visited the site and reported it to the governor-general in Guatemala. Fourteen years later, Charles III ordered the governor-general to have the place examined and collected on behalf of the Crown, and general Antonio del Río was assigned to the task. Although he only spent a little over a month surveying, clearing, making drawings, and collecting things, his report still stands as the first arguably scientific archaeological investigation conducted in the Americas—even if it wasn't anything like what we would call "archaeology" today. More like antiquarianism with careful notetaking.

As impressive as the feat was for being the first more-or-less systematic dig accompanied by a technical report rather than, say, random gouging in the earth accompanied by maps that say "cave in cañon with trees," it was still more random than systematic. And there was certainly gouging of a sort. Del Río and his men smashed and blasted their way through solid walls just to see what, if anything, was behind them, doing a lot more ruining to the ruins than even the jungle had. But in doing so, they also managed to capture a lot of attention for the place.

A surveyor and architect named Antonio Bernasconi and a draftsman named Ricardo Almendáriz both accompanied Del Río, making a detailed map and careful drawings of the place as it was being ransacked in a manner eerily similar to how technical excavations take place today. These, along with additional drawings by another draftsman named Luciano Castañeda who visited the site in 1807, filled out a book called *Description of the Ruins of an Ancient City: Discovered Near Palenque, in the Kingdom of Guatemala, in Spanish America*, an English translation of which appeared in London in 1822. Two more editions followed over the next decade as interest in the place grew. It's safe to assume the British took all this like a slap in the face.

After that, investigations of the place continued pretty much unabated right up to the modern day, including archaeologists from Mexico's National Institute of Anthropology and History reporting the exciting discovery of a small statue of the Mayan maize deity Hun Hunahpu in 2023.

◆ ◆ ◆

The British were already at war with the French when Charles III ascended to the throne in 1759, the very year that the British Museum opened, and the Brits appeared to be in the lead. The Spanish and the English had warred once already from 1585 to 1604, mostly over trade disputes vis-à-vis the New World colonies, although it was never formally declared and basically ended in a truce. Seeing the French starting to lose to the British in the latest naval dust-up and fearing what that imbalance of power might entail, the Spanish king openly talked about jumping into the fray on the French side. After some hemming and hawing on both sides, war was declared between Britain and Spain in 1762, a few years after France limped off the field. It comprised the last two years of the Seven Years War and included no small amount of proxy wars carried out among colonial settlers under their respective European flags.

The Spanish lost.

Old Blighty won Canada during the war, along with Cuba and the Philippines—which they immediately traded back to Spain in exchange for Florida. The British now controlled the entire eastern third of North America, from the icy top of Quebec to the swampy bottom of Florida and all the way west to the Mississippi River. And they had paid a fortune fighting for it.

This would have some consequences a decade later. Something or other involving tea.

◆ ◆ ◆

The natural sciences as a whole underwent a bit of a revolution in Europe and the United States after this period, although institutionalization would be a better term for it. During the late seventeenth and early nineteenth centuries in Europe, the Enlightenment radically reoriented both politics and natural philosophy. British philosopher John Locke, although not a scientist himself, helped lay the foundation with his *Principia Mathematica and Essay Concerning Human Understanding*, in both of which he asserted that human nature was variable, and that knowledge is obtained through accumulated experience rather than by accessing some fundamental store of dogmatic Truth.

That's the Cliff's Notes version of it, at least.

In reality, the Enlightenment was neither a unified nor a uniform movement, with ideas and practices varying wildly by region throughout this period. However, the one thing these fellows all did have in common was wealth. The investigation of the natural world during this period was the pastime of rich and privileged men who were free to wonder about frivolous things like how far away the moon is. It was more of a hobby for snobs than it was a serious endeavor conducted for the good of humankind or a steady paycheck.

Although I will say this for the Enlightenment scientists: they were even better than modern ones when it comes to getting the word out. Public lectures became remarkably popular during the 1700s, offering scientists who weren't engaged at universities or other institutions a way to share their knowledge and ideas with an increasingly interested public. Start times and lengths varied greatly, but they were most often conducted after traditional working hours—for obvious reasons—and attendance ranged well into the hundreds.

This practice was particularly useful to women, who were barred from formal universities and other institutions until the following century. They attended these public lectures in droves.

Not surprisingly, there was a premium on showmanship. Hold ing the public's attention is, has always been, and will always be the bane of scientists and other academic specialists. In the 1700s, this was often accomplished by leaning heavily on demonstrations of things like the principles of physics in practice. Advances in the field of electricity offered exciting new ways of wowing spectators than some boring old lecture, up to and including a popular demonstration by Jean-Antoine Nollet and others called The Electrified Boy. It involved a young lad hanging from the ceiling, stretched out parallel to the floor, on silk threads. The demonstrator would then electrocute him. Because he was suspended in the air using non-conducting material, the electrocution would be harmless, but would also turn him into a magnet. If the crowd wasn't sufficiently wowed by this, a young girl would sometimes be invited from the audience to touch or kiss the boy on the cheek, causing sparks to shoot between them.

All of this was considered useful for the growth of science and the good of society.

◆ ◆ ◆

Back in Enlightenment Europe, the surging popularity of science combined with booming economies in France, Britain, and Spain—because of worldwide theft of labor and resources from Indigenous peoples—helped to spur the institutionalization of science. Universities dated back to just after AD 1000 in Europe, so they weren't anything new, but a helping hand from the Industrial Revolution meant a prolific surge in learning institutions. German universities in particular emphasized an educational ideal focused on constructing a common culture, with high academic minister Wilhelm von Homboldt stating at the time:

> Just as primary instruction makes the teacher possible, so he renders himself dispensable through schooling at the secondary level. The university teacher is thus no longer a teacher, and the student is no longer a pupil. Instead, the student conducts research on his own behalf and the professor supervises his research and supports him in it.

American educators during this time were especially fascinated with this German—or, more accurately, Prussian—model, which is why it looks so familiar to anyone who's attended college in the States. Institutions like Cambridge and Oxford also began emphasizing the importance of research rather than regurgitation, arguably even more than the German schools did since they were still under state control. Broadly speaking, though, science became the focus of universities in the eighteenth and nineteenth century.

In the Americas, the earliest universities were established

by Spanish, British, and French authorities on the lands they'd conquered a few hundred years before, mostly for the purpose of educating their respective colonists while also propagating monotheistic religion. Because what's education without a heaping dose of religion? The first universities in the New World were the University of Santo Domingo, established in 1538 in what is now the Dominican Republic; and the University of Michoacán, established in 1539 in what is now Mexico. Then came Harvard in 1636, William and Mary in 1693, Yale in 1701, Princeton in 1746, and King's College (now Columbia) in 1754. Most of these were established by religious denominations. It wasn't until the Morrell Act of 1862, which granted each state parcels of land they could use to finance new schools, that the Prussian ideal of "academic freedom" was fully incorporated into the American university system. Cornell and MIT were both direct results of this.

Secularization continued apace in Europe, meanwhile, with—in this order—Italy, Spain, and France shifting their universities from sponsorship by religious denominations to sponsorship by the state. They even started admitting women during the latter half of the 1800s. The study of non-scientific but nonetheless scholarly stuff was added to curricula during this time, including courses in literature, languages, economics, psychology, and sociology.

◆ ◆ ◆

The nascent practice of archaeology, meanwhile, was still considered an amateur pastime by most professional scholars as late as the mid-1800s in Europe, and it fell to an army officer and ethnologist named Augustus Pitt Rivers to do the heavy lifting of developing it into a formal science.

Ethnology is the comparative analysis of different peoples and the relationships between them, and it dates to the late 1700s in Europe. Foundational ethnologist Adam Franz Kollár described it in 1783 as "the science of nations and peoples, or, that study of learned men in which they inquire into the origins, languages, customs, and institutions of various nations, and finally into the fatherland

and ancient seats, in order to be able better to judge the nations and peoples in their own times."

It's the study of human groups, in other words. That's all. It relies on another process called ethnography, or the cataloging of cultural traits, for this type of study to be possible. The whole process gained a lot of steam through the end of the Colonial Period in world history, as colonial powers became increasingly nervous about losing control of their colonies—the term "ethnology" was officially coined seven years after the American Revolution—and started thinking it might help things if they understood the people they were subjugating.

Pitt Rivers may or may not have had this sort of attitude, but he was wild about excavation, and he spent seventeen field seasons digging sites from the Roman and Saxon periods using highly methodical and meticulous means that were remarkably advanced for the time. He is often called the world's first scientific archaeologist for this reason. Leaning on the evolutionary writings of Darwin and Spencer, he inferred stages of "evolution" in artifacts, often arranging them in his displays from what he perceived as crudest to most advanced, and in doing so laid the foundation for the principle of seriation.

At about the same time, a fellow named William Flinders Petrie conducted his own impressively scientific investigations at the Great Pyramid of Giza. Despite lots of wild ideas floating around at the time, and even wilder ones about space aliens floating around to this day, Petrie was able to use fine-grained analyses of architectural practices and trends to establish the baseline data still used for studying the Egyptian pyramids today.

Within the hallowed halls of academe, the earliest example of academic archaeology that I can find is that of Olof Verelius in Sweden, who was named "Professor of the Fatherland's Antiquities" at Uppsala in 1662. Although he mostly focused on transcribing and interpreting sagas, like any good Scandinavian in those days, he also published a handbook of Swedish runic inscriptions—though subsequent historians note that he was mostly wrong about them.

Much later, the Institute of Archaeology of the Jagiellonian University at Kraków was founded in 1866. Prehistoric archaeology and ethnology emerged together in Britain at the University of Cambridge in 1904 with the establishment of a Board of Anthropological Studies. The creation of a Diploma in Anthropology at Oxford in 1906 took anthropology away from the realm of sociocultural studies, and teaching in prehistoric archaeology began there in 1946 with the appointment of the first Professor of European Prehistory. And so on.

In sum, archaeology in Europe was founded primarily in studies of geology, history, and "the classics" (that is: ancient Greece and Rome) with just a tiny smattering of evolutionary ethnology. And that legacy can be seen to this day in archaeology's place in European universities. By contrast, formal archaeology in the United States catalyzed with the broader field of anthropology, or the comparative and supposedly objective study of human groups, based at least partly on the notion that Native Americans didn't really have a "history" to speak of.

To quote M.J. Shott, who in turn was paraphrasing Bruce G. Trigger: "Perhaps North American archaeology's submergence in anthropology was an assertion of European superiority over native cultures."

Yeah. Perhaps.

◆ ◆ ◆

This period of increasing scientific literacy also birthed the career of one Dr. Samuel George Morton, a man of singular influence and awfulness. His role in the science of race serves as a useful springboard for studying that "science" in toto.

Morton, like famed naturalist Louis Agassiz, was a pioneer in the science of natural history in the early United States. Morton, like Agassiz, was also profoundly racist. He argued vehemently against the theory of monogenism—the single creation story of the Bible—in favor of polygenism, a theory that posits the creation of multiple races of humans in different parts of the Earth. This was the time when secularization of universities was just getting going, and it lagged in the States because religion has always been a bit of a *thing* here.

Morton poured the foundation of what would eventually become the anthropological expression of race science by being the originator of "American School" ethnology, which claimed that the differences between human groups was one of species rather than culture. Leaning on evidence from the Bible, he posited that all the different human races were created separately and given specific sets of inherent characteristics.

The scientific concept of human biological subsets didn't actually start with Morton. Non-scientific assumptions about groupings and people and the implications thereof probably go back to the dawn of our species, and it was Carolus Linnaeus—inventor of the binomial classification system that gave us names like *Turdus ignobilis*—who first proposed in the early 1700s that there were four "varieties" of humans based on what were then considered the four major continents: Europe, Asia, Africa, and the Americas. Subsequent race scientists like Morton took this idea and ran with it, right off the cliff of reason and into the yawning abyss of madness.

However, Linnaeus isn't often criticized for having invented race science for a couple of key reasons. First, he never used the word "race," believing instead that *Homo sapiens* is a single species comprising several clustered varieties—which is more or less true. Second, his explanation for those varieties was based entirely in extrinsic geographic factors rather than intrinsic value judgments, like how darker skin becomes much more prevalent as one nears the equator—which is also more or less true. He wasn't *entirely* correct, since we now know a host of other selective pressures are also at work, like cultural selection, sexual selection, resource stressors that flip epigenetic triggers, etc. But he was on the right track.

One of the more frustrating things about studying the history of science is realizing just how often the so-called march of progress does an about face and starts marching backward for a while. Geniuses like Linnaeus and Darwin made observations in the sixteenth and seventeenth centuries, respectively, that are still largely credible today—only for people like Morton to come along afterward and use their brilliant ideas in awesomely ignorant ways. It's like someone using the greatest global communication technology ever created to bring back archaic race science or reinstate Medieval serfdom. Sometimes we slip backward for a bit.

The invention of race as a thing is a bit like that. It's far too convoluted a topic to cover in this book, let alone this chapter, but the aspect of greatest importance here is that the process was a lot more recent than most people seem to realize—that and how it was almost entirely economical. The old Christian versus non-Christian distinction held up less and less during the Colonial Period as more and more locals became missionized, which in turn made it difficult to keep track of who was justifiably exploitable for cheap or free labor. To that end, the first official instance of race as a legal category was the 1681 Servant Act in the British colony of Jamaica, which described the privileged class as "white" instead of "Christian." This charter was almost immediately copied for use in the colony of South Carolina, also British at the time, and spread from there on the mainland.

Racial categorization was then embraced in the French colony of Saint Domingue in the late 1700s, followed quickly by creation of legal racial apartheid, mainly because of white plantation managers realizing that many freed slaves were becoming wealthier than they were. Prior to those few years, the quickest way for a newly arrived working-class French guy to jump up in social class was to marry into the family of someone who'd bought their freedom and then invested wisely—often in slaves of their own. Nobody batted an eye at their respective skin tones. After the new race-based laws went into effect, however, batting eyes at skin tones became legally mandated, and people officially determined to be of colored or mixed heritage were barred from the full rights of white citizens. This was a critical component of the Haitian revolution in 1789.

Such was the state of things when Morton was born in Philadelphia a decade later.

In addition to writing and lecturing about how God stamped human pedigrees with quality judgments discernible at a glance, Morton also conducted field science, including the inspection of several mummies from Egypt. He subsequently concluded that European-derived "Caucasians" and African-derived "Negroes" were already distinct races over three thousand years ago, so that must have been the case at the dawning of creation—which, according to biblical scholars at the time (and a few special cases today), had occurred maybe three thousand more years before that. He claimed that skull capacity was directly related to intelligence, reasoning that the more brains you have the more wits you've got, and went on to amass what was at the time the world's largest collection of human skulls.

Based on extensive comparative analyses of this collection, Morton also concluded that Caucasians had the biggest brains, Negroes had the smallest, and American Indians were right in the middle. He then further subdivided the human species into a more elaborate ranking system, with Caucasians as the superior race—Teutons and Anglo-Saxons at the top, Jews in the middle, Hindus at the bottom—and basically everyone else jumbling beneath. The Chinese he called a "monkey race" and the black Hottentots were like "the lower animals," according to studies of the man by archaeologist and historian David Hurst Thomas.

This was all according to God's master plan, Morton insisted. The Caucasian race was first and fairest, and they would always reign supreme because anything else would be antithetical to the proper functioning of God's universe.

As ridiculous as this all seems now, or at least as ridiculous as I hope it seems, Morton and his ideas were both immensely popular at the time. This is at least partly because he often made politically useful pronouncements about where the different human races fit with regard to each other. Contemplating how a lot of ancient Egyptians had dark skin like the people in most of the rest of Africa, for example, Morton quipped: "Negroes were numerous in Egypt but their social position in ancient times was the same that it now is, that of servants and slaves." All that based entirely on the shapes of their skulls. Pronouncements like that made him extremely popular in the pre-Civil War United States for both pro-slavery and abolitionist types, the former because it justified slavery and the latter because it justified treating freed slaves like garbage.*

Prolific artist, slave trader, and bird murderer John James Audubon contributed a not-insignificant amount to Morton's skull collection, by the way. While embarked on journeys into the western American wilderness in the 1840s, Audubon made a prodigious habit of robbing the graves of Native Americans killed by smallpox and Mexican soldiers killed in the Mexican American War.

In one particularly illustrative instance, according to his curated journals, Audubon came upon a chief who'd been reverentially interred in a tree scaffold (a lot of Indigenous peoples on the Plains "buried" their dead by wrapping them in blankets and laying them out on raised poles or in trees). The old fellow was called The White Cow by his Assiniboine clan, and his body was wrapped in two bison robes and an American flag. Audubon and his assistant yanked him out of the tree, sawed off his head, and left the body, blankets, and flag behind to rot on the prairie. This looted cranium and scores of others he bundled off to Morton.

Morton's skull measurements also provided what he asserted was evidence for racial stereotypes, which also helped justify the brutality of colonization here and abroad. This included the notion that Native Americans were designed by God to be "averse to cultivation, and slow in acquiring knowledge; restless, revengeful, and fond of war; and wholly destitute of maritime adventure," in his own words. Never mind the robustly seagoing Inuit, Haida, Mi'kmaq, Inupiaq, Inuvialuit, Chumash, Aztecs, Maya, and pretty much every other Indigenous population that lived near water prior to European conquest. Africans, meanwhile, he described as "joyous, flexible, and indolent; while the many nations which compose this race present a singular diversity of intellectual character, of which the far extreme is the lowest grade of humanity."

The upshot is that human races are outdated, unscientific, ignorant, prejudiced, and ultimately useless made-up categories that are

* This isn't often taught in schools, but many—possibly most—abolitionists in the early United States didn't want to abolish slavery because it was unfathomably cruel. They wanted to abolish slavery because doing so would open up paying jobs for white people. Thomas Jefferson, who famously wrote "all men are created equal" in the Declaration, also wrote in Notes on the State of Virginia about how the greatest evil of slavery is that it makes white men lazy.

nonetheless still employed by the likes of jumped-up social media influencer Graham Hancock, who argued as recently as 2000 that "the Americas were inhabited by a variety of ethnic groups—Negroid, Caucasoid, and Mongoloid." His argument is based entirely on a cherry-picked assemblage of rock carvings that kinda sorta look like African or European people if you chug a beer and then shake your head really hard.

The publication of Darwin's *On the Origin of Species* in 1859 dealt a serious blow to this pernicious nonsense about ranked racial categorization, and his subsequent *The Descent of Man* challenged it even further, but as Hancock and his ilk demonstrate it never went away entirely. Czech-born American anthropologist Aleš Hrdlička, who is often regarded as the "father of physical anthropology," had much to do with its survival in the post-Darwin world.

Hrdlička was the 1903 founder and first curator of physical anthropology at the US National Museum, later renamed the Smithsonian Institution National Museum of Natural History—or simply The Smithsonian. He also founded the *American Journal of Physical Anthropology* in 1918. Hrdlička was intensely critical of African hominid evolution, insisting instead that human beings must have evolved in Europe because that's where the earliest human skeletal remains had been found at the time, although not many people were with him on that.

Out of all of Morton's disciples, Hrdlička is also especially relevant to the history of American archaeology because he insisted that Native Americans had only been here for about three thousand years at the most. He and his colleagues blackballed anyone seeking institutional support for studies of deep antiquity in the Americas, which is why it fell to Black cowboy George McJunkin to blow that apart with his chance finding of a bison kill from approximately ten thousand years ago in Folsom, New Mexico in 1908.

Not surprisingly, Hrdlička was also an advisory member of the American Eugenics Society in 1926, and his work—along with Morton's craniology, Agassiz's efforts to rank and segregate different human "species," and the pseudoscience of phrenology that synthesized itself out of both—was a big help to the Nazis. It is in this supposition, that Native Americans were themselves relative newcomers to the Americas because of misguided notions of racial and cultural evolution and what's written in the Bible and much other nonsense besides, that a lot of early anti-Indigenous racism was cooked.

It wasn't the only source, of course. History has shown again and again how the process we now call fascism—which originally referred specifically to Mussolini's regime, but at this point refers more broadly to efforts by a ruling elite to consolidate unilateral political power—requires a common enemy to rally the people to its cause. Screaming about how "the Indians" are the root of all evil and need to be stamped out differs little from screaming the same thing about "the Jews," "the Muslims," "the immigrants," or "the trans . . . es." It's a recipe that probably goes back to the dawn of civilization.

In this case, anti-Native propaganda was an extremely useful tool for uniting the original thirteen colonies under a shared American identity. The colonies weren't united by much, apart from being British subjects and rather grumpy about it, and rallying the cause for independence was hard going at first. What ultimately tipped the scale for the dissenters was, in large part, fearmongering about Native Americans in colonial newspapers like this 1755 edition of the *Virginia Gazette*:

> Amidst the shrieks of women, the wailings of children, the hideous shouts of savages, and the dreadful din of arms, to what method of opposition would we betake ourselves? Distracted with fear, and the prospect of death in a thousand forms, should we not fall an easy prey to an unrelenting adversary? And what heart can conceive, what language describe the sequel? Virgins defloured by merciless savages: Children pluck'd from the fond grasp of a screaming mother, and deashed by barbarians against the bloody pavement, less obdurate than the unpitying murderers: The recking scalp, stripp'd from the hoary head.

Most damning of all to their readers, these publishers also caterwauled about how the British were using "Indians and [freed] Blacks to help quell the rebellion." In fairness, it was partly true.

A version of this would find its way into the Declaration of Independence about a decade later, where the authors charge that King George III has "excited domestic insurrections amongst us and has endeavoured [*sic.*] to bring on the inhabitants of our frontiers, the merciless Indian Savages, whose known rule of warfare, is an undistinguished destruction of all ages, sexes and conditions." Which is very much in contrast with the merciful and humane treatment of Indigenous peoples at the hands of European colonists—right?

This thinking informed a lot of the earliest archaeology in the United States and is often regarded as a historical hindrance to understanding the deep history of the continent. In the first annual report of the executive committee of the Archaeological Institute of America, for example, the authors lament that "the study of American archaeology relates, indeed, to the monuments of a race that never attained to a high degree of civilization, and that has left no trustworthy records of continuous history. It was a race whose intelligence was for the most part of a low order, whose sentiments and emotions were confined within a narrow range, and whose imagination was never quickened to find expression for itself in poetic or artistic forms of beauty."

In the fullness of time, American archaeologists would be pitted against this propaganda and its attendant philosophy by attempting to depict pre-contact Native Americans as what they really were: people. Happy ones, sad ones, angry ones, charming ones, hunters, farmers, warriors, cowards, healers, builders, thieves, artisans—the works.

Much of the history of American archaeology is a legacy of Sisyphean efforts to prove to the American public that Native Americans are, in fact, fully human. This position contrasts with a lot of very old scientific and government documents testifying the opposite. That shouldn't be much of a hindrance, given the very-oldness of those documents, but in a country where people still worship the Constitution as a living document rather than a shaky set of guidelines written by slaveowners who didn't even have ballpoint pens, it has indeed proven to be one.

◆ ◆ ◆

Curated historical writings can, in sum, be a minefield of horrors. But they can also shed much-needed light on beneficences that have been lost and mostly forgotten, including the tendency of archaeologists and others in the related field of naturalism to write for a general audience rather than exclusively for an academic one. Apart from providing a signaling strategy for didactic egos, specialized language can also be a barrier of entry to non-specialists, acting as a sort of "if you can understand this gibberish, you're good enough to receive its gospel" gauntlet.

Meanwhile, writing in a 1928 report for *Southwest Museum Papers*, Monroe Amsden notes how an archaeological reconnaissance in northern Sonora begins "mounted on three fairly sorry saddle-horses, driving four sore-backed pack-mules, one of which is twenty-eight years old (and looks it)." He also goes on at length about camping etiquette, food—lots of beans and biscuits—and water, and how challenging it is to thrash through jungles of mesquite.* At one point in the tale, he "praised the Mexicans and their federal government highly for the interest they take in preservation of their ruins" to a local farmer, who responds to the flattery by leading Amsden to see and record a few sites near his fields.

Amsden was largely following in the footsteps of Adolph Bandelier, another early luminary in American archaeology who plays a bigger role in the next chapter, and his own reports aren't any less narrative in tone. "The landscape of the Southwest is striking at all times," he notes in his final report for the Papers of the Archaeological Institute of America in 1879. "The plains of Eastern New Mexico are impressive through their immensity and absolute rigidity. They are far from producing the feeling which is created by the ocean. A

* My favorite passage in Amsden's report is probably this one: "As usual, we arose this morning, cooked, ate, washed the dishes, packed and rode on our way. Life in camp is romantic, no doubt, but to the camper it soon becomes plain hard work—a 'dog's life,' as it is sometimes called. The best part of a pack-trip begins the day it ends." This appears in a formal report printed by an august academic institution.

liquid level is never absolutely at rest; the mind, as well as the eye, is always kept on the alert for something to occur, even on the calmest day." About Sonora, and the northern Sierra Madre specifically, he reports how "the cave villages on the Arroyo del Nombre de Dios, in the mountains west of Casas Grandes, lie in a region covered with beautiful pine forests."

Closer to home—for me, at least—is Frederick H. Chapin's *Land of the Cliff-Dwellers*. The volume is a record of two summers Chapin spent in the field, published in 1892. "Drawn thither both by a love for the mountains and cañons and by an amateur's interest in archaeology," Chapin reports, "my narrative will include the twofold experience of the climber and the interested seeker for new archaeological wonders." He even refutes that absurd claim about Native Americans not having poetic or artistic expressions of beauty expressed by the executive committee of the American Institute of Archaeology, remarking on the artistic specialties of various Southwestern peoples and noting how fellow archaeologist Jesse Walter Fewkes devoted considerable attention to Zuni music.

Language like this can be found throughout the pages of many historical reports, books, and edited volumes by American archaeologists, many of which are curated online at places like the Hathi Trust Digital Library.

That sort of language is all-but gone from archaeological reports, these days, but the sentiments themselves are not. Writing for *The Archaeological Record* in 2017, my good friend and former coworker Jamie Hollingsworth recounts: "I've wanted to be an archaeologist since I was a little kid. I grew up camping and exploring all over the American Southwest—being outdoors and exploring seemed like second nature . . . Classic nerd, I know."

Jamie is half Diné and half Scandinavian, or "Navajo-wegian" as she likes to call it, and did a master's thesis on the relationship between archaeology and the Indigenous community. Outside of that, before the need to support her two sons prompted her to find a more lucrative career, she was the fiercest advocate for public outreach I knew in the archaeological realm. To that end, she filmed and uploaded a video series called Dig It in which she asks archaeologists to talk about their favorite aspects of the discipline.

In one of those videos, Great Basin archaeologist Lisa Krussow reports that what she loves best about archaeology is "being outside all day and finding cool artifacts." Pacific Island archaeologist Chris Filimoehala echoes that sentiment: "I've definitely been fortunate enough to have the opportunity, as my career moved into the Pacific, to work in some very remote, isolated, fascinating places." Julie Kramer talks about getting to work in a variety of places and learn from different cultures. Jamie even had me do one of those videos, ten years ago as of this writing, and my testimony was largely the same: the thrill of clamoring through vicious plant life, negotiating jagged rocks, and avoiding venomous beasts to find oneself staring at some gorgeous old thing.

The next step is recording it, which can be tedious. Then incorporating the find into a report, which can be even more tedious. Then sharing the report with interested parties like the Tribes and State Historic Preservation Officers, often in the form of tedious meetings. And then, depending on the nature of the find and the sorts of things that are threatening it, advocating for its protection by government agencies and conservation groups. That part can be tedious to the point of stupefying.

The thrill of discovery keeps most of us coming back again and again. That and the novelty of getting paid to do things like hiking, camping, taking pretty photos, and playing in the dirt—activities a lot of other people pay their own money to do. It almost feels like cheating.

But the biggest motivator for many of us is continuing the fight against people like Morton, Hrdlička, and the late-1700s journalists who breathed fire into genocidal efforts by portraying Native Americans as monstrous villains the way all fascists do with one group or another. Every time I collaborate with an Indigenous individual or group to help understand and preserve irreplaceable material heritage, it's like another big middle finger right in their faces. That keeps me going more than anything else about this practice. The rest, the thrills of adventure and discovery and getting published and all that, is just icing on the cake.

CHAPTER 2

NATURALISTS AND NATIONALISTS

The history of archaeology and the history of Western science have a lot of overlap, but they also developed in markedly different ways along wildly different timelines. The two wouldn't start openly cavorting in the United States until about the middle of the twentieth century, save a few earlier rendezvous—like when Swedish historian Gustaf Nordenskiöld introduced amateur archaeologist Richard Wetherill to the concept of stratigraphy in the 1890s.

Natural philosophy was the dominant form of studying nature and the physical universe in Western society before natural science took its place in about the year 1900. It's most often associated with Aristotle starting in about 400 BC, chiefly because he was the first one to start formally writing about it, although the idea was kicking around Greece for a while before that. In practice, it just means carefully observing nature and trying to suss out direct cause and effect relationships between variables.

As a branch of philosophy, naturalism was also germinated in the same soil as religion.

◆ ◆ ◆

The relationship between Christianity and natural philosophy was a complicated one, prior to this time, with some Christian philosophers—like Thomas Aquinas—seeing what would become natural science as a means of interpreting scripture. Others, however, considered natural philosophy a scary chimera of pagan Greek meddling, putting things like the burgeoning scientific method on par with a pantheon of "false gods" who couldn't keep it in their pants.

The Catholic Church went as far as to drive a hard wedge between theology and natural philosophy or science with the Condemnations of 1210 through 1277, essentially mandating that scientists shouldn't meddle with theology and had better stay in their lane. Stephen Jay Gould would later echo this sentiment in an essay on what he called Non-Overlapping Magisteria, or the notion that science and belief can peacefully coexist provided they try not to play in each other's sandboxes overmuch.

The Condemnations took the form of lists of things that were considered naughty, ostensibly for crimes like pantheism but more realistically because these nosy scientists were starting to find evidence that poked serious holes in the Official Story. Not unlike how a lot of the people condemned for "communism" during the 1950s were actually labor organizers trying to let everyone know how much they were getting screwed over. The Condemnation of 1210 included a total ban on the books and commentaries of Aristotle on pain of excommunication, something Umberto Eco later turned into a major plot point in his excellent historical fiction *The Name of the Rose.*

More pointedly—and more than a little hilariously—the Condemnation of 1277 expressly forbid anyone from repeating the Aristotelian proposition that a soul separated from a physical body cannot suffer from bodily fire. Which makes sense. How could an incorporeal soul with no nervous system possibly "burn" for eternity? I can see why they wanted that one nipped in the bud.

Then came the 1500s and a whirlwind of overhead punches to accepted Western worldviews. Christopher Columbus, a mostly incompetent and objectively horrible man from the Republic of Genoa who had to beg the Spanish for three ships after the Genoese doge laughed in his face, nonetheless managed to prove that there were entire continents full of people and animals not accounted for in the scriptures. Astronomical observations by the likes of Copernicus, Tyco Brahe, and Galileo Galilei also demonstrated that the Earth was not the center of the universe—or, at any rate, that the Sun was the center of our local solar system—and was furthermore just one of many planets.

That last one dealt a serious blow to biblical assertions about the basic shape of reality, but also proved many of Aristotle's own ideas about heavenly bodies and how they operate to be totally wrong. Galileo, Kepler, Hobbes, Locke, Bacon, and others began wandering away from both theological recapitulation and Aristotelian natural philosophy, not taking the road less-traveled so much as cutting a new one through the weeds. Bacon in particular had a radical vision of how this new emphasis on unencumbered scientific inquiry should look: Supported by the state, rather than the church, and informed by collaborative research rather than according to some extraneous agenda or other. Radical notions, at the time—and still alarmingly radical in the United States in 2026.

Natural philosophers came more and more to see the natural world as comprising mechanisms of all shapes, sizes, and levels of complexity—but mechanisms, nonetheless. By the end of the 1600s, the scientific revolution was off and running, although religious notions weren't jettisoned from science in their entirety, even to this day. The reason we still talk about "laws" in science, like the law of gravity and the law of thermodynamics, is because these were understood to be cosmological constants, i.e., God's laws about existence. Thou shalt accelerate toward the Earth at a rate of 9.81 meters per second squared.

The concept of scientific laws that emerged in seventeenth- and eighteenth-century physics gradually supplanted this idea, leaving little room for divine action in explanations of how things do things. But use of the word "laws" in science remained canon.

This move to adopt method-driven natural science over more fluffy-minded natural philosophy resulted in numerous discoveries of discrete, law-abiding mechanisms underlying all their questions. Things like laws of gravity and laws of thermodynamics and the like. And the more this happened, the more their obsession with mechanism and order became dogmatic—something that would represent a problem for the early practices of ethnology and scientific archaeology. A problem we have yet to shake.

Because these early academics considered Native Americans to be backward, or degenerate, or somehow unfavorable in the eyes of the Christian deity, their graves—and bodies—were considered fair game for plundering, at least in the English colonies. Early naturalists were thrilled with this attitude, regarding Indigenous people to be part of the "natural" as opposed to "human" world and, therefore, candidates for scientific investigation without moral scruples.

◆ ◆ ◆

Meanwhile, the Spanish took a somewhat less nuanced approach to the deep history of the Americas. Throughout Mexico and Peru, starting in the 1500s, the Spanish had a policy of destroying, defacing, or simply hiding any material vestiges of Indigenous people's pre-Christian history. Special efforts were directed at erasing Aztec identity and sovereignty from the planet's surface. The general theme was one of enforced forgetting or cultural erasure, with the hope that Indigenous people would eventually forget all about their "savage" roots and go forward into the future as good little Christians in the Christian land of El Virreinato de Nueva España. It was also a lot easier to ignore the immense pre-Hispanic monuments in places like Meso- and South America because it only took a few decades or so of neglect before the encroaching jungle made them vanish—something a bit harder to pull off in the arid American Southwest.

This is an unfortunate but common tactic throughout history whenever there's a totalitarian regime change. In ancient Egypt, the pharaoh couple Akhenaten and Nefertiti were all-but obliterated by subsequent pharaohs after they tried to install monotheism in the 1300s BC. Julius Caesar did the same to a lot of places that he conquered during the first stage of Roman expansion, simply wiping several entire societies off the map when they refused to cooperate, so that now the only record of their existence that remains is in Roman military records. The Taliban and China would eventually do something similar to long-standing emblems of Buddhist culture in Afghanistan and Tibet, respectively.

All this ground to a halt south of the border by the mid-1700s, followed by that brief period mentioned in the last chapter when the Spanish tried to go blow-for-blow with the British in both warfare and archaeological plundering. Neither went especially well for them.

Things took a more interesting turn in the Americas, however, when the period of colonialism gradually—and far from uniformly—gave way to the period of independence therefrom. Thomas Jefferson's report on the burial mound excavation, for example, included a claim that Native Americans were the "First Americans" in an obvious attempt to transform them from victims of colonialism into national symbols of the new republic.

However, the Spanish had taken a lot more inclusive attitude toward the Native peoples—if not their material history—at least after some grossly genocidal bumps early in the process. Although the prevailing philosophy among the English colonists was that Indigenous people were somehow less than human, the Spanish Crown had convinced the Catholic Church to proclaim that Indigenous people are indeed human and possessed of human souls. Souls that needed saving. One result of this was a lot more mingling between Spanish and Indigenous people. By the early 1800s, a rapidly increasing number of Mexican citizens were of part-Indigenous and part-European ancestry.

Because of this, by the time of Mexico's struggle for independence from Spain in the early 1800s, a large number of Mexicans were studying and publicizing the surviving monuments of groups like the Aztecs and Mayans as points of nationalistic pride. This led to the usual partitioning among society members along totally made-up and often very muddled "racial" lines, although that was all the rage in the Americas by then.

Legal racial categories were abolished when the First Mexican Republic was established in 1824. A national museum was also created because of this the following year and was reorganized in 1831 with the addition of a library on natural history, written history, and archaeology. A law was also passed in 1829 forbidding the exportation of Mexican antiquities to other countries. This had much to do with the fact that by the early 1800s, according to one of the only official census efforts for which we still have copies—that of Guadalajara in 1821—less than half the city's population was considered Spanish, approximately 40 percent were considered Indigenous, and about 10 percent were considered *mestizo*. Less than 2 percent of all sampled individuals gave Spain as a birthplace.

Thus, pride of place had taken hold in Mexican culture by the early 1800s, with most of the population identifying as either Creole Spanish or altogether non-European. This is how archaeology became a tool of nationalistic pride south of the border. The incredible monuments of the Aztec, Mayan, and earlier Teotihuacan cultures that were destroyed or obscured by earlier colonial authorities now became symbols of Mexico's non-European ancestry, which was pretty bad ass. It helped fan the flame of independence, if nothing else, and inadvertently helped some of those sites get restored and protected.

This attitude was heaped particularly high on the Aztecs and their material and cultural histories. The term Aztec is itself a shortening of the Nahuatl phrase *aztēcatl*, meaning "person from Aztlán," one of their points of origin as identified in Mixtec cultural narratives. According to this narrative, the god Huitzilopochtli led their ancestors to central Mexico from a homeland located someplace to the north called Aztlán or "land of the white herons." Chicano activists would adopt this concept as a sort of metaphor for Mexican American identity later in the twentieth century, but at the time it served to help Mexican authorities and independence boosters anchor their claims to the land extending from the Yucatan Peninsula all the way up to the southern border of Canada.

The state of Nuevo México—which at the time encompassed most of the present-day American state of New Mexico and all of Arizona, along with sections of Texas, Colorado, Kansas, and the Oklahoma panhandle—was particularly rich with archaeology that looked, to their eyes, more Mesoamerican than not. Most Native American groups at the time of contact were seen as foragers, after all, but here in the greater Southwest a bunch of them were found living in huge stone houses with the crumbling remains of other stone houses scattered all over the place. Moreover, they were found cultivating maize and beans, herding turkeys, and even having scarlet macaws in their iconography and material history.

There was no denying it, as far as Mexican officials were concerned. Places like Aztec Ruin in modern New Mexico and Montezuma Castle in modern Arizona were *clearly* built by the ancestors of the peoples who developed into the mighty Aztec empire—which is why those places are still called that today.

◆ ◆ ◆

Meanwhile, over in the Old World, it was also the use of archaeology as a tool of nationalism in Denmark that helped set the tone for "prehistoric" archaeology in both Europe and the Americas in the early nineteenth century.

Patriotism in Denmark was heightened at the time, helped in no small part by the British bombing the hell out of them in 1801 and 1807 because they were allies of Napoleon. Bolstering this was a growing interest in the concept of evolution, which long predated Darwin among Enlightenment intellectuals—he just came up with the theory of descent and adaptation by natural selection. It was already understood by many intellectuals at the time that evolution is indeed a thing that happens, and it appears to happen to societies as well as organisms. This position was endorsed with particular zeal by an antiquarian named Christian Jürgensen Thomsen.

In 1807, after the second round of British bombs were done shaking everyone up, a Danish Royal Commission for the Preservation and Collection of Antiquities was established, and they immediately set about collecting antiquities from all over Denmark. In 1816, they retained Thomsen to catalog and prepare this immense collection for exhibition at the National Museum of Antiquity. His first problem was how to arrange them.

Thomsen decided to arrange them all chronologically by subdividing the "heathen" period into successive stages of stone, bronze, and iron. He was no doubt inspired by first-century Roman poet and philosopher Lucretius, who was supposedly the first to propose subdividing pre-literate historical ages by metals, which would be a fun way to do it if we still did. We'd be living in the Rare Earth

Metal Age right now, following the Steel Age, which followed the Aluminum Age, and maybe the Gold Age before that since my own ancestors were invading everywhere on the planet to find it . . .

This three-part scheme is still in use in Europe today, at least to a point. Stone Age, Bronze Age, and Iron Age remain the basis for understanding the deep history of at least mainland Europe for kids and freshman before getting hit with the brutal reality of just how incredibly complex history really is.

With adoption of Lucretius' three-tiered system of social evolution also came his problematic concept of progress. He conceived the process of cultural progression or evolution to be analogous to the life history of a human being. According to a poem he wrote,

> For the nature of the world as a whole is altered by age. Everything must pass through successive phases. Nothing remains forever what it was. Everything is on the move. Everything is transformed by nature and forced into new paths . . . The Earth passes through successive phases, so that it can no longer bear what it could, and it can now what it could not before.

The general conception of the world's creation by Roman thinkers at the time was that all humans and animals were spontaneously created from the materials of the Earth by the goddess Venus—hence the word *mater*, meaning "mother," being the etymological root for words like "material" and "matter." Once we'd been birthed by Venus, the human species was then expected to grow and mature the same way that individual humans are, in a very definite direction with very definite stages. From embryo to infancy to childhood to adulthood in the case of biological life history; something analogous in the case of sociocultural history.

Thus the idea came bundled to Thomsen, after passing hands through successive generations of intellectuals. Most historians agree that he was the first to take this idea and put it into action, arranging the prehistoric artifacts placed under his care into the first true chronological system of pre-literate antiquities. He was also the first to perceive and recognize "typologies" or constellations of shared traits, and assign them to different layers or soil strata where they were encountered during excavation. An unmistakable trend emerged from this process: the earliest or Stone Age artifacts were almost always found beneath the Bronze Age ones, which in turn were almost always found beneath the Iron Age ones.

In one fell swoop, Thomsen minted the concept of archaeological seriation, the concept of archaeological typology, and the concept of relative dating—where you don't have an absolute (that is: calendrical) date for your excavated material but you do know that this came before that. Much like how modern biology involves the grand synthesis of Darwinian evolution by natural selection with Mendelian population genetics, modern archaeology wouldn't look the way it does without the grand synthesis of general Euro-American antiquarianism with the Danish concept of regarding the material history of pre-literate peoples as essentially "readable" under proper analysis. It would, however, take another generation before the British caught up with the Danish.

It fell to John Lubbock, 1st Baron Avebury, to incorporate the three-age system into British archaeology and "improve" it with the addition of that other burgeoning social science: ethnology. In his 1865 book *Prehistoric Times*, Lubbock subdivided the Stone Age into older (Paleolithic) and newer (Neolithic) phases, while leaving the Bronze and Iron Ages unsliced. He cast the whole model as schema for the natural and inherent developments of human culture, from that of "non-metallic savages" to the fully civilized people who looked and acted suspiciously like himself. A later addition by Hodder Westropp was the Mesolithic, or "middle Stone Age," which was quickly picked up by geologists at the time, although it would take some years for archaeologists to find it in the material record.

Westropp also further subdivided the Stone Age into three phases and five stages. The first stage, now called the Lower Paleolithic, contained stone artifacts that were "roughly knocked into shape." The second phase included flint flakes that were knocked off cores, starting with a mode that consisted mostly of scrapers and heading toward a mode that included projectiles. The third and more advanced stage comprised flint flake tools that were "carefully chipped into shape." The fourth and fifth stages represent the Neolithic, which includes things like axes with finely ground edges.

You can see the comparative metaphor of the life history of a human or other animal heavily influencing interpretation of these findings, and not without good cause. The earliest artifacts were indeed core tools rather than flake tools. The flake tools themselves get more complicated over time. Hammering and chipping gives way to more refined methods of grinding and shaping and so on. What this doesn't tell you is anything about the people creating them.

Drawing a direct line from "these tools are primitive" to "these people were primitive" is the problematic bit. The smartphone in my pocket bombarding me with spam calls is astronomically more complicated than the rotary phone my grandparents were still using when I was a toddler, but that doesn't mean my grandparents were brutish savages compared to subsequent generations. Knowledge simply accumulates over time, and technology often becomes increasingly more complicated as a result, but the people utilizing both are still fully formed People the whole way through.

Nonetheless, the idea of rigid orthogenic stages of cultural evolution was an appealing one at the time, especially considering the legacy of colonialism. Which is why it was so excitedly adopted and expanded by nascent evolutionary archaeologists. The belief that progress is an inherent aspect of the human condition was codified in the work of nineteenth-century American scholars like Lewis Henry Morgan in the 1870s, whose Barbarism-Savagery-Civilization schema* helped underscore widespread mainstream belief in the biological inferiority of Native Americans at the time.

What's more, the rapidly declining numbers of Indigenous individuals—through things like disease, enslavement, and outright

* For reasons I don't quite understand—probably owing to my fundamental disdain for psychology—humans seem inordinately attracted to schema whose components come in sets of three. Three strikes and you're out, comedy comes in threes, the Holy Trinity, the three pillars of sustainability, the three branches of government, popular film and literary trilogies, etc. Whatever it is you're selling, if you package it in sets of three, you'll find at least a few buyers.

slaughter—gave these thinkers the impression that Native cultures were going extinct, which further jived with the concept of cultural progress being analogous to Darwin's recently published notions about adaptation. Species that fail to evolve go kaput. The fossil record is full of them! Never mind that this posits the process of evolving as a zero-sum, do-or-die form of gradual improvement rather than a non-directional process of adaptation to environmental specifics. Evolution was a form of progress, in their eyes—and if you don't evolve you perish, so it stands to reason that societies that fail to progress are doomed to oblivion. And so Indigenous peoples in the Americas came to be regarded as living fossils in mainstream colonial mindsets owing to the comparative primitiveness of their material culture. Again, this hasn't entirely gone away.

◆ ◆ ◆

As for why the peoples of the New World hadn't "progressed" beyond what Europeans considered primitive technology: reasons are legion, and chief among them is the fact that progress itself is a bit of a myth. Progress is a relative concept—you progress up a hill, or toward a goal, or you get tougher or healthier or richer compared with other people. Without a stated goal, you don't really progress. You just sort of move along.

Concomitant to this is how they didn't really need to progress in the Western sense. Necessity is the mother of invention, after all. Absent a cultural mindset obsessed with one-upmanship, why devote all your free time and energy to developing a fancy new gadget when the ones you have already work just fine?

Behavioral ecologists refer to this as an expression of what they call the technology-intensification model, which posits that innovation only occurs when it makes economic sense to invest energy into doing so. The model involves a great deal of complicated math derived mostly from studying other animals and then shouting that it also applies to humans—and I happen to agree with them on this point—but for simplicity's sake I like to think of it as the Three Little Pigs model.

We all know the story. Three pigs, one builds a house of straw, one builds a house of wood, one builds a house of brick, and then a wolf blows the first two down. It's a classic Western fable with a classic Western lesson: always do the biggest and bestest you can at all times because life is one big competition and if you lose it's your own fault. But what if there wasn't a wolf? If there's three months in a summer, and it takes one month to build a straw house, two months to build a wood house, and three months to build a brick house, then building a straw house in a wolf-free forest would give you the biggest advantage. You could spend the next two months gathering food, working out, finding a partner, and just generally living your best piggy life while the overachiever spends the entire summer building a brick house just to spend the winter starving alone inside it.

You do not, in other words, need a sledgehammer to swat a fly. You don't even need a flyswatter—just make sure to wash your hand afterward. And you don't need to develop extravagant means of travel and murder when there's no pressing need to cross entire continents at rapid speed or blow great masses of people to bits.

◆ ◆ ◆

Meanwhile, not very long before Darwin published his *Origin*, the United States engaged in a war with Mexico that would culminate in the US–Mexican boundary jumping south by about seven-hundred miles. The land that would become the American Southwest was full of communities that predated those of the founding fathers on the east coast, by literally thousands of years in the case of the Pueblo communities at places like Hopi and Acoma. And, according to archaeologist and author Stephen H. Lekson in his excellent *A History of the Ancient Southwest*, these people "had historical claims (and sometimes legal title) to the land [they occupied]. Or did they? Were the Indians latecomers to a land originally home to greater civilizations now vanished? Aztecs perhaps?"

This is where the long-standing Mexican story about a homeland called Aztlán located someplace to the north collided with the popular (then as now, sadly) notion that Indigenous peoples of Contact-era North America had moved in after some earlier, more advanced civilization departed. The "Indians" of that time were considered by white scholars as too primitive to have learned how to build things like stone houses all on their own, and what's more they had all these Mesoamerican crops and birds all over the place. Something special must have happened there before all these fellows turned up.

This attitude pervaded a lot of both academic and mainstream literature at the time, eventually becoming Mormon canon and the underpinning of a lot of modern conspiracy theories. It was also a political exigence. If it could somehow be proven that Indigenous groups in the American Southwest—in particular the Pueblos, with their impressive stone villages—were "merely imitators, not heirs, of the long-departed Aztecs, then Americans were justified in displacing [them] from the Southwest's best agricultural lands" to quote Lekson again.

To that end, Adolph Bandelier—a student of Lewis Henry Morgan—was sent to the Southwest to resolve this issue. The Archaeological Institute of America wanted to know once and for all if the ancient sites of the American Southwest were indeed Aztlán. Bandelier concluded that they most certainly were not. His results, published as the *Final Report of Investigations Among the Indians of the Southwestern United States*, hit shelves just in time for the four-hundredth anniversary of Columbus' arrival.

This, too, wound up having nationalistic consequences, at least of a sort. Bandelier's intellectual progeny, including Edgar Lee Hewett and Charles Lummis, were *proud* Southwesterners who despised the primacy of New England philosophy and politics dominating the entire country. They manifested this by building a distinctly regional intellectual architecture, including the founding of departments and institutions, creation of numerous monuments, and composition of a body of writing that anchored the ancient Southwest firmly in The Southwest rather than in broader American history.

Lummis was particularly appalled at what he identified as the East Coast notion that the American Southwest had anything to do with the Aztecs. Writing in his 1925 book *Mesa, Cañon, and Pueblo*, Lummis fumed that "Montezuma—who was the war-chief of an ancient league of Mexican Indians, and emphatically not 'Emperor of Mexico,' despite Prescott and the Romantic School—never had anything more to do with our Southwest than Napoleon or Caesar did. The talk of Aztecs in New Mexico or Arizona is wholly absurd and without a shadow of foundation." He's here railing against a fellow named William Prescott, a Massachusetts-based historian who'd published a book in 1843 called *History of the Conquest of Mexico* which strongly hinted that Aztlán was in the American Southwest.

I've got a copy of *Mesa, Cañon, and Pueblo* that I happened to find in a thrift store, years ago, and a striking amount of Lummis's prose still holds up today. The opening paragraph is especially poignant:

> Our years come insensibly upon us, unmeasured, not half realized, till, on a sudden, we notice that the children have grown up! "It seems only yesterday"—but today, children no longer, they stand tall as we are; aye, or perhaps tower over our gray heads. And their talk is no more prattle—they are speaking of a changed world, and maybe of babies of their own.

I hear you there, Charles.

On the topic of The First Americans, he also pulled no punches. The chapter begins with Lummis noting that "many brutal and many foolish things have been said by man; but probably the most idiotic as well as the most brutal of all the sayings that have passed into proverb is, 'The only good Indian is a dead Indian.'" He ends that paragraph with one of the most salient sentences I've ever seen: "Race hatreds are the most ignorant and the most harmful of all human passions."

Again, this was published in 1925, a full ten years before that most ignorant and most harmful of all human passions brought us the Holocaust. Lummis wasn't predicting it or anything—he was just commenting on the racially motivated genocide already perpetrated in North America that would end up inspiring it.

Lummis would go on to use examples from ethnography and archaeology to argue that Indigenous peoples of the Americas were not ignorant savages but fully sophisticated people whose civilization just happened to differ from those of Europe. So much so that notions of their having non-local roots is insultingly ludicrous. "Where did they come from—these First Americans, these prehistoric [Aborigines] of the soil we have mostly stolen from under them? They came from—Here! No fable dies harder than the Protean myth that the American Indian derives from the orthodox 'Cradle of Mankind.'"

No, indeed. Versions of it can still be found even now.

◆ ◆ ◆

We've got some fun tales here in the States, to be sure, although I would argue the best—and often the most humorous—case studies of absurd nationalism in archaeology all come from elsewhere. But they're relevant here, nonetheless.

Nationalism and archaeology have been close bedfellows in a lot of areas and instances since at least the eighteenth century, with Mexican scholars pointing at ancient Indigenous monuments and even Thomas Jefferson trying to make some weird point about how the Moundbuilders imply that colonists should be proud to be Americans. Although one could argue that the practice predates formal archaeology by a considerable gap.

Not unlike Khaemweset and his efforts to restore and glorify Egyptian Old Kingdom material history over three thousand years ago, Aztec civic leaders did something similar, pointing to the crumbling remains of the mighty city-state of Teotihuacan. Teotihuacan predated the Aztec capital city of Tenochtitlan by about a millennium before it fell into rapid decline—because of the climate, or because of a volcano, or because of civil unrest; nobody is sure—nearly a thousand years before.

The name of Teotihuacan was given to it by the Aztecs when they found the place and its awesome but crumbling temples in the 1400s, and it roughly translates to "the place where the gods were created." Aztec architecture and religious iconography closely follow that of Teotihuacan in what appears to have been another case of using archaeology, or at least material history, to anchor a then-extant culture into a deeper history of the place. This despite there being no direct ties between the two societies.

The overarching theme is that interpretations of material history can be used just about any way people want to use them, given that material history differs from written history in that it's, well, unwritten. This means it can also be manipulated for nationalistic purposes, often in the form of identifying one's own ethnic group with some ancient group based on what may or may not be confident evidence. Sometimes those groups don't even exist. Nationalistic archaeology has therefore historically been a sort of revolving door for pseudoscience in archaeology, or "pseudoarchaeology," and to a certain extent it still is.

Pseudoscience was not invented in the modern era. Not even close. Pseudoscience, generally defined as statements or practices that claim to be rooted in scientific fact but are incompatible with the scientific method, probably dates back to the invention of modern science itself—typically pitted between 1572 and 1704.* Early examples include spiritualism, homeopathy, and phrenology, the latter of which played a big role in the Nazi atrocities. Eugenics, which the Nazis also loved, could be considered early-ish pseudoscience as well. Later examples include creationism, ancient astronauts, flat Earth theory, adrenal fatigue, blood-type diets, the teachings of L. Ron Hubbard, numerology, palmistry, dowsing, parapsychology, some silliness about jet fuel and steel beams, the whole alpha/beta male thing . . . I could go on.

Pseudoarchaeology is no different. Given that archaeology is the investigation of the past by analyzing physical remains in the present, pseudoarchaeology comprises statements or investigations of the past rooted in pure speculation without any objectively verifiable

* Astrology and acupuncture are holdover examples that predate the scientific era in that they claim to be rooted in natural systems whose existence are not objectively testable, making them arguably the earliest examples of pseudoscience. But that's a tricky line of reasoning. It makes more sense to say they started out as folk wisdom and then refused to surrender when the scientific method came out swinging.

evidence. Usually because it flew away in a spaceship, or it sank beneath the waves, or the government or some nefarious organization is covering it up, or it got buried by a volcano, or an asteroid blew it all to hell, or our instruments aren't sensitive enough, or some other "only I can see and read the golden tablets" kind of nonsense.

Most studies of pseudoarchaeology list it as just another example of pseudoscience, usually falling between "parapsychology" and "psychic surgery" if the list is alphabetized. But it's really not an example of pseudoscience so much as a branch of it, complete with its own methods, models, devotees, and loads and loads of examples. I already mentioned one above, the dreaded ancient astronauts myth, but at least that one is barred from entry to the hallowed halls of academia. Not all of them are.

Take the case of Piltdown Man. In 1912, an amateur archaeologist named Charles Dawson claimed to have discovered the "missing link" between apes and humans—in England. His find, purportedly part of a human-like skull in the Pleistocene gravel beds near the village of Piltdown in Sussex, was reported to Arthur Smith Woodward, Keeper of Geology at the Natural History Museum at the time. The two men worked together making further discoveries in the area, including a set of teeth, a jawbone, more bits of skull, and primitive stone tools.

The results of their find were reported later in that year at a Geological Society meeting, where they announced they had found evidence of a human ancestor living in England roughly half a million years ago. This came after the discovery of Neanderthals and *Homo erectus* elsewhere in Africa and Eurasia, which understandably made Victorians and their ideas about Anglo superiority a bit nervous. So, for that and related reasons, most of their academic audience accepted their story in good faith. Racists throughout the country rejoiced at having found evidence that the deepest roots of human anatomical modernity were British.

It wasn't until about three decades later, after new dating technologies were introduced to the field of archaeology, that the biggest flaw in this narrative was exposed: the bones were actually fifty-thousand years old. Dawson and Smith Woodward's date was "off" by a whole order of magnitude. Once that crack appeared, other people leapt in to enlarge it, including Oxford University's biological anthropologist Joseph Weiner and human anatomist Wilfrid Le Gros Clark. They teamed up with Kenneth Oakley, the researcher who'd used radiometric methods to re-date the bones, and together the gang concluded that the skeletal remains came from at least two separate individuals: a human and an ape (most likely an orangutan).

They published their findings in 1953 in *Time* magazine. The article related how the Piltdown Man fossil was actually a composite of three different species—a medieval human skull, a five-hundred-year-old orangutan jawbone, and chimpanzee teeth. Someone, maybe Dawson, had then foisted the illusion of age onto this chimera with an iron solution and chromic acid. It was an elaborate hoax, whose staying power was anchored partly in the scientific supposition that large brains preceded modern diets (hence the large orangutan jaw and chimp teeth), and partly out of desperation to retain the notion that all human evolution led inexorably to London.

That seed proved the hoax's undoing, and a technical article fully refuting the find was accepted for publication in the scientific journal *American Scientist* two years later.

Insidious ignorance of this nature leeched into American politics way before then in a variety of ways, but nowhere more overtly than in the form of Andrew Jackson, a top contender for the evilest president we've ever had—up until recently anyway.

Among other things, Jackson was responsible for the Indian Removal Act of 1830, which authorized the president to grant lands located west of the Mississippi River to Tribes located within the existing states in exchange for their homelands. Most of them said "no." Over the next decade, around sixty thousand Native Americans from at least eighteen groups were moved by force instead, with the southern Tribes winding up mostly in Oklahoma and the northern Tribes winding up mostly in Kansas. An unknown but presumably very high number of them died as a result. This is the reason there are so few Native American reservations and communities east of the Mississippi to this day.

Although many American citizens at the time supported this legislation and its attendant actions, significant opposition popped up almost immediately. The act only passed by a hair's breadth, and opposition to the policy by civilians, religious organizations, and a handful of senators lingered on.

This was all to Jackson's considerable chagrin.

In his Second Annual Message—what we now call the State of the Union Address—he excoriated bleeding-heart ne'er-do-wells by asking: "What good man would prefer a country covered with forests and ranged by a few thousand savages to our extensive Republic, studded with cities, towns, and prosperous farms . . . and filled with all the blessings of liberty, civilization, and religion?" Pondering the *non sequitur* of committing genocide in order to create a space full of liberty is a fun mental exercise.

Within that same paragraph, Jackson bemoans those who "wept over the fate of the aborigines" and praised the forced and bloody removal of Indigenous peoples from the eastern states as a "happy consummation" of Indian policy. After all, the Native Americans themselves were relative newcomers to these lands and were furthermore guilty of perpetrating far worse crimes on an earlier race of white people—the ones who built all the temples and mounds and whatnot. "In the monuments and fortifications of an unknown people, spread over the extensive regions of the West, we behold the memorials of a once powerful race, which was exterminated or has disappeared to make room for the existing savage tribes," Jackson proclaimed.

His argument was basically this: Why should we be nice to these brown people when they were so ruthless and bloodthirsty toward the entirely fictional white people that we invented out of whole cloth to justify our own ruthless and bloodthirsty treatment of them?

Thus were the seeds of "white genocide" planted in the American body politic, to paraphrase journalist Alexander Zaitchik in a 2024 article for Observatory. Thomas Jefferson had observed with his own eyes how descendants of the archaeological Moundbuilders were still around and knew exactly why the mounds were built, and every effort to prove the existence of a vanished civilization predating the Native Americans beyond mere speculation turned up empty—then as now. But it was a popular idea, and popular ideas have a habit of sticking around whether they're realistic or not.

Fast-forward to the era of Piltdown Man, and pseudoarchaeology no longer appeared in American politics as such. Discoveries like Folsom and Clovis had much to do with this, but so did the simple fact that it had already done its job. Many of the laws and policies this type of insidious lunacy inspired have yet to be repealed, and some of them are currently enjoying a comeback tour.

Where it didn't cease to appear was in popular culture.

◆ ◆ ◆

Modern examples of that sort of mental gymnastics are typically benign in comparison. We can be proud, at the very least, that pseudoarchaeology—especially versions of it with a nationalistic bent—are largely barred from both politics and academia in the United States today. Emphasis on *largely* rather than *entirely.*

Take the cosmology of the Church of Jesus Christ of Latter-Day Saints (also known as the Mormons). Their story begins when the Earth was created shortly after Jesus won a fight with Lucifer to become the chosen savior of the soon-to-be humankind. Then came the standard biblical story about Adam and Eve and the apple of knowledge in the Garden of Eden, followed by a lot of wandering around, before the LDS version picks back up with an Israelite named Lehi journeying from the Middle East to Mesoamerica around 600 BC. His descendants became two tribes, the Nephites and the Lamanites, the latter of whom are allegedly Native Americans.

The Lamanites are presented as "ferocious, blood-thirsty" people in the *Book of Mormon*—not surprisingly, given the cultural and political climate when the book was published in 1830. The Nephites were pure and more industrious, but they became obsessed with wealth and power, so they weren't exactly ideal people either. Jesus himself appeared here in the Americas shortly after his death in AD 33, and preached pacifism to the Nephites and Lamanites for a good long while, but they eventually ignored him and set about warring with each other again. In about AD 385, a Nephite prophet named Mormon started writing all this stuff down on golden tablets that could only be read in the presence of a special seer stone.

Mormon died soon after during a climactic battle against the Lamanites, during which nearly all the slightly nobler Nephites were destroyed, and his son Moroni wrote a few more things on the golden tablets for about thirty-six years before he also died. Roughly two thousand years later a guy from upstate New York named Joseph Smith found the golden tablets and the seer stone, without anyone else laying eyes on them, and translated them into the *Book of Mormon*.

So that, canonically, is why there's impressive temples and solar calendars and so on in places like Tikal, Tulum, and Chichén Itzá. They weren't constructed by Indigenous peoples of the Americas, who seemed to early Mormons to be far too primitive to pull that off unassisted. White people built all those things, after heading west through the Pacific Ocean against prevailing westerly winds and currents that stymied even the best-trained mariners for more than two millennia afterward and before being killed off by the Lamanites in so thorough a manner that not one single vestige of their presence has ever been found. For all that, the Lamanites were cursed with darkened skin, stamping them as spiritually impure and *de facto* second-class citizens forever after. This, in turn, shaped LDS policy—and, by extension, Utah state policy—toward Indigenous peoples and their status as being basically unworthy of managing or even occupying the lands where they'd dwelled since time immemorial.

Actual Mormon history commenced in the 1830s during the Second Great Awakening in the early United States as Americans struggled to figure out who, exactly, they were. They weren't Native Americans, of course—but they weren't Europeans either. They'd just fought two whole wars over that. The newly minted Americans were struggling for a sense of identity, and people oozed out of every conceivable corner to offer one. Quakers, Shakers, Spiritualists, the Reformed Mennonites, the Unitarians, Adventists, Christadelphians, various Amish groups, and others popped up during the early- to mid-nineteenth century like Wack-a-Moles.

Smith founded the religion in a part of New York about an hour north of my own birthplace, and not long after which the whole community was forced to flee to Ohio where he was charged with banking fraud. Rather than submit to the arrest, he and his congregation hustled to Missouri, where the faithful believe the Garden of Eden was located. Mormons bought up a lot of land in Missouri that was recently "liberated" from its Indigenous inhabitants thanks to the Indian Removal Act, which Andrew Jackson justified with the same type of pseudoarchaeology Mormons were espousing, before being run off again.

The Mormon caravan then stopped in Illinois where Smith was killed in 1844 before ultimately landing in Utah on July 24, 1847.* Over one hundred enslaved people were brought with the Mormon emigrants, who were also encouraged to purchase or enslave Native children so they could forcibly educate those children into the faith. Brigham Young explained this initiative in 1851 after the founding of the township of Parowan:

> I spoke upon the importance of the Iron County mission and advantage of the brethren fulfilling it. I advised them to buy up the Lamanite children as fast as they could, and educate them, and teach them the gospel, so that not many generations would pass ere they would become white and delightsome people, and said that the Lord could not have devised a better plan than to have put us where we are, in order to accomplish that thing. I knew the Indians would dwindle away, but let a remnant of the seed of Jospeh be saved.

The rampant Native slave-trading stoked a lot of Indigenous hostility toward the Mormons, not surprisingly, culminating in attacks like the massacre of Captain John W. Gunnison and a number of his men in Millard County in 1853. That's less than a decade after the Mormons arrived.

---

* This date is still celebrated as a state holiday in Utah, officially as Pioneer Day to the faithful and unofficially as Pie-and-Beer Day to the unfaithful.

Policies gradually changed after that, with polygamy and slavery and, eventually, canonical racism being officially abolished by 1977, although their stance on non-heterosexualities hasn't shifted. Nor has widespread teaching that the so-called Lamanites are at least part of Native American ancestry.

◆ ◆ ◆

However, to be fair to the Mormons, this notion that the mysterious and majestic aspects of a non-white culture must be proof of earlier occupation by an advanced civilization of white people wasn't invented by them. Its roots are deep, and its usages are legion.

Greek philosopher Plato wrote lavishly about a vanished civilization called Atlantis that was more advanced than any known civilization at the time—nearly three-thousand years ago, for the record. Atlantis was described in his works *Timaeus* and *Critias* as a naval empire that ruled over the entire Western world, until it pissed off the deities living atop Mount Olympus by attempting to conquer Athens and was wholesale scuttled in response.

Atlantis never actually existed. It was a fictional fabrication crafted by Plato to serve as an allegory of the hubris of nations, the population-scale equivalent of Icarus eschewing caution and flying too close to the sun—or any other purely metaphorical narrative.

Not many people in those days believed there was a real man named Icarus who built enormous wings using feathers, stray blanket threads, scraps of clothing, and beeswax to fly out of prison, any more than people who read The Lorax these days believe a guy named The Once-ler caused an ecological collapse in Thneedville by chopping down all the Truffula Trees. It's just as likely not many people in Plato's time thought the purely symbolic civilization of Atlantis was real, either. But a lot of others came to believe it subsequently.

Much later, in 1759, French Enlightenment author and philosopher Voltaire published *Candide*, a satirical treatise on—among other things—trying to find happiness and perfection in a world full of unpredictability. It also includes the character Pangloss, who provides what has evolved into the greatest send-up of confirmation bias in studies of evolutionary adaptation.

> "It is demonstrable," said [Pangloss], "that things cannot be otherwise than as they are; for as all things have been created for some end, they must necessarily be created for the best end. Observe, for instance, the nose is formed for spectacles, therefore we wear spectacles . . ."

From this, the term "Panglossian" was coined by Stephen Jay Gould to refer to any instance where biologists argue that because they see a pattern suggesting optimal behavior, costly signaling, or what have you, there's a fair-to-good chance that it's just projection of the researcher onto behavior they think forms a pattern conforming to their theories. Behavioral ecologists hate this.

Voltaire also made much of the wisdom of the Far East in his book, but not to pedestalize or fetishize those cultures—at least not entirely. Again, the book is a satire, and Voltaire's point was to show Europeans that they shouldn't act all high and mighty all the time, as if they and they alone are the pinnacle of God's creation and therefore deserve mastery over all the Earth just because they have the greatest numbers of both telescopes and cannons. Candide ends up finding the happiness for which he searched his whole life in Ottoman Turkey following some coruscating stuff about his beloved becoming uglier by the day and a heap of mystical Eastern philosophy on the nature of good and evil. It was all supposed to be a big joke.

But a lot of Enlightenment thinkers missed the joke, as did people who came after them. Occultist grifter Helena Blavatsky, for one. Writing in the mid- to late 1800s during the rise of what historians broadly categorize as Spiritualism, the Russian-American author and pseudoscience enthusiast openly and, somehow, convincingly mused that the great peoples of the Far East were indeed endowed with secret ancient wisdom, most of which was "rooted" in now-lost continents. This is the theosophist concept of Root Races, or stages in human evolution according to cosmological creative thinking, and one of those roots was—and I wish I didn't have to keep typing this—Atlantis.

In her fictional cosmology, the superior race of humans evolved along a specific trajectory that ultimately ended in disaster for them. There were the Polarians, the Hyperboreans, the Lemurians, the Atlanteans, and the Aryans. The original Polarian race reproduced like amoebas—because Blavatsky thought sex was a recent and abominable adaptation—and the succeeding Hyperborean race occupied all the places now covered in ice. When the ice sheets came, they fled, stopping over at Lemuria (the South Pacific) before moving to Atlantis roughly 100,000 years ago. Then Atlantis sinks and what are now the Aryans flee to other locales, where they lose their magical powers through the practice of frivolous miscegenation. It's all a bunch of hilarious nonsense.

But the philosophy at the heart of this hilarious nonsense had a definite appeal for certain types of thinkers soon after she published them in her seminal book *The Secret Doctrine*. The idea was that all the really great things in the world were the work of the Aryans, or the fully realized *Homo sapiens* race at the absolute top of its game tens of thousands of years ago, but that the Aryan race had become diluted through time by mixing their superior blood with the inferior blood of lower races living in the regions they came to occupy. It's not hard to draw a line between that part of European history and historic American archaeologists frantically looking about for who *really* built the mighty temples of places like Chichén Itzá, since the racially inferior Mayans certainly could not have.

This is also the mystical-theosophist-pseudoscientific foundation of Nazism. Seriously. That's the myth underlying the motivation to kill millions of people in order to back-breed humanity into its purest form.

Behold, the master race.

◆ ◆ ◆

The term "Aryan" itself derives from the Indo-Iranian word for "noble," and was predicated on the notion that Proto-Indo-Europeans were a distinct race separate from—and superior to—all the other human races purported to exist at the time, which is a moving target at best. The roots of this hypothesis go all the way back into the late 1700s and the search for the linguistic origins of the Proto-Indo-European language families, but it was adopted with gusto by Nazi scientists in the 1930s as a *cause célèbre* for their supremacist race science—especially after Voltaire published his book about how Westerners shouldn't feel superior to the great minds of the East and people like Helena Blavatsky took that message entirely the wrong way.

Nor did the Nazis' specific brand of pseudoscience fail to include its own measure of pseudoarchaeology. In 1938, party leader Heinrich Himmler sent a team of five researchers to Tibet to search for the origins of the Aryan race. Adolf Hitler believed that ancient Aryans had most likely entered India from the north about a thousand and a half years before the 1930s, having thereafter committed the crime of mixing with non-Aryan peoples throughout Eurasia and losing the racial attributes that made them superior to everyone else. That would mean about AD 430, or roughly three decades before the fall of the Western Roman Empire, so you'd think Roman historians might have noticed a thing like that.

Hitler and the Nazis also believed the bit about how the point of origin of their mythic superior race was Atlantis, where people of the "purest blood" had once lived before fleeing to the Himalayas when their island home sank beneath the waves. In 1935, Himmler created a unit called the Bureau of Ancestral Heritage within the *Schutzstaffel* or SS, the elite guard of the Nazi regime. Its task was to find out where the *Übermenschen* of Atlantis had fled after their homeland went all *überschwemmen*, using the fancy new science of archaeology to find and trace evidence of their migration before falling into disgrace through miscegenation in places like India. The 1938 expedition to Tibet was directed to find evidence of this.

The men themselves were a hoot. According to historian Vaibhav Purandare, one of them was a hunting enthusiast who'd accidentally shot his wife in the head while blasting at ducks from an unsteady boat. Another one was an anthropologist obsessed with phrenology whose role in the expedition was, in a very literal sense, headhunting.

They got lucky in their travels because of the Nazis' clever adoption of the swastika as their party symbol. Swastikas are among the oldest complex symbols known to humankind, with versions popping up all over the planet, including in Indigenous cultures here in the Americas—where, according to Hopi Tribal Registrar Alfred Lomahquahu and several Diné fellows I know, they represent what we call the Big Dipper constellation circling around the North Star. The constellation—technically an *asterism*—rises in a different and predictable configuration throughout the year, and then rotates around the unmoving North Star every night in a pattern that looks remarkably swastika-like.*

How the swastika first came to the attention of what would become Nazis is another fun twist in the history of archaeology in Western culture. Back in the 1870s, a German amateur archaeologist named Heinrich Schliemann commenced an earnest search for the ancient city of Troy—immortalized in Homer's epic poetry as the place where pantomime horses reached their military apotheosis—after finding a cache of ancient artifacts in what is now called Hisarlik, Turkey. Believing that the mighty kingdom of Troy lay at the lowermost stratigraphic levels of the discovery location, overlaid by more recent and frankly unimpressive ruins, Schliemann assembled a large team and spent a few years blasting haphazardly downward.

In so doing, to paraphrase classicist Kenneth Harl of Tulane University, Schleimann's excavation accomplished what the Greeks could not: leveling the walls of Troy.

To understand this uniquely baffling circumstance, it's important to remember how easy it is for people to take historic hyperbole and run wild with it. Troy was an ancient city—blocky walls, garbage piles, stables, privies, etc. But "Troy" in the minds of adventurous treasure hunters of yore was something more like El Dorado or, lord help me, Atlantis. It was larger than life, with towering minarets, streets paved with gold, all that sort of stuff. It had

* In a . . . let's call it *interesting* twist, a group of Diné, Hopi, Apache, and Tohono O'odham representatives gathered in Tucson in 1940 to ceremonially denounce the Nazis' "acts of oppression" and foreswear the use of swastikas in their "blankets, baskets, art objects, sand paintings, and clothing"—something they'd done for hundreds or thousands of years up to that point.

to be. Why else would Homer write an epic poem about it? All these boring buildings and uneven roads and other crumbling nonsense lying around must therefore be some more recent and degenerate settlement, Schliemann reasoned, with the glory that was Troy glittering quietly beneath it.

To make a long story short, he really did find the lost city of Troy, so he gets credit for that, even if he and his team completely destroyed the remains of Troy while searching for the remains of Troy by digging for the remains of Troy underneath the remains of Troy. In the process, Schliemann found immense numbers of ceramic vessels with swastikas on them.

And so the symbol passed into Prussian culture as emblematic of, in effect, the magnificence of peoples long past.

In Hindu culture, the swastika was and remains a symbol for good luck or fortune, and this is also true for Hindu spinoffs like Buddhism—the dominant belief system in Tibet for over a thousand years before the daffy mythologies of spiritualism were even invented. For this reason, more than probably any other, the ragtag team of Nazi archaeologists deployed by Himmler were accepted warmly in Tibet, all the while gathering skull measurements, actual skulls, and thousands of artifacts to build their case that the Buddhists and Hindus of the region were the perverse and degraded offspring of wayward Aryans getting frisky with the locals.

The efforts of these plucky adventurers to find archaeological evidence of a mythical race of super humans from the mythical civilization of Atlantis among the actual peoples of the Tibetan Plateau were cut short by the war, but a lot of the materials they collected can still be found in German and American museums. Stories like these gradually morphed into notions of Nazis as bloodhounds for mystical ancient artifacts in the *Indiana Jones* films, where they get punched, kicked, stabbed, run over, shot, melted, and turned to dust in very satisfying ways.

The myth of an Aryan race still endures in some circles, however—despite having as much objective reality as Atlantis, or Piltdown Man, or the Easter Bunny—and people in the real world continue to suffer because of it.

These and similar beliefs came to the Americas in the same colonial package as rats, smallpox, and the Bible. Certain types of researchers maintained a dogged and remarkably earnest search for evidence of lost tribes of white people and/or literal aliens to explain how the Indigenous peoples they saw as subhuman were nonetheless able to do so many impressive things. When they can't find any hard evidence, slick bullshit suffices.

So, to recap, a bunch of wildly unrealistic fiction provided subsequent policymakers with an excuse to pass ridiculous laws and inspired subsequent researchers to engage in desperate searches for evidence. Which they never find, because it doesn't exist, because it's all wildly unrealistic fiction. This is how you end up with Nazi archaeologists, totalitarian theocracy, and unhinged anti-vaxxers being appointed Secretary of Health and Human Services.

◆ ◆ ◆

Pseudoscience and pseudoarchaeology are both alive and well today. While they aren't exactly welcomed with open arms by most of academia, they still make their way there at times, with people conducting research, earning degrees, and publishing supposedly peer-reviewed papers with such compelling scientific evidence as "perhaps the materials disappeared" or "this petroglyph kinda looks like a horse." It could be just laughable and annoying, if it happened in a vacuum where no other humans dwelled, but belief underlies conviction, conviction informs politics, and politics results in policy—some of which have proven to be extremely harmful.

The Mormon creation myth that includes horses and chariots in Mesoamerica when a group of ancient white people started building all the impressive architecture also informs the culture of millions of voters to this day. It's not just wacky-but-ultimately-inconsequential gibberings by imaginative thinkers with questionable agendas and heavily biased or nonexistence oversight. These things can and do have an impact on the real world.

Bunk science is intentionally misleading and potentially dangerous stuff. biblical scholars believing their book trumps the established science of evolution is fine when it's done in the comfort and privacy of their own homes, but when the pseudoscience of creationism is forced into schoolbooks as a valid alternative, we veer down a dangerous path. Same with pseudoarchaeology. The fact that *Ancient Aliens* will have been on the air for fourteen years when this book hits shelves is troubling, as is the popularity of Netflix "documentaries" like *Ancient Apocalypse* and *Queen Cleopatra*—the former of which is entirely motivated by Graham Hancock's belief that actual archaeologists are part of a worldwide conspiracy to hide the truth about our species' history, and the latter of which is a vanity project by Jada Pinkett Smith that asserts the entire nation of Egypt is wrong about its own past.

These aren't on the same scale as Andrew Jackson using pseudoarchaeology as an intellectual substructure for his genocidal nationalism, or the Nazis using pseudoarchaeology to argue for the existence of a superior race to which our species could return if we filtered all the inferior ones out of the gene pool—both of which have resulted in acts of heinous brutality. But they are playing the same sport. The one that uses phony versions of the past as a motivator for how we treat people in the present.

CHAPTER 3

COLLECTORS AND CHRONICLERS

The next phase in the earliest iteration of American archaeology involves a lot of C-words: collectors and chroniclers, but also cavalier attitudes toward Native Americans that gradually gave way to curiosity about their cultures. Underlying all that, however, was control. Control of the lands, first and foremost—and, as a second-order priority, control of the history inherent to those lands.

History is a living thing, after all, as I am often wont to repeat. I don't mean a living thing in the sense that it eats and breathes, of course. I mean living in the sense that it grows, changes, and evolves over time. It's a domain of narrative about the past that's created by human understanding—which also grows, changes, and evolves over time. It "lives" in that it carries the breath of life we impart into it. And the predominant Western mindset is that all living things need to be controlled, especially if there's something about them that's scary.

Throughout the bulk of the nineteenth century, American archaeologists—whose country now extended from sea to shining sea—didn't give much additional thought to the people that first inhabited it. Much of the practice of archaeology is, after all, the study of material residue from the distant past as a means of anchoring one's own culture into the deep history of a given location. And, except for a few colorful chaps arguing for mysteriously vanished Eurasian progenitors of people like the Maya, early Euro-Americans knew well enough that their culture wasn't anchored into the deep past of the Americas.

That's part of the reason, anyway. The other part was proactive reticence to investigate the matter by those best-equipped to do so.

Intellectual curiosity has, until quite recently, been the playground of the extremely privileged. We used to speak of "a gentleman and a scholar" because most of the time those words were synonymous. A scholar, from the Latin *scolare* which means approximately "leisure," was a person who could fritter away the days of their lives studying curiosities instead of working for a living.

Sometimes this meant being born into wealth, while other times it was the result of patronage or the dumb luck of getting "discovered" by rich people who appreciated their talents. Tycho Brahe had as one of his patrons a man named Peder Oxe, a Danish finance minister and Steward of the Realm. Galileo, Kepler, and Copernicus were also enjoyers of patronage, with Galileo having even provided the moons of Jupiter as a "gift" to the Medici dukes who thanked him with a title and court position. So, in case you were wondering, several of Jupiter's moons are owned by the Italians.

The same was true here. Thomas Jefferson is often credited as the first American archaeologist, and he also owned an immense plantation and at least six-hundred human beings during his life. Benjamin Franklin engaged in numerous studies of electricity, in addition to inventing bifocal glasses and central heating, after becoming fabulously well-to-do as a publisher. Even the rough and rugged Wetherills of Mesa Verde, ranchers though they were, had most of their biggest archaeological expeditions funded by the heirs to the Bab-O Soap fortune.

Along with all this goes the basic fact that people with a lot of wealth and privilege don't typically love being presented with evidence that they're standing on someone else's property, so they don't often go out of their way to look for it.

◆ ◆ ◆

That concept of personal property—and the differing philosophies underlying its interpretation—deserves some attention as it, too, winds up playing a major role in the life history of American archaeology. The very idea of "owning" land is a foreign concept in most Native American philosophies. Instead, to paraphrase Diné conservationist Talia Boyd, many or most Native perspectives about the land describe it as a transactional relationship, more like the Western concept of ecology than that of ownership. And, as such, it implies responsibilities the way that any healthy relationship does.

This serves as an even better heuristic for understanding how wide the chasm stretched between Indigenous and early American philosophies. No group of people is ever a monolith, but in general terms you've got one side who don't believe ownership is a natural component of any relationship and another side who think even connubial relationships consist of a man and his stuff.

Renowned journalist and war correspondent Sebastian Junger meditated on these points in his 2021 book *Tribe: On Homecoming and Belonging.* At one point, Junger relates how "it may say something about human nature that a surprising number of Americans—mostly men—wound up joining Indian society rather than staying in their own." This was a trend that went in only one direction when it wasn't being forced.

Take the infamous case of the HMS *Bounty*, a British vessel that sailed to Tahiti in 1787 under Captain William Bligh to gather breadfruit plants for provisioning British slave colonies. After five months in Tahiti, during which the crew mingled with the local Tahitian tribespeople and even married a few of them, Master's Mate and Acting Lieutenant Fletcher Christian led a mutiny that saw the captain and just under half the men offboarded while Fletcher and the other half sailed back to the islands. There's a 1984 film about the event called *The Bounty* that does a remarkably solid job of reenacting the tale.

But it happened a lot more often than that. This is one of those weird little tidbits in American history that doesn't often appear in mainstream history books: a downright shocking number of early European colonists and Euro-Americans either left home to join Indigenous communities in what they were pretty sure was a better life or were captured as prisoners by Indigenous warriors and just chose to stay with them. For all the criticism it otherwise rightfully warrants, *Dances with Wolves* absolutely nailed the ways in which Native American lifestyles appealed to historic white dudes. It wasn't long before loads of American women, regarded as little more than washing machines and brood mares in Puritan America, followed suit.

In one instructive instance, Junger reports how a white woman named Mary Jemison was captured by the Seneca in early 1755 and became so enamored of Seneca life that she "hid from a white search party that had come looking for her." Jemison would end up marrying two Indigenous men in succession, raising the children born thereby, and later narrated the content of a book called *Narrative of the Life of Mrs. Mary Jemison* that recounted her life and why she chose to remain with the Senecas rather than return to the oppressive American colonial culture. The fact that she calls herself "Mrs. Mary Jemison" is itself a cheeky assertion, since married women were legally regarded as Mrs. [Husband's Full Name].

Sentiments like these were a big part of why newspaper publishers and other propagandists in the late 1700s stoked anti-Indian fire as a tactic to attempt to consolidate sentiments across the colonies, the same as Nazis did with the Jewish community in the 1930s and far-right groups do with immigrants and the LGBTQ+ community today. The other reason for that ramped-up campaign to depict Native Americans as nothing but bloodthirsty brutes was to try to stem the tide of colonists realizing life was better without cops, taxes, or churches.

This tide was halted at last when most Indigenous groups were driven off their ancestral lands for good with the end of the Indian Wars and the official closing of the American West a little over a century after Jemison was captured. By that time, everywhere was owned by somebody, be they private citizens, domestic or foreign companies, Tribal governments in the form of reservations, or the federal government on behalf of the citizenry in the form of public lands.

This precipitated one of the biggest differences between American and European archaeology. Material history and other resources located on public land is *de facto* public property, which implies those things are "owned" by the public. Ten miles to the west is land owned by the state, and ten miles to the east is land owned by Fred

Johnson. This creates a fragmentation of material history that simply doesn't occur—at least for the most part—in the Old World. Many times I've seen the boundaries of archaeological sites with sharp edges and corners that absolutely did not exist when those sites were occupied during ancient times, and it's because the researchers didn't have permission to cross into someone else's property.

Things are a bit different in Europe. Excavating or damaging sites located on private land in places like Greece and Sweden, for example, is forbidden by law without government permission. Federal law No. 245 in Russia, passed in 2013, made all movable archaeological objects in the ground, on the ground, or underwater officially state property. There's a similar statute in Belarus. In Italy, ownership of artifacts vests in the Italian government based on the idea that the primary proprietor of cultural heritage is the national public.

Looming over these and other country-specific examples is the Valletta Treaty of 1992, formerly known as the European Convention on the Protection of the Archaeological Heritage, which aims to protect the material heritage of Europe "as a source of European collective memory and as an instrument for historical and scientific study." It included a mandate to establish certain codes of conduct and permitting methods whether on public or private land. As of 2018, it was ratified by forty-six states, including all but two of the forty-four member states of the Council of Europe, plus the Holy See and Luxembourg.

Not so in the United States. Not for a whole bunch of reasons.

◆ ◆ ◆

The concept of private land ownership as we know it today really started in England with the Norman conquest of 1066, when William the Conqueror declared that the whole of terrestrial Britannia was, in effect, his. He then parceled the land out to various nobles, friends, and relatives, and of course the Church.

Much of this land was known as either "waste" or "commons," land that was technically owned by one toff or another but was open for use by the public for farming and grazing, and at the start of the

1500s this was about thirty percent of mainland England. However, starting in the twelfth century and then ramping up like crazy in the sixteenth century, a process called "enclosure" saw the closing of the commons by a series of legislative acts carried out by the aristocracy and gentry, effectively depriving access by commoners and reducing the commons from thirty percent down to right around three percent.

Dispossessed and disenfranchised people often fall back to default communal survivalist settings. This is one of those rare cases of seemingly universal behavior among humans, although it tends to play out in very different ways than people expect. The *blitzkrieg* strategy of the German military during World War II, for example, was predicated on the assumption that if you cause extreme panic in a given population by bombing the shit out of them, they'll become ungovernable animals and tear each other apart. In fact, the aerial bombing campaigns had the opposite effect: it created a sense of solidarity, because being part of a community in resistance to widespread and monstrous aggression gave them a sense of comradery that everyday life in Western culture just doesn't encourage.

This is repeated over and over in human history, right up to the present. Media coverage in the wake of Hurricane Katrina, for example, portrayed the post-deluge situation as lawless chaos and looting, because that's the sort of thing American media salivates over, when in fact most of what emerged in the immediate aftermath was entire neighborhoods of people helping each other out and "looting" food that was otherwise going to sit on store shelves and rot.* Things went rapidly and unexpectedly sideways, in other words, and rather than cowering in fear or sucking the marrow out of each other's bones they worked together to address the calamity.

In Merry Olde England, people who were no longer able to farm or hunt following what was essentially privatization of public lands—something for which we should probably start preparing ourselves here in the modern US—turned to whatever means they could to get by, including things like theft, thuggery, and prostitu-

* Not that this prevented mainstream journalists from characterizing them as howling savages, of course. Tradition is tradition.

tion. Trading sheep for people in the commons meant that people were flocking like sheep into the cities, and they were treated like vermin in response. Although, they often helped each other out and formed entire coalitions to do so. A lot of historians think this is one of the major roots of "gangs" in Western culture.

Something similar occurred in North America up to about 1763, when England finally held a commanding grasp on the entire eastern seaboard after removing most of the other colonists from the region. Land ownership had morphed into a defining characteristic of the American colonies, given how the English were in the Americas practicing English things, and a lot of the push for westward expansion was the result of non-landowners seeking to escape the same sorts of enclosure practiced back in their homeland—something that was fiercely resisted by the Crown at the time.

The imperative was to "learn from the abject failure of the British to slow frontier settlement" by creating an entire society of farmers, which would "postpone the dreaded emergence of a propertyless proletariat of white people," in the delightful words of historian Alan Taylor. This was fundamentally reliant on the systematic acquisition of Indigenous-occupied land by whatever means necessary, as well as the forced subjugation of imported African peoples into slavery.

The latter edict was a result of earlier experiments to force Indigenous peoples into slavery often ending with them dying of imported diseases or simply disappearing into the wilderness they knew so well, along with a general consensus that enslaving white people via indentured servitude—the very thing that injected most of the founding population into the colonies in the first place—was morally reprehensible.

When the United States adopted and then ratified its federal Constitution in 1789, it declared that "[t]he Congress shall have power to dispose of and make all needful rules and regulations respecting the territory or other property belonging to the United States." The Constitution does not define "public lands," exactly, but lands that were not under private Euro-American or state ownership were generally considered public or common at the time of the Constitution's adoption. Bear in mind this was before the Louisiana

Purchase and the war against Mexico, so we're talking about the lands extending from the coast to the Mississippi and from Quebec down to the northern border of Florida.

◆ ◆ ◆

Because of all this, some lands inhabited by Indigenous peoples were considered "public" land despite being very obviously occupied, albeit not occupied by many. By this point, Indigenous groups in the east—especially in New England, where colonization by the British was densest—had already been dispossessed of much of their land.

With the adoption of the Constitution and the acquisition of land through the papal Doctrine of Discovery, among other means, the federal government became an immense landowner by the early nineteenth century. In 1812, the year we very nearly stopped being an independent nation thanks to a few gripes over trade and government policies toward the Natives, the federal government began the process of disposing (that is: turning over for private development) portions of that land. To that end, the General Land Office (GLO) was formed, an agency that played a vital role in westward expansion.

The GLO was surveying and disposing of government land into private lands, wherever it made sense to do so, and thereby created the earliest legislative distinction between public and private lands. During its existence, the GLO administered two of the nation's most significant land ownership and disposal laws: the Preemption Act and the Homestead Act. By 1849, the GLO had become part of the Department of the Interior, and in 1946 it was reborn as the Bureau of Land Management.

Meanwhile, purchase of the Louisiana Territory from France in 1803 prompted then-President Thomas Jefferson to conceive and support the Lewis and Clark Expedition, which aimed to explore the northern plains and Pacific Northwest from 1804 to 1806. Its stated purpose was to survey and map the newly acquired territory—people these days tend to forget how big the "Louisiana Purchase" was, but it extended from modern-day Louisiana all the way to Vancouver—and to find navigable transportation routes.

So little was known of the interior Americas at the time, and Europeans were still so shaken by the discovery that the Americas existed at all, that Jefferson confidently expected the explorers to find dinosaurs on their expedition. This makes more sense when considered alongside the fact that dinosaurs were only formally described by scientists about a century earlier, and a lot of intensely religious Americans simply couldn't wrap their heads around the idea of an Earth that was millions of years old and included whole hordes of species that God allowed to go extinct. Some of them still can't.

They didn't find any dinosaurs, but the Lewis and Clark Expedition was a remarkably successful endeavor for its time. One that would not have been nearly as successful without the support of Indigenous communities and individuals who guided Lewis and Clark along the way, including one who ended up being "commemorated" on the Sacagawea golden dollar coin that contains exactly zero gold. A more fitting metaphor I cannot imagine.

◆ ◆ ◆

Back in the 1800s, many Americans believed strongly in Manifest Destiny, a religio-nationalistic myth purporting that Americans and their institutions had special standing with God. Because of this, their mission was to redeem or "reclaim" places like the vast American West and make it into an agrarian paradise for Americans by decree of the Almighty Himself. It was basically an American spinoff of the Doctrine of Discovery, which had its origins deep in European history.

As with so many other ills that accompanied Western colonialism—patriarchal hegemony, cutthroat capitalism, religious impunity, officialized heteronormativity, fascistic militarism, and so on—it all more or less began with the original colonists, the Romans. Long before the empire was Christianized by Constantine in AD 313, the Romans considered themselves an intensely moralistic lot. Yes, they were militaristic to the point of all-but worshipping the art and craft of warfare, but they always insisted on having a moral justification for doing so. The ancient fetial law (*ius fetiale*) decreed that "no war was acceptable to the gods unless it was waged in defense of one's own country or allies," according to Roman historians. An appeal to the gods was thus an essential exigence for legitimizing any war to the fanatically religious and superstitious Roman citizens.

Naturally, this allowed for quite a lot of whimsy on the part of expansionist generals like Gaius Julius Caesar, who used the hasty migration of several Gallic tribes in his direction (they were, in fact, fleeing from Germanic attackers on their own northern border) as reason enough to "defend" far-away Rome by conquering and subduing the lot of them. This was the first major act of imperial expansion by Rome, and it set a bit of a precedent. The fact that Caesar was massively in debt to the Gauls at the time was, of course, pure coincidence.

As it was for Jupiter, so it became for the godheads that followed Him as trends and political allegiances shifted along with the religions attached to them. In AD 274, emperor Aurelian made the worship of Latin deity *Sol Invictus* (literally "Unconquered Sun") the official religion of the empire. Worshipers of Sol Invictus celebrated a holiday called *Dies Natalis Solis Invicti* ("Birth of the Invincible Sun") every December 25th to mark the celestial turn toward springtime, and when Constantine decided to Christianize the empire a little later, he wisely kept this popular holiday on the calendar so the people wouldn't tar and feather him. That's how we got Christmas.

By the time of Constantine, the Roman empire occupied pretty much all of modern-day Europe, and when the western half "fell" by AD 476 it did so into the hands of culturally Romanized locals. This would come back to haunt Europe in a big way when Hitler and Mussolini decided it was time to get the old *Senātus Populusque Rōmānus* up and running again some fifteen-hundred years later.

During the Medieval Period that followed the dissolution of the Pax Romana, a lot of distinctly Roman notions and ideas were still very much in vogue, including the list of colonialistic grievances mentioned above. These beliefs and practices weren't retained because they were ethical, or even sensible. They were retained because, as a carefully constructed architecture of ideas, they were very effective at keeping the powerful in power and keeping the lower classes at each other's throats so they wouldn't rise in revolt.

To that end, going back as far as the 1100s, papal doctrines or "bulls" decreed to anyone who was interested that Christian monarchs could seize any land not held by other Christians. This was the legal, spiritual, and political justification for things like expanding one's kingdom, deposing rival monarchs, dispossessing or enslaving pagan locals, and genocide. One such bull, issued in 1455 and aptly titled "Romanus Pontifex," granted the Portuguese a blanket sanction and operative monopoly on the trade of enslaved Africans. Thirty-eight years later, in 1493 (one year after Columbus arrived in Hispaniola), Pope Alexander VI issued a bull called "Inter Caetera" that gave God's alleged assent to Christian explorers' seizure of lands in the New World, as well as the conversion, enslavement, or massacre of whomever happened to be living there.

The latter has been dubbed the *Doctrine of Discovery* by subsequent historians. British comedian Eddie Izzard* joked that imperialism occurred through the "cunning use of flags" in the 1999 stand-up special *Dress to Kill*. "No flag, no country!"

Izzard's timeless hilarity aside, it really was that simple. Millions of native peoples in the Americas, Australia, New Zealand, and parts of Africa and Asia were told simply that their brutish presence was not up to the *official* standards of land ownership as handed down to enlightened Europeans by Himself above. This was especially true in the Americas, where—again—the philosophies of many, if not most, Indigenous groups didn't even recognize land ownership as a thing.

What happened next—aside from the direct genocide of countless people via brutality and the indirect genocide of countless more through the spread of disease—was a widespread, systematic severing of people from the lands with which they'd maintained a close, intimate relationship for millennia.

* To head off any quibbles: Izzard uses feminine pronouns and goes by either Eddie or Suzy, these days, but maintains that the choice is up to the speaker. She was Eddie when that comedy special was recorded, so it makes for an easier reference to cite.

Severing that deep-rooted ecological connection was only implicit in the Doctrine of Discovery, chiefly because the founding principles of ecology didn't really calcify until the 1700s. It took that long for Western scientists to realize things weren't just, you know, kind of there in the world, but instead existed in transactional relationships with everything around them. Eventually, however, understanding this relationship—and the power that can be gained by severing it—evolved into full-fledged national policy. Hence the mass re-location of many Indigenous communities in the United States and Canada to places far away from their ancestral homelands, where they would, in true Pax Romana fashion, feel too disconnected and disconsolate to rise in revolt.

◆ ◆ ◆

Thereafter, land ownership became a defining aspect of what it meant to be American, not because of British enclosure of the commons but as a reaction against it, with all the land that wasn't privately owned being owned by the government for use by all citizens in perpetuity without the risk of pesky aristocrats snatching it all up. It was to be a whole continent of farmers who possessed their own homes with freedom to graze and till the commons, beholden to neither tyrants nor oligarchs, united in cause while independent in spirit, with liberty and justice for all. Supposedly.

The implications of this land ownership stuff in the early twentieth century led to a strict and distinct dichotomy of policies vis-à-vis archaeology: material history located on public land was given federal protection starting in 1906 with the Antiquities Act, while material history located on private land was—and mostly remains—completely at the mercy of the landowner.

The former situation had much to do with Richard Wetherill and his brothers, who began excavating the mighty cliff dwellings of Mesa Verde in the late 1800s and popularized the whole shebang at the World's Columbian Exposition in Chicago in 1893. Wetherill's diggings at Chaco Canyon in particular enraged Edgar Lee Hewett of the Smithsonian Institute, and much of the wording he provided for the Antiquities Act was specifically intended to give Wetherill the boot.

History is written by the victors. As hackneyed and threadbare as that statement has become, it is nonetheless a fundamental truth—one that bedevils succeeding generations of historians to no end. The legacy of the Wetherill family is a useful case study in this regard. Richard and his brothers weren't singled out as exceptional rascals so much as singled out as outstanding and handy scapegoats for what were actually general trends at the time, sometimes in direct opposition to their own views and practices.

As historian Harvey Leake asserted in a clarification piece written for *The New York Times*, the Wetherills were always thinking about historic preservation to a much greater degree than most people in their day. And disinterested they were. In the mid- to late 1800s, the bulk of professional American archaeologists were East Coasters schooled at places like Harvard on European-style studies of material history. Although the mounds of the Mississippi River valley were known to them and remained a focus of much puzzlement despite Jefferson having confidently asserted in the 1700s that at least some of them were tombs built by the ancestors of the Natives still living nearby, most white American scholars still assumed Native Americans were relative newcomers without any real history worth exploring.

Back in Mancos, the Wetherill family immediately set upon two seemingly contradictory trajectories: excavating the cliff dwellings and pushing for their protection. The excavation part was regrettable, and although it was done to the highest possible standard of the day—and was not illegal to boot—it's still a huge and ugly mistake that occurred in historic times from which we can learn important lessons today.

Topmost among those lessons: just because something is legal doesn't mean it's the right thing to do. Slavery was legal. Driving while intoxicated was legal. Beating your children was legal. Beating your *wife* was legal. In today's world, thanks to the Reagan administration's revocation of the FCC's fairness doctrine, it's legal to portray monstrously biased propaganda as "news." None of which strikes me as especially right things to do. Laws can be tricky like that.*

Wetherill patriarch Benjamin Kite, or B.K. for short, got the other ball rolling with a series of letters written to the then-fledgling Bureau of American Ethnology. "We are particular to preserve the buildings, but fear, unless the Gov't sees proper to make a national park of the Cañons, including Mesa Verde, that the tourists will destroy them," he wrote in one. The Bureau responded to say they regrettably couldn't do anything about it.

Meanwhile, Benjamin's son Richard continued to expand his search for antiquities throughout the greater Mesa Verde region, eventually arriving in Chaco Canyon where he found that many of the rooms of the great Pueblo Bonito and a nearby burial mound had already been ransacked by looters. He decided to stay in the canyon both to facilitate his own efforts there, and to keep watch over them. He and his wife filed homesteading paperwork and made a few purchases until nearly the whole place was theirs, and then set about the dual tasks of ranching and excavating—hiring mostly local Diné laborers for both. One of them would end up murdering him.

Through it all, he considered himself a temporary custodian or caretaker while entreating the government to take over management of Chaco and its archaeology, saying that "it was the duty of the present generation not to permit the wrecking and destruction of these communal houses by pothunters whose sole object it is to unearth their curious and varied contents and sell them" in a letter Leake has curated in his collected files. Richard and his wife expressed eagerness to swap some or all of their holdings with the federal government if it meant the place would be turned into a park or reserve—to no avail.

By the late twentieth century, spurred at last by the passage of federal legislation that came about in the 1990s, the Smithsonian

* My favorite example of this fact: an 1879 revision of the Constitution of the State of California mandated that all laws be written exclusively in English (the original 1849 version was bilingual). California then passed a law outlawing fellatio and cunnilingus in 1914, during a period when hypocritical puritanism was making its first of now two resurgences. This led to a contentious legal battle in 1918 because those are not, in fact, English words.

alone owned up to having a total of nearly *twenty thousand* full and partial Native American corpses in its storage cabinets. This casts Hewett's rage toward Wetherill in a rather different light, considering he was head of that institution at the time.

Wetherill certainly didn't dig them all up. Not even close. He was part of a larger systemic problem, much of it by design rather than unintentional in nature, but he also happened to have especially rich locales like Mesa Verde, Chaco, and the canyons of what is now Bears Ears National Monument more-or-less all to himself for a while. He treated that richness the way his upbringing and the dominant culture taught him to treat it, even going beyond it in some cases to incorporate scientific methods that hadn't yet caught on elsewhere in North America.

Still, when all is said and done, it adds up to what we now consider grisly and unforgivable behavior. Most of us, anyway.

Looming over this anecdote about the Wetherill clan and the rapacious excavations of places like Mesa Verde, Chaco Canyon, and Grand Gulch is the basic fact that all three places are what is considered federal or public land. The exception to this is a 161-acre portion of Chaco that fell within a homestead claim filed by Richard Wetherill in 1901, which was initially disallowed but was finally enacted in 1907 with all the major archaeological sites cut out of it. He relinquished his claim later that same year on the assumption that it would all be turned into a national park—which did indeed happen toward the end of the century.

The major archaeological sites were always located on public land, in other words—even when the land immediately surrounding them was in dispute. Thus they became focal points of controversy. Had they been located on private land all along, there's a good—and grim—chance nobody in any official regulatory office would have even heard about them.

◆ ◆ ◆

Granted, Wetherill and his ilk weren't exactly researchers, although they did attempt to incorporate the best scientific ideas of the day into their diggings. A more accurate term for their work would be "collectors." Because that's what they did. They went to sites in places like Mesa Verde and Bears Ears, collected all the best artifacts and human remains they could find, and then passed them along to museums located back east.

This is probably the closest professional—or, at least, semi-professional—archaeology got to the plotline of the *Indiana Jones* films. Hence the old "it belongs in a museum" aphorism quoted ad nauseum thanks to the third film in the franchise, which long predates the current "it belongs right where you found it" version.

The late 1800s through early 1900s were the heyday of archaeological collecting in American archaeology, especially in the Southwest. The first person to make a collection of archaeological materials in southeastern Utah was Bluff resident Charles Lang in about 1880. Charles McLoyd and Charles Graham excavated extensively throughout what is now the Bears Ears area starting in the early 1890s, with Richard Wetherill following soon after.

Then came a harebrained expedition through the region for a magazine called *The Illustrated American*, which involved the Peabody Museum funding and overseeing a disastrous trip throughout the northern Southwest by Mississippian archaeologist Warren K. Moorehead and his misfit crew. *The Illustrated American* Exploring Expedition, as it billed itself, amassed an immense collection of archaeological materials, along with creation of numerous maps and photographs—all of which were destroyed when the magazine's New York office burned down a few years later. All that survives from that ridiculous episode are fourteen publications from the field.

Compounding the issue were the efforts of a handful of federally funded expeditions to carefully map the entire region so recently obtained from Mexico. There's a colorful history of rivalries between the groups, which numbered four at one point, but it was the effort led by Bernard V. Hayden that helped spur public interest in the archaeology of the Four Corners area. Hayden had with him a fellow named William Henry Jackson who was arrestingly talented at both drawing and photography, creating illustrations and photographs of topographic and archaeological features encountered during the mapping expedition whose detail holds up to this day. Many of them were displayed during the Great Exposition in Philadelphia in 1876, astounding audiences with the impressive architecture Jackson had managed to capture on paper. This effort effectively laid the kindling to which Wetherill set a torch in Chicago seventeen years later.

These collection efforts gradually became more systematic over time, engendering what archaeological historians often call the Descriptive Period of the science, although the name of the game was still getting as much as one could.

Professor Andrew Kerr, who took over curation of the University of Utah's collection in 1915 after the genial Byron Cummings retired, is a prime example of this. Kerr made it his sole mission in life to amass the largest collection of antiquities of any institution on the continent, and in so doing went as far as to train locals in the Four Corner region to dig sites for him. He paid them two dollars a pot—or about $60 in 2025. One of the men he hired was the grandfather of Earl Shumway, one of the most notorious looters in the history of the Southwest.

Looting in general ramped up considerably through the early twentieth century. The illicit antiquities trade has a rich history both here and abroad, although calling it "illicit" does put a bit of an unfair spin on the practice since doing so wasn't technically illegal until relatively recently. It didn't become illegal in the United States until passage of the Antiquities Act in 1906, for example, and then only on public lands. Meanwhile, an economic collapse in the late 1800s, combined with popularization of the well-preserved* antiquities of the Southwest through Jackson's visual media and public displays of collections like those of the Wetherills convinced a lot of people in the arid region that there was money to be made digging ancient treasures out of the ground.

Tension between the people digging up antiquities so they could sell them just to make money and people digging up antiquities so

* This is one of those unfortunate "a blessing and a curse" situations. The Southwest is where most of the greatest surges in the development of American archaeology have occurred because the arid climate is so conducive to preservation. It's also where the greatest surges in archaeological looting have occurred, for precisely the same reason.

they could ship them to institutions with official government charters is, in short, what led to creation of the Antiquities Act. But it couldn't have happened if another historical character hadn't laid some additional groundwork by encouraging governmental interest in Indigenous peoples as more than just enemies to be exterminated: a one-armed military veteran named John Wesley Powell.

◆ ◆ ◆

Major Powell was born in 1834, fought in the Civil War and lost his arm—like my own war-hero grandfather did fighting the Nazis a little over a hundred years later—and then went ahead and set the tone for early and subsequent exploration of the Colorado River and its tributaries. Powell had extensive military training in science and engineering, but he was also interested in the natural sciences and human history, along with the fledgling science of evolutionary biology. Best known for leading a series of history-making trips down the Green and Colorado Rivers from 1869 through 1871, he went on to become the director of the Bureau of Ethnology—later renamed the Bureau of American Ethnology, because nationalism—at the Smithsonian Institution.

Like other scientists of his time, Powell was utterly convinced of the "racial inferiority" of the Native Americans. He appears, however, to have had immensely greater respect for them than most of his contemporaries. He would go on to publish expansive ethnographic studies on Native peoples and languages in his later roles at the Bureau and the Smithsonian. The BAE under Powell's direction was also the first federal agency in the United States to make any substantial investment in archaeology.

The Bureau was founded in 1879 as a rider on a bill that founded the United States Geological Survey, showing how long that sort of thing has been going on in American politics, and Powell was its first director. According to authors David Meltzer and Wallace Stegner, in their own separate portraits of the man and the agency, Powell's own political craftiness was at the heart of all this. He quietly established the Bureau under the protective aegis of the

Smithsonian Institution, and secured an operating budget that was small enough not to get him noticed by the wrong people but big enough to accomplish his lofty goals vis-à-vis American Indians: to ease their acculturation and capture data of ethnological interest before they all disappeared.

It was mostly later, and mostly because of pressure from Smithsonian Secretary Spencer Baird, that Powell started funding large-scale archaeological investigations. Baird was primarily interested in building the Smithsonian's collections, much as Andrew Kerr would be about a quarter-century later in Utah, and a budget amendment in 1881 specified that a certain amount of the yearly budget needed to go to what they called "mound research." Powell contended that the amendment caught him off-guard.

The often-strained relationship between Baird and Powell continued like this for some time, but Powell was at least congenial about it. He considered anthropology to be a "common ground for the physical sciences, language, history, and even literature" according to Meltzer, demonstrating that he was more of a lumper than a splitter. So, although he didn't much care for archaeology himself, he didn't seem to mind it either, and he ponied up with funds whenever Baird proposed new schemes to expand the museum's collections. This made the BAE the first instance of American archaeology being a holistic practice that incorporated other sciences, including anthropology, although at the time it was an isolated one—most universities still practiced European-style archaeology, and the rest of American archaeology was made up of non-professionals like the Wetherills.

This was still the era when American scholars believed that some "lost race" had existed in the Americas prior to the Indigenous groups encountered by Europeans when they got there. Who they were and how they died out was a topic of much debate, but since the American Indians were still around and they didn't seem to be building or occupying any impressive earthworks at the time, the fate of the mysterious peoples who built things like the mounds of the Mississippi River valley was usually pinned on them. William Cullen Bryant lamented as such in 1833:

The red man came—

The roaming hunter tribes, warlike and wild,

And the mound-builders vanished from the earth.

The solitude of centuries untold

Has settled where they dwelt.

Powerful stuff. Powerful, racist, factually incorrect stuff that people like Andrew Jackson used to great advantage.

The BAE and the rest of the burgeoning field of American archaeologists in the 1800s set about solving this "riddle" in radically different ways, based on their respective interpretations of what archaeology was and how it was supposed to work. Frederic Ward Putnam, curator of the Peabody Museum of Archaeology and Ethnology—who, it should be noted, was a kindly man who regularly hired both women and Native Americans when nobody else would—had crews working at places like Hopewell and Serpent Mound. It was also Putnam who deployed Moorehead on the ill-fated *Illustrated American* expedition.

The BAE had crews working pretty much everywhere else.

Putnam and the Peabody crews were operating on the assumption that different peoples had occupied the Americas during the Pleistocene, and extant Indigenous peoples were most likely an amalgamation of at least four previous occupations between the two major time periods. The BAE researchers, on the other hand, took the "living fossil" approach of starting with observations of living Native peoples and using archaeology to work backward in order to reconstruct their history. This approach included them taking as given that no major changes had occurred among Indigenous peoples of the Americas for however long they'd lived there—which, then as now, didn't really square with the fact that some of them lived in portable wikiups while others constructed towering architecture.

Still, in the end, the BAE approach won the day, since Putnam was never able to find any substantial evidence to show that no less than four distinct human "races" had occupied the continent at various times. Shocking, I know.

This all took place almost exactly a century after Thomas Jefferson excavated one of those mounds to try to address this very same conundrum, noting at the time how it really seemed to him like the local Native Americans treated the mounds as part of their own heritage. Putnam wasn't unaware of this in his own day, and he acknowledged that the mounds were probably built by the ancestors of Native folks he saw all around him, but that just didn't seem like the whole story to him. There must have been some other, mysteriously vanished people who played a major role.

Putnam was not alone in this spirit of recalcitrant stubbornness. It's a mainstay of archaeology to this very day. I had a professor in my graduate school program less than a decade ago laugh derisively at the idea that Indigenous heritage in the Americas goes back a lot further than the Clovis period, or about twelve-thousand years ago. This despite how there are sites with confirmed dates nearly twice as old all the way down at the southern tip of South America, and in 2023 scientists applied several rounds of rigorous radiometric testing to a set of footprints in New Mexico that all substantiate a much deeper antiquity in North America as well, not to mention the beliefs of Indigenous peoples themselves.

This is not a dig on that professor or anything. Cognitive inertia is a bastard. Aristarchus suggested in 200 BC that the sun is the center of what we now call our solar system, an idea that was mostly brought up as a party joke until Copernicus proved it over a thousand years later. Even then it was only accepted by a few people, and Giordano Bruno was burned at the stake in 1600 for endorsing it (along with some other heretical naughtiness). Ignaz Semmelweis was literally institutionalized and tortured to death in a mental institution after he suggested in 1847 that doctors could prevent infection by washing their hands between patients. Alfred Wegener was openly derided for telling his colleagues in 1920 that continents sat atop plates that moved around from time to time.

We kind of suck at changing our minds, even when presented with substantial evidence. This has interesting effects in, among other places, voting booths.

Anyway, Putnam was just as wrong in his day as my professor was in mine. The BAE archaeologists proved him wrong yet again when they later concluded that, no, there was no Paleolithic occupation in the Americas that was identical to the Paleolithic Period in Europe, principally because Europe and the Americas occupy different parts of the planet. The pieces were gradually moving into place for the final showdown between the two dominant methodological approaches: the European school and the American school.

◆ ◆ ◆

Meanwhile, there was another component in the development of American archaeology that flourished in popularity during this time: the idea of the Vanishing Indian. It was the guiding principle that drove most of what Powell was trying to do, and it deserves a lot of focus to understand how the discipline evolved. To bring that focus into context takes a bit of a historical run-up.

Since the early nineteenth century, the concept of mysteriously disappearing communities, races, or civilizations has enjoyed at least modest popularity among wealthy societies. This is at least partly because human beings love a good mystery, to the point where they'll create mysteries that don't even exist just so others can have fun trying to solve them. But it was also due to the discovery of extinction not long before the first ostensibly professional archaeologists took to the field in the Americas.

The assumption among just about all European intelligentsia was that the world was made perfect. God made everything, after all, and it's not like Him to make mistakes. It just didn't make sense to them that an almighty creator would create things just to then throw them in the existential recycling bin. Extinction as a concept didn't begin to attract even moderate attention in Western intellectual circles until 1796, when paleontologist George Cuvier presented a paper called "On the species of living and fossil elephants" in which he made the bold claim that woolly mammoths must be extinct because otherwise we'd see them walking around.

This dovetailed nicely with the budding science of geology in which "catastrophism" was then very much in vogue. This was the notion, again based largely on biblical tales like that of the great flood, that the Earth has largely been shaped by a series of sudden and cataclysmic events that are worldwide in scope. Not surprisingly, it was also Cuvier who championed this view, and his assertion that animals have gone **poof** in the past made this concept even more appealing.

Such thinking was eventually replaced with the theory of uniformitarianism thanks to people like Charles Lyell, which posits that slow incremental changes are really the cause of Earth's makeup, but the catastrophists of the Enlightenment weren't entirely wrong either. We are now certain that an asteroid strike wiped out the dinosaurs, while the eruption of several mega-volcanoes known in the geologic record are associated with even bigger die-offs. In fact, the largest mass extinction known in the fossil record occurred at the end of the Permian Period a quarter of a billion years ago, owing to what most scientists think was one hell of a volcanic eruption that dumped incalculable levels of sulfuric acid aerosols into the stratosphere and carbon dioxide into the atmosphere, effectively causing global climate change that was downright brisk in geologic terms.

◆ ◆ ◆

Interpreting the fossil record to mean that whole species of plants and animals can and, in a geological sense, very often do pop out of existence was one of those historical milestones that doesn't get enough play in modern textbooks. And it really should. When top-tier thinking types in Europe fully digested this information, it accompanied a much smaller realization that would only grow with time: one of the "catastrophes" associated with extinction is us. The dodo bird was hunted to extinction by about 1662,* and the Steller's sea cow was hunted to extinction in 1768, so we'd already killed off several species of animals before Cuvier announced that doing so was even possible.

* Sort of. Sailors did consume dodos from time to time, but apparently they tasted awful and were more like starvation food than something regularly pursued with gusto. But they also brought pigs, dogs, and rats to Mauritius Island, and that's what really sealed the dodos' fate.

Nor was this concept lost on anthropologists, who noted that two more recent waves of extinction were curiously correlated with mass human migrations around the globe. Chief among these was the Pleistocene Extinction, when megafauna disappeared on every continent but Africa between about ten and twelve thousand years ago. Then there was the Holocene Extinction, which started with the expansion of European colonies (along with their germs and rats and dogs and so forth) in the 1500s and hasn't really slowed down since.

The effects of human activities on global climate and ecosystems from the commencement of industrial modernity has led some scholars to propose a geological epoch known as the Anthropocene, and the concept has become gospel in Reddit forums and coffee shops, but most experts dismiss it out of hand—mostly because none of its boosters can decide when it actually starts. At the dawn of the Holocene? At the start of the Industrial Revolution? With the Trinity nuclear bomb tests? With the Vietnam War? All of these are real proposals by people with real doctoral degrees, and if you choose one, you'll anger devotees of the others, so most formal institutions simply haven't bothered.

People started thinking about our own extinction and how we might bring it about long before now, however. Plato may not have intended to kick a hornet's nest of conspiracy theories that buzz around to this day when he created the vanished civilization of Atlantis in the seemingly naïve assumption that everyone would always know it was just a metaphor, but he did so nonetheless.

The notion that cities and nations can disappear wasn't exactly new to Enlightenment thinkers, either, since by then European and Asian historians had done a fair job of real-time chronicling how places like Carthage were totally destroyed by the Romans and places like Pompeii were totally destroyed by a volcano. The disappearance of Atlantis slotted neatly into these *actual* disappearances like a cuckoo egg in a warbler's nest. But recall that the later Enlightenment is also when scholars minted the concept of that other cuckoo's egg known as race science. People weren't just people, in their minds. People were a conglomeration of different subspecies of people, and some of them probably have gone extinct over time.

This notion wasn't helped by the discovery of Neanderthal fossils in Forbe's Quarry in 1848, followed fairly quickly by discovery of the type specimen in the Neander Valley in Germany in 1856. The remains of early humans dating to at least thirty thousand years ago were then found in a place called Cro-Magnon in France in 1868, marking the first discovery of anatomically modern humans in Europe at the same time as Neanderthals. But we're still here, and Neanderthals quite obviously aren't.

Because of this, in the words of British archaeologist Julia R.R. Drell in a 2001 paper, there was an "expulsion of Neanderthals from 'humanity' in the nineteenth century and first half of the twentieth century." Neanderthals were an extinct race of not-quite-humans, in other words, and therefore proof positive that some human races simply aren't fit to survive.

Furthermore, because these early thinkers associated Neanderthals with what they conceived as "primitive" racial traits located someplace on the continuum between animal and human, their conception of Neanderthals was also heavily influenced by colonialism. Neanderthals were repeatedly compared to—and understood through analogy with—the people Western scholars considered most primitive at the time, especially Australian Aborigines. Here, to their immense gratification, was (literally) rock-hard evidence that certain races are doomed to extinction owing to their fundamental backwardness and incapacity to evolve. This was very useful for alleviating guilt over the unspeakable horrors of colonialism.

◆ ◆ ◆

The effect all this racism and extinction stuff had on American archaeology and its parent discipline of anthropology is not at all surprising, and it manifested in two forms.

Euro-Americans had long mused already about how the builders of the great Mississippian mounds and the mighty temples of the Mayan heartland couldn't possibly have been what they thought of as the lowly savages found upon their forebears' arrival. This is a big part of what prompted Joseph Smith to found an entire religion around the daffy notion that they were built by an advanced civilization of white people not entirely unlike those of Atlantis, all of whom managed to disappear without a trace before more white people could show up and look for them. The gaping absence of evidence was neatly addressed by word from the Old World over the next several decades that there were indeed extinct proto humans buried deep in the ground, so who knows what else might be down there?

That was one manifestation—factual support for the otherwise cockamamie notion that someone preceded Indigenous peoples in the Americas, and their remains simply hadn't been found yet. This made taking such a claim on faith a much easier sell not only for Mormons but for everyone else who believed an advanced civilization predated extant Native Americans. You could watch a Netflix "documentary" about it as recently as now.

The other manifestation was the notion that some forms of *Homo sapiens* were simply too primitive to evolve and thus doomed to wind up in the extinction bin alongside Neanderthals and *Homo erectus*, whose fossils were also being found by the late 1800s. The forms they had in mind were, unsurprisingly, *Homo sapiens* whose culture and appearance differed most radically from whoever was doing the thinking.

This notion was specifically applied to Indigenous peoples in the United States, and the explanatory roots for why that happened aren't hard to trace. Darwin had stated "when civilized nations come into contact with barbarians the struggle is short, except where a deadly climate gives its aid to the native race" in his 1871 book *The Descent of Man*, which is a fairly straightforward synopsis of the legacy of colonialism, although he didn't appear to be celebrating this facet of colonialism so much as lamenting it. But that certainly didn't stop a lot of his readers from celebrating it.

Henry David Thoreau wasn't so ambiguous. He wrote toward the beginning of his posthumously published *The Maine Woods* of a "woebegone Indian" disembarking from his canoe near Oldtown with "a bundle of skins . . . and an empty keg" to fill with whiskey. "This picture will do to put before [the reader] the Indian's history," Thoreau concludes; "that is, the history of his extinction." It was a sentiment that nicely jived with Darwin's contention when it hit shelves a decade later.

Native Americans were, in other words, doomed to extinction because they are fundamentally incapable of adapting to modernity. Something many Americans at the time saw as both an inevitable destiny and a handy way to score free real estate.

◆ ◆ ◆

Because of all this, by the mid- to late 1800s, most Americans subscribed to a germinating theory about what scholars call the Vanishing Indian. It would come to full flower during the Jacksonian Era.

Despite how much of the disappearance of Native peoples from North America had nothing to do with their inherent characteristics or conscious choices so much as introduced diseases and genocidal government policy, a lot of American thinkers at the time considered their declining numbers to be part of the Manifest Destiny myth. They also believed that, in the event not all the Indigenous peoples themselves went extinct, their cultures surely would in the face of elective or forced assimilation into Western culture. Because of this, a lot of them set about the self-appointed task of preserving the cultural knowledge and materials of American Indians before they disappeared, including Powell and his colleagues.

Moreover, since these people were largely perceived in mainstream culture to be headed for total oblivion on account of some internal flaw of theirs—not to mention ongoing efforts by the American government to hasten the onset of that oblivion—early anthropologists also didn't put much faith in Indigenous peoples to preserve their own traditions. And there was a grim sort of logic to that. It's hard to imagine people preserving anything after they've been exterminated. Thereafter began a systematic effort to gather as much material from them as possible and transfer it to the seemingly more secure holds of museums.

Although the collectors believed they were using these objects to showcase the memory of a vanishing people, the objects themselves were mostly taken from very definitely not-vanished people, many of whom believed that public display was disrespectful and potentially harmful to viewers. This would end up being a big component of the 1990s push for federal legislation specifically aimed at repatriation of human remains and sacred items, an effort that continues to this day. Sort of.

This form of salvage anthropology was often undertaken in decidedly underhanded ways, as scientists scrambled to preserve these supposedly disappearing cultures by digging up graves, showing up to important ceremonies with cameras, and so on. One collector, Alanson Buck Skinner who collected for the American Museum of Natural History between 1910 and 1914, earned the nickname Little Weasel for his tendency to use deception and outright lies to fleece Indigenous peoples out of their ritual objects. This and more led acerbic Lakota scholar and author Vine Deloria Jr. to write in his amazingly titled 1969 book *Custer Died for your Sins*:

> Into each life, it is said, some rain must fall. Some people have bad horoscopes, others take tips on the stock market. But Indians have been cursed above all other people in history. Indians have anthropologists.

The archaeological version of this wasn't wildly different, although unfortunately it has lasted a lot longer. Warren K. Moorehead's curiously doomed journey to dig up and collect as much material history as he could for the World's Columbian Exposition was literally titled "In Search of a Lost Race." The simple, observable fact that the direct descendants of the people who'd built the pueblos and cliff dwellings Moorehead was plundering lived no more than a few miles away was apparently an unheeded one.

Skipping ahead a century, we have a 1975 book about the artwork found on Mimbres black-on-white pottery with the title *Art of a Vanished Race: The Mimbres Classic Black-on-White*. Granted, 1975 was fifty years ago as of this writing, and it was a time when documentaries like *Footprints in Stone* were produced to prove that humans and dinosaurs walked side-by-side in Texas. But 1998 certainly wasn't fifty years ago, and that's when the fourth edition was printed with the very same title. As usual, descendants of whomever crafted the Mimbres material culture can be found living nearby. I've eaten their frybread. But the "vanished" aspect (to say nothing of the "race" aspect) was a popular hook, and popular hooks generate sales.

This attitude has not entirely abated even now. On the official website of The History Channel, that remarkable bastion of shameless pseudoscience and occasional howling lunacy, an article dating to October 23, 2020, by Jesse Greenspan bears the title "Here's Why These Six Ancient Civilizations Mysteriously Collapsed." Included on the list are both the Maya and the "Anasazi," an outdated term for the peoples associated with most architectural archaeological sites in the northern Southwest.*

Yet the article itself is remarkably accurate, with Greenspan noting how the Maya "never disappeared" but rather dispersed from their city-states at the end of the Classic Period, and how the modern-day descendants of the Anasazi "include the Hopi and Zuni peoples, some of whom consider the term Anasazi offensive, preferring instead to say 'ancestral (or ancient) Puebloans.'"

The choice of "Mysteriously Collapsed" in the title is therefore entirely misleading, but since authors don't often have final say over the titles of their publications, I can only assume it was written that way simply to draw attention. They didn't collapse, in other words, but simply changed over time, including at least one period of relatively massive change. Similar critiques have been thrown at Jared Diamond for his bestselling *Collapse: How Societies Choose to Fail or Succeed*, which spotlighted the Maya, Ancestral Pueblo (specifically the imperial zenith of the Chaco system in the 1100s), and peoples of Easter Island as examples of societies that "collapsed" because they all stupidly chose to overtax their environments.

* To a point, anyway. Pueblo scholars dislike the term because one interpretation of it is "old enemy," while speakers of the Diné language—from which Anasazi is derived—insist that it simply refers to the "old ones" or ancestors they share with some of the Pueblo groups. Ancestral Pueblo has become the official term and it's the one I use for this reason, but it's worth noting that most of my Navajo friends despise it. That's the problem with officializing terminology in what is effectively a foreign language.

None of that is true, although to be fair to Diamond a lot of what we know now simply wasn't known by Western researchers at the time he wrote them down. At least some of the groups in the Mayan culture area appear to have gotten sick and tired of increasingly complex city-states being constantly at war with each other, and decided maybe the whole imperialism thing was a shitty idea. The mighty Ancestral Pueblo empire that radiated outward from Chaco Canyon wasn't really an "empire" in the Western sense, more like a vast sociopolitical network, and it fragmented into smaller and less stratified societies like those of Mesa Verde and the Hopi villages because—again—imperialism of any sort turned out to be a dumb idea in the long run.

As for Easter Island (more accurately Rapa Nui), it was Western contact that caused them to go into harsh and rapid decline after early European sailors brought rats and disease to the island but before other Europeans showed up to take note of the Indigenous inhabitants' consequently dilapidated condition. They were doing just fine until then.

The effect of this sort of idea on mainstream culture I'll cover shortly, but the effect it had on the broad field of anthropology was to inspire a lot of ostensibly well-intentioned people to want to save at least the *memory* of Native Americans from the extinction that otherwise awaited them. Collecting their material history was one major aspect of this; chronicling their cultures and behavior through the lens of the "living fossil" myth was the other.

◆ ◆ ◆

This obsession with the notion that entire civilizations or "races" can just vanish off the map was therefore always a fishy one, and it mostly involved straight-up myths like that of Atlantis or the lost cities of Cibola and Quivira that inspired a lot of murderous Spanish adventures in the 1500s. But it reached a fever pitch in mainstream culture with the 1885 publication of H. Rider Haggard's *King Solomon's Mines*. A book to which we owe a lot—for better or worse.

Indiana Jones is so much the canonical archaeologist of mainstream culture that he's all-but synonymous with the word. Tell any ten random strangers that you're an archaeologist and you're likely to get anywhere from five to fifteen Indiana Jones-based comments in return—along with a few questions about dinosaurs and at least one about aliens. Lesser known is the fact that Indy himself was "inspired by" (read: a blatant rip-off of) the character Harry Steele from the 1954 film *Secret of the Incas*, which starred Charlton Heston in a black leather jacket and raffishly cocked fedora hunting for lost ancient treasure in the Andes.

Seriously, it's uncanny how little effort George Lucas and his team put into outright stealing costume and story elements from *Secret of the Incas* for *Raiders of the Lost Ark*, but since both films were owned by Paramount Studios, they just quietly shelved the former when the latter made a much bigger splash. The chief difference between Indiana Jones and Harry Steele is that Indy killed a whole bunch of Nazis, including a clean dozen in *Last Crusade*, so he gets extra points for that. Otherwise it's the same character.

However we regard him, Harry "Indiana Jones" Steele was himself largely inspired by the fictional character Allan Quatermain in *King Solomon's Mines*. Quatermain was probably the first of what we'd now call an "adventurer" in modern literature, someone who intentionally goes out of their way to become embroiled in dangerous shenanigans for the amusement of readers. It follows the burly badass as he leads an expedition into the African jungle in search of a white guy who disappeared looking for the titular mines, and stumbles upon a lost civilization that possesses tremendous wealth.

The book is pretty racist, not surprisingly—although not as racist as one might expect. It opens with Quatermain explaining who he is and why he's telling this story, and no more than six paragraphs in he explains how he hates the N-word because he's met African natives who are gentlemen and "mean whites with lots of money who are not."

The rest of the story I won't bother recounting here, but it involves finding a lost world of people living in a primitive state with impressive stone architecture way out in the African jungle and the protagonist winding up with some diamonds. Stories like these would gradually morph into the men's adventure literary genre of the 1940s through 1970s. Magazines with titles like *His World, True Men,* and *Man's Adventure*; and featuring stories like "Crushed by Eight Giant Arms of Hell" and "Blood for the Harlots of Horror" and "We Found the Paiute Gold!" Yes, those are all real.

People who say fiction doesn't influence real-world behavior have either never investigated the matter or never lived in the real world. Popular media is inspired by culture, of course, but it inspires culture right back—which is why so many Dalmatian puppies get adopted (and then abandoned) every time Disney re-re-remakes *101 Dalmatians*. Bartenders routinely have to speed dial new drinks whenever one of them is featured in a piece of pulp media, something with which I have harrowing memories thanks to the cosmopolitan craze that accompanied the first *Sex and the City* film. And it's possible that as many as thirty people have died looking for the Lost Dutchman's Mine in the Superstition Mountains of southern Arizona despite the whole thing being a wild pulp fantasy based on zero actual evidence.

In addition to arguably being the first instance of popular Western fiction in which the main character gets embroiled in exciting adventures just for our amusement, *King Solomon's Mines* is also regarded by most experts as the first book in the "lost world" genre of fiction. Popular cultural attitudes at the time played heavily into its popularity, and consequently inspired follow-up works like Edgar Rice Burroughs' *The Land That Time Forgot*, Arthur Conan Doyle's *The Lost World*, Rudyard Kipling's *The Man Who Would Be King*, and H.P. Lovecraft's *The Mountains of Madness*, to name just a few. Much of the Indiana Jones canon is concerned with lost civilizations, including one that involved aliens, and Michael Crichton's 1980 novel *Congo* is pretty much just *King Solomon's Mines* with weird gorilla/chimp/human hybrids standing in for native Africans.

Closer to home, David Roberts' 1996 book *In Search of the Old Ones: Exploring the Anasazi World of the Southwest* did the same thing for the recreational archaeology subculture—a sort of sub-subset of American archaeology that is really the material heritage equivalent of birdwatching—that *King Solomon's Mines* did for the lost worlds genre of fiction.

This made it doubly ironic when Roberts' publisher asked him to put out a ten-year follow-up book, and he titled it *The Lost World of the Old Ones: Discoveries in the Ancient Southwest.* But again, as with the aforementioned History Channel article, Roberts doesn't say anything especially inaccurate about the ancient Southwest, and certainly nothing about "lost worlds" as the title would imply. It just sells. It's a title that sells because the notion of mysteriously vanished civilizations has, itself, yet to vanish from popular Western consciousness.

Meanwhile—despite literal efforts by the US Government and a few religious institutions to bring it about—neither Native Americans in general nor the majority of their cultures have actually gone extinct. Although this hasn't stopped people from claiming that they have, both here and elsewhere.

Earlier in the same year that I drafted this section, UNESCO was forced to retract a document published in 1982 that stated that "Tasmanians are now an extinct race of humans" thanks to the genocide of British colonists. True, the British *tried* to erase the Aboriginal Tasmanians from the face of the Earth, and they did succeed in killing off all individuals of sole Tasmanian descent by 1876. But descendants of Aboriginal Tasmanians who intermingled with white sailors in the early 1800s are still around today, and they don't really like being called an "extinct race of humans," especially not by so august an institution as UNESCO in a report that wasn't pulled for revision until August of 2023.

◆ ◆ ◆

The race to understand the Vanishing Indians and their cultures ahead of their seemingly inevitable extinction gradually became the modus operandi of an entire government agency. As mentioned, under the direction of Major Powell, the BAE and its crack team of mostly ethnologists enshrined what was probably the earliest version of explicitly archaeological science. Other institutions would soon follow.

Although these efforts were directed at funneling the main bulk of American archaeology toward the purviews of austere and official institutions, another of those curious quirks in the history of the practice started to emerge as a result: avocational archaeologists.

These are archaeologists not formally affiliated with any institutions or companies, at least not where their work is concerned, but who nonetheless practice actual archaeology instead of just looting with notes. The Council of Allied Societies defines them as "citizen scientists who actively participate in the gathering and understanding of the archaeological record, who follow the ethical guidelines set forth by [the Society for American Archaeology] and the national mandates that include NAGPRA, ARPA, NHPA and individual state preservation policies." We'll come back to these later on.

The practice itself predates all those acronyms and the laws they signify. An argument can be made that Richard Wetherill was an avocational archaeologist, since he wasn't affiliated with any institutions but was also as scientifically diligent as he could be for that time and place. He also wasn't breaking any laws at the time—at least not until Hewett and Lacey used him as their type specimen for why such a law needed to exist—so "looter" doesn't quite fit him either.

While most archaeologists were jostling for institutional credibility, a handful of renegades apparently continued to work outside the realm of professional affiliations. In reality, the story is much more complicated and interesting than that.

In 1919, a newly formed organization called the National Research Council created within its purview a Division of Anthropology and Psychology, and one of the projects they were directed to undertake was the creation of the Committee on State Archaeological Surveys. The committee mostly intended to address the fact that, as implied by the Wetherill example, enthusiastic non-professional archaeologists continued to manifest their enthusiasm in rather destructive ways. Their goal was to encourage the non-professionals to work *with* professionals in the area, giving them a level of accreditation while hopefully spreading the word further afield among the public.

The balancing act, then as now, was involvement of the public while maintaining at least some semblance of professional standards. For that reason, a lot of what they did—and still do—isn't technically archaeology so much as adjacent to it.

Reporting in 1924 on the activities of the Wisconsin Archaeological Society, for example, celebrated Southwest archaeologist A.V. Kidder* notes how the group owned and operated two mound sites as state parks, and had developed interpretive signage for other sites located in the region. In the same report, Kidder also reports on how the State Historical Society of Iowa managed to develop a bibliography of all the archaeological work conducted in the state up to that year, an impressive clerical feat that nonetheless involved neither blunted trowels nor muddy boots.

Public interest in archaeology hasn't really waned since then, although direct interactions between both professional and avocational archaeologists and the public hit a few snags and developmental challenges that have grown into a rift in the last century—one that was stuffed with some unfortunate filler in recent decades. One such example was a 1958 censure by the Society for American Archaeology—an organization founded in 1934 that was intended to wed amateur and professional archaeologists under one umbrella—against the state of Arkansas, whose Parks and Publicity Commission had published a brochure encouraging the public to visit the state and "dig for Indian relics." The Arkansas Archaeological Society was founded out of the snafu in 1967.

Relevant to this is the development of federal protective legislation that applies only to federal lands or to projects relying on federal funding. Most states do have some form of historic or archaeological preservation laws, but they apply only to state lands.

Arizona has a set of statutes within the Arizona Antiquities Act nicknamed the "burial laws" (ARS. 41-844 and 41-865) which "strictly regulate the removal and disposition of human remains

* A number of archaeologists go by their first two initials, for some reason. Alfred "A.V." Kidder, known as Ted to his friends, was among them—as are R.G. Matson, H.R. Wormington, A.T. Hill, J.O. Brew, J.O. Kinnaman, and my dear friend and colleague K.C. Carlson, to give just a small sample. It's the reason I started doing it.

and associated funerary objects on state-owned or state-controlled lands and private properties, respectively" in the official words of the Arizona State Museum. But even that only applies to human remains and funerary objects.

Because of this, amateur or avocational archaeologists became the primary source for archaeological research on private lands and remain so to this day. Private landowners possessed of both archaeological resources on their land and a rasher of goodness in their hearts often turn to avocational individuals or non-profit groups to investigate them, interpret them, or conduct mitigation to salvage them before the plows or bulldozers show up.

In time, conservation organizations would start to rival—and, in some cases, eclipse—state archaeological societies when it came to salvaging or preserving material history located on lands not controlled by state or federal agencies, and these days most state archaeological societies are more like social clubs for people who want to gather and geek out about the distant past. I routinely give talks for these groups all over the Southwest, and they're usually a lot of fun, chiefly because they've got a ready-made audience of people eager to hear what researchers have to say.

But the overarching prime mover is the subject itself. People are fascinated by archaeology. They'll show up for it, if you give them a chance to do so.

◆ ◆ ◆

Major Powell's own journals and the diaries of his crew members discussed archaeological sites that present-day researchers have either found or continue trying to find to this day. This is true of many historic reports, but theirs are especially enticing because of the lurid prose they often employed describing what they found—and much else besides.

One of those diaries, written by assistant topographer Frederick S. Dellenbaugh when he served with Powell as a youth on his second journey down the river, was published as *A Canyon Voyage* in 1908 and includes a lot of details you don't often find in the official reports.

Details like "at first we put the bacon into rubber, but it spoiled the rubber and then we saw that bacon can take care of itself, nothing can hurt it anyhow, and a gunny-sack was all that was necessary."

I guess they made tougher bacon back then. In 1910, charismatic archaeologist Earl Morris used a square of bacon rind to replace a burned-out bearing in his Model T in the Lukachukai Mountains after the vehicle broke down. A replacement that lasted the rest of the field season. Upon hearing about this, friend and fellow archaeologist Neil Judd was moved to proclaim, "You don't get bacon rind like that anymore!"

Food is always a bit of a *thing* in fieldwork. While chatting with legendary archaeologist Bill Lipe in Bluff in early winter 2020, just before the pandemic went into overdrive, I learned that one of the camp cooks on his famous Cedar Mesa Research Project in the early 1970s wasn't just living in camp to serve up hearty fare to hungry archaeologists—he was also there ducking a murder charge.

"Food was good, though."

Life in camp certainly isn't the worst of it. Camp meals are fun to prepare, and when I worked for in the private sector, the members of the field crew would each pick a night or two as their night to cook group meals. I always made jambalaya because it's one of the few dishes I ever learned to cook, being a bartender who dates chefs rather than a chef myself, and I actually won an award from my fellows for consistently making a dish they loved (the award was a role of tinfoil). One coworker always brought pre-made chili, usually more than one version, and another once managed to pull off an incredible Japanese stir-fry over the temperamental communal propane stove.

And always booze—except in the case of the Mormon field workers—in abundances that could sometimes be staggering to behold. I once counted no fewer than forty combined liters (or just under eleven gallons) of wine in bottles and boxes piled up underneath a pine tree at the start of a field session in northern Utah that involved only six people, and when I mentioned this to the crew chief she smirked and responded, "I guess you haven't looked in any of the coolers yet."

So no, life in camp isn't the worst of it. Life in cheap motels is the worst of it. Cooking in most motel rooms is frowned upon to the point of carrying stiff penalties, which doesn't stop people from bringing camp stoves or single-pot electric ranges into their rooms—they just try to keep quiet about it.

One memorable evening, a notoriously wily coworker was using a Jet Boil in her room in one of those roadside motels where all the rooms are lined up side-by-side, and a manufacturer glitch in the fuel bottle's nozzle caused the whole thing to erupt into flame. Panicked, thinking quickly, and not thinking too far into the future, she opened the door to her room and kicked the little stove out of it as hard as she could, propelling a tumbling fireball along a screaming arc out into the middle of the busy parking lot.

Camp stoves were officially banned from all company field vehicles bound for motels after that.

Back in Powell's day, according to Dellenbaugh, food supplies on lengthy field excursions consisted of flour, beans, dried apples and peaches, coffee and tea "with, of course, plenty of sugar," and an abundance of seemingly indestructible bacon. Powell's own narratives are scanty regarding such trifles, concerned as he was with bigger-ticket items like mapping the Colorado River, although his own journals and reports show that it was increasingly on his mind as they journeyed.

As their food stores dwindled through usage, swamped boats, and an out-of-control campfire that destroyed a lot of it in one go, the men supplemented their stores with game and wild plants. They would also steal from gardens they happened across, and on one occasion it cost them dearly. They'd pilfered the garden of an interpreter in Green River, but the vegetables—including potatoes—weren't ripe yet. Underripe potatoes contain not-insubstantial portions of a toxin called solanine. All but two of Powell's men cooked and ate the bitter potato greens, and then puked and pooped themselves senseless afterward.

These examples aside, there's an art and craft to field food that really makes it one of the uncelebrated highlights of our discipline. When the Diné woman whips up Navajo tacos the first night, the hippie couple pass around pillow-sized burritos the second night, the dude from New Yorks ladles up pasta with rich red sauce and fire-roasted meatballs the third night, the Colorado cowboy hands out seared steaks and Dutch oven potatoes the fourth night, the Mormon who did his mission in India pulls off a campfire kebab masala on the fifth night, the girl from Arizona lays out an entire table of fajita options on the seventh night, and the exhausted crew chief forgoes cooking and drives into town to grab everyone pizza and beer on the last night . . . Those are the times when you start to wonder if you should bother going home at all.

Home is where the heart is, after all. But home is also where the office is. Powell seems to have rued that aspect of the process in his own day, preferring to work in the wild rather than in the office, and the gradual officialization of American archaeology would soon enough yoke the rest of us with the same burden.

CHAPTER 4

SALVAGERS AND SCIENTISTS

By the time the twentieth century was in full swing, more and more of American archaeology was tending toward officialdom. Efforts to wrangle the snarled practice carried out in wildly various ways across the continent centered mostly on institutionalizing it, by which I mean corralling it into institutions with official charters and standard operating procedures rather than consigning it to the laughing academy. That would come later.

Edgar Lee Hewett, co-author of the Antiquities Act along with John F. Lacey, is often regarded as the chief builder of institutions in early American archaeology, although one of the more curious quirks from this period is how he stole one. The oft-mentioned Archaeological Institute of America, or AIA, was founded in Boston in 1879 by Charles Eliot Norton "for furthering and directing archaeological and artistic investigation and research." He was a professor of art at Harvard, in addition to being an author, social critic, progressive activist, and the guy who coined the term "Western civilization." He served as the first president of the AIA, and it was under his direction that Bandelier was sent to the Southwest to debunk the notion that the sites in places like Chaco and Mesa Verde were built by the Aztecs.

Hewett, an Illinois man by birth, had set his sights firmly on the Southwest for both research and preservation goals by the late 1800s, and he was aghast at what some of the earliest institutions were doing to the place. As archaeologist and author Steven Lekson puts it in *A History of the Ancient Southwest*, Hewett "was furious. He saw the greatest sites of his generation destroyed and the best artifacts freighted to museums back east." By the turn of the century, Hewett lamented that "Smithsonian collectors had [already] been shipping railroad carloads of archaeological and ethnographic objects from the Southwest to Washington DC for two decades." Even more went to New York and Boston.

These early institutions sprang up for a variety of reasons, but by 1916 at the latest, they were nearly united in standardizing methods of collection and classification. Institutional archaeology had begun to grow and expand with the passage of the Antiquities Act of 1906, which set the trend of establishing professional qualification requirements for conducting archaeological work on federal lands; it expanded further with the 1916 creation of the National Park Service, the one and only federal land management agency whose mission is preservation rather than mixed-use management.

A common archaeological approach of this time was to place sites in chronological order based on temporally diagnostic artifacts, a process more formally known as *seriation* or the establishment of a chronological series, which dates back to the early 1800s with Christian Jürgensen Thomsen in Denmark. Archaeologists hypothesized that distinct groups of people would be represented by distinct artifact collections that could be traced through time. That, in other words, material cultures or artifact traditions were effectively synonymous with literal cultures—a useful but flawed basis for the study of human history.

To understand how this works, think of a list of items common to whatever actual culture with which you identify yourself. For me, as of this writing, it would be smartphones, video-capable watches, plastic soda cups large enough to drown in, and jeans that give the impression of having been washed in a cotton thresher. An assemblage of such items in a site would indicate that the site's occupants were associated with mainstream American culture in the early 2020s. Simple enough, yeah?

The thing is: a different array consisting of a rotary phone, a temperamental quartz watch, a small paper cup, and jeans of a notably smaller size that still give the impression of having been washed in a cotton thresher would more accurately peg the site to the 1980s—but it's still mainstream American culture. It's just that technology evolves, while fashion trends come and go (and often come back again when trendsetters run out of fresh ideas), within any given society.

That's the problem with using the material culture or "culture history" method on its own to reconstruct history. Lumping artifact traditions into discreet material cultures only tells you about the artifacts themselves: how and when they were used, where they may have come from, or how they were traded around the landscape, that sort of thing. It can tell you a bit about the behaviors of people associated with them—if they were farmers, say, or if they ate a ton of shellfish. Using that as a basis to pretend you know all about the so-called Shellfish Eaters as people is, on the other hand, problematic to say the least. But that's where it all started.

To that end, similarities and differences among sites and culture areas were discussed at great length, while the social or individual behaviors behind the artifacts were not considered in any detail. The focus was instead on lists of artifact attributes that showed some sort of patterning. To achieve chronological goals, special care was needed in the methods of excavation so that stratigraphic sequences could be documented. The level of detail in data collection was considerably greater in comparison to that of earlier practices.

As archaeology gained acceptance as an increasingly officialized discipline in the US, researchers received professional training from universities, which were by then establishing anthropology departments. However, opportunities for employment in the growing field were limited to universities and museums, with a few precious positions also available at the National Park Service. Most projects conducted during this period were also funded by universities and museums, though professional societies like the AIA were coming up strong.

In 1905 and 1906, Hewett toured various cities on behalf of the AIA, drumming up interest in archaeology and establishing local chapters of the institution. He'd been appointed Director of American Archaeology by the AIA for this purpose, as well as to establish a School of American Archaeology, which the AIA originally intended to be in Mexico to study the highly complex civilizations of Mesoamerica.

Instead, in 1907, Hewett established the School of American Archaeology in Santa Fe, later renamed the School of American Research and now known as the School for Advanced Research, which has always struck me as odd because they dropped "archaeology" out of their name entirely while keeping it their sole focus. The details of how this came about are convoluted but suffice to say that Hewett was a shrewd politician. Members of the AIA and affiliated institutions who wanted the school in Mexico went away shaking their heads and licking their wounds.

A few years after establishing the school, Hewett inherited the Museum of New Mexico as an agency thereof. From there he launched a series of field schools, the first formal ones in the country, attracting such future American archaeology luminaries as A.V. Kidder from Harvard. Oddly enough, Kidder would eventually decide that Hewett's little institution wasn't up to the task of studying the whole of Southwest antiquity on its own and helped others to convince John D. Rockefeller to fund a competing institution in Santa Fe. It was called the Laboratory of Anthropology, or simply The Lab to the fellas.

Hewett wasn't pleased about this, unsurprisingly, and openly rejoiced when the Great Depression forced Rockefeller to redirect his funds, causing The Lab to limp along in dire straits until Hewett died in 1946 and the Museum of New Mexico scooped it up to save it from bankruptcy. When the School of American Research and the Museum of New Mexico parted ways in 1959, the Laboratory of Anthropology became the Museum's research wing.

◆ ◆ ◆

Stories like this abounded in those days. Mad scrambles to make everything official and institutionalized ran smack into the basic human tendency to see their own way as the best way to do things, resulting in competition between institutions that reverberate today in infuriating ways. Here in Arizona, the Arizona State Museum (or ASM) was established in 1893 and came to prominence under director Byron Cummings, who would later become one of the staunchest defenders of archaeological preservation in Utah. It grew even more under Emil Haury, who took over as director in 1938 after working with another institution called Gila Pueblo, which was started around the same time as Hewett's school. In 1950, Gila Pueblo abruptly stopped doing research of any kind, and its collections and archives were all transferred to ASM.

All this meant that by the time of the National Historic Preservation Act in 1966,* which directed every US state and territory to appoint State Historic Preservation Offices (or SHPOs, pronounced like "hippos") to oversee all things archaeological, ASM was already an enormous and deeply entrenched figure of authority in Arizona archaeology. And so it remains.

In every other state in which I've worked as a professional archaeologist, museums are regarded solely as curation and public-interaction facilities while SHPOs are responsible for permitting projects, overseeing management of resources, acting as storehouses for reports, and so forth. That's also true in Arizona—but only on federal lands. If you've got something like a road or a pipeline or even a big archaeological site that extends between federal and state lands, you get to deal with both of sets of agencies, along with their respective standards, practices, personalities, and idiosyncrasies. This is more annoying than most would even dare to fear.

In places like Utah and Idaho—actually, in every state but Arizona—where the SHPO is the primary non-Tribal institution of archaeological authority, site numbers are all either loosely or tightly based on the Smithsonian trinomial system of state number, county monicker, and sequential number. So, for example, 42SA000420 is the 420th site recorded in San Juan County in Utah (state number 42 for arbitrary reasons). They don't do this in Arizona because of the ongoing fragmentation mentioned above, so every institute and agency within the state has its own numbering system, as does ASM itself.

* Relevant and interesting side note: the effort to create and pass NHPA was actually started by what my colleague Kim Ryan calls "a bunch of old ladies whose focus was saving Victorian houses." This is why the National Register criteria we still use today are geared almost entirely toward historic structures, with application to ancient sites being a bit catch-as-catch-can in nature.

Consequently, a historic road or prehistoric trail that crosses numerous jurisdictions can have official site numbers like AR-03-12-08-1337(USFS)/AZ BB:15:0567(ASM)/AZ BB:15:022(ASU)/AZTFO-2024-0004(BLM). I've seen a few that are even longer than that.

◆ ◆ ◆

Regarding regulations, animosity toward what they perceived as uncouth despoilers spurred a lot of early professional archaeologists to begin nudging Indigenous material history toward the cognitive radar screens of early historic preservationists. Preservation or management of archaeological sites and materials overlaps with archaeology as a research process, but they are not one and the same, and among the unfortunate truisms of archaeology in general is that its methods are usually destructive. You have to dig a site to find out how it's layered in terms of historical sequences, after all. You have to evaporate materials in a laboratory to get radiocarbon dates or mass spectrometry data about stable isotope ratios. You have to be able to see the sequence of rings in a log to count them.

Archaeologists have addressed this issue over time to minimize the destructiveness of their research methods, especially after the early 1970s when my dear friend and mentor Bill Lipe—along with his colleague Hester Davis—proclaimed a "crisis" in archaeology. They noted how the rate and scale of development projects in the US, coupled with archaeology's own innately destructive process, was rapidly destroying material history throughout the country. Non-destructive analysis has become both a goal and a shibboleth for newer-generation archaeologists.

Back in the early days, though, it was all digging and chopping and, on occasion, blowing things open with dynamite. Early archaeologists weren't unaware that these are destructive behaviors, of course, but the practice had only recently hardened into a profession after several centuries of haphazard antiquarianism conducted as an intellectual or nationalistic pastime. The conflict, therefore, was between the professionals and the non-professionals—defined, then as now, as those who don't have institutional affiliation. If we loot and plunder, it's for the good of all mankind, but if they loot and plunder it's because they're bastards.

The primary connective tissue with the early historic preservationists was the "nationalistic pastime" bit. Most historians generally agree that organized historic preservation efforts in the United States began in the nineteenth century as a nationalistic endeavor. Citizens, groups of citizens, local governments, and scholarly societies sought to preserve places that commemorated important events in American history, like Civil or Revolutionary War battlefields.

The federal government started getting involved in the practice of preservation toward the end of the 1800s with the establishment of Yellowstone National Park in 1872 and the creation of Casa Grande Reservation in 1891 (later to become Casa Grande Ruins National Monument in 1918). However, generally speaking, preservation of places important to American history was generally not considered an important function of the federal government until several decades later, and only federal properties were protected in any case.

Nationalistic ideologies of historic preservation meant that pre-contact sites were "generally considered to have no historical importance for the Euro-American dominant local communities" according to Ian Milliken, and antiquarian research still consisted of the finding and studying of objects of museum quality. However, with the end of the 1800s and the evolution of antiquarianism into professional archaeology, prehistoric places and objects began to be regarded as providers of information rather than simply interesting curios.

Co-occurring with the early historic preservation movement was the early conservation movement in the United States. The roots of that aspect of American history are complicated, but the short version is as such: By the early 1890s, Theodore Roosevelt and John Muir, along with a literal club of other wealthy white men—called the Boone and Crockett Club—had grown very concerned that their favorite hunting, hiking, and birdwatching places were being wrecked by development and cattle. So, they sought to stymie that.

The idea of restricting development in wilderness areas because it's nice to have wilderness areas was kind of a new one at the time, although Yellowstone was withdrawn from public auction by Congress in 1872 because reports from the Hayden Expedition made it clear the place was crazy cool. Hayden believed in "setting aside the area as a pleasure ground for the benefit and enjoyment of the people" and warned that certain types of people would "make merchandise of these beautiful specimens," according to historian Marlene Deahl Merrill.

So, the notion that some places should be set aside for protection on the grounds that they simply deserve it wasn't entirely the creation of Roosevelt or Muir, but they became its biggest champions and deserve some credit for that. These gentlemen and the rest of Roosevelt's Boone and Crockett Club, as well the rest of the nascent conservation community in the US, still represented the interests of wealthy white men—period. Indeed, primary membership in the Club was initially limited to no more than one-hundred wealthy men who'd successfully hunted "in a fair chase" at least one specimen of the three largest game animals of North America. Rumor has it Muir started the Sierra Club instead of just joining the Boone and Crockett Club because he wasn't rich and didn't like murdering big animals for sport.

◆ ◆ ◆

Not surprisingly, given all these points and a myriad of others I don't have time or space to list out here, women are woefully underrepresented in the mainstream history of conservation in this country—despite playing a number of crucial roles. This is especially true in the narrow realm where conservation and archaeology overlap.

Virginia McClurg and Lucy Peabody are wholly responsible for getting Mesa Verde protected as a national park starting in the mid-1880s, for example, although it's always important not to make humans into idols because nobody is infallible. McClurg proved this when she dropped out of the Mesa Verde National Park fight in frustration before Congress got around to creating it, redirecting her efforts to help with the creation of an eyesore of a tourist trap in Manitou Springs—a "cliff dwelling" built with materials snatched from actual archaeological sites in the vicinity of Dolores, Colorado. The park wouldn't have happened without all the work McClurg put in before that, but it was Peabody who really carried it over the finish line, with help and encouragement from our old pal Hewett.

Alice Fletcher was another one. She was a researcher at the Peabody Museum starting in 1880, and in that capacity helped Frederic Ward Putnam bring about protections for Serpent Mound. She also has the unique distinction of representing not one but two "firsts" for women in American academics: the first to hold any sort of fellowship at Harvard, and the first to chair a scientific position on the American Association for the Advancement of Science (AAAS). It was in this latter position that she petitioned Putnam in 1887 with a call for the federal government to "set aside certain portions of the public domain in the southwest territories in which are characteristic remains of former and present aboriginal life and holding them as national reserves."

According to archaeologist and historian Rachel Morgan, Fletcher also preempted the inevitable backlash to this idea. "Many of the most remarkable ruins and dwellings are upon land [of] little value to the settler, so that the claims of archaeology do not interfere with local prosperity," she's quoted as saying. "They are daily in more and more danger from the curiosity and zeal of traders. If they are not speedily preserved many will be irrevocably lost."

Fletcher was joined in this cause by Matilda Coxe Stevenson, and the two were selected by the AAAS to serve under Putnam on the Committee for the Preservation of Archaeologic Remains on the Public Lands. The Committee submitted a report in 1888 recommending that the government withdraw for protection the archaeological districts of Chaco Canyon, Canyon de Chelly, Canyon del Muerto, Walnut Canyon, and a few others in Arizona. Unfortunately, as Morgan wryly concludes, "it all came to nothing." The AAAS and the Committee were ignored.

The story comes full circle at this point, because the AIA—the institution founded in Boston in 1879—established a Standing Committee on American Archaeology at about this time, and Fletcher and Stevenson's boss Frederic Ward Putnam served on that as well. They submitted three bills lobbying the feds to create sweeping legislation for protection of archaeological resources on public lands, although these also died in committee by 1900.

As luck would have it, Edgar Lee Hewett met John F. Lacey when he was visiting Washington, DC that very year. The three proposed bills had been passed along to the Secretary of the Interior and commissioner of the General Land Office by Lacey, chair of the House Committee on Public Lands. After Hewett established himself in the Southwest and worked himself into a frothing rage over the continued efforts of non-professionals like Richard Wetherill trying to excavate every site in the region, he zeroed in on Lacey as the person most likely to help put those efforts to an end. He took him on a tour of places that included what is now Bandelier National Monument before heading to Switzerland to pursue a doctorate at the University of Geneva.

Hewett's dissertation served as the basis of a 1904 report submitted to the General Land Office in which he broke the entire Southwest into a series of archaeological regions or districts, each of which he summarized in terms of its general content and research or preservation needs. Hewett specifically called out four districts that were in dire need of legislative protections: Mesa Verde, Chaco, the Pajarito Plateau, and the Bluff District. All but the last one received it within about a decade or so. It would take the Bluff District until 2016 to receive broad legislative protection in the form of Bears Ears National Monument, a momentous and contentious event.

The role that Alice Fletcher played in American archaeology and anthropology during the early Institutional phase didn't stop with her helping to draft encouraging but ultimately doomed early versions of cultural resource protection bills, however. In the words of archaeological historian Don Fowler, Fletcher "played many major roles in American anthropology and Indian affairs for nearly four decades, from about 1880 to 1910." She was an active part of early feminist and temperance movements while a teacher in New York City, and became interested in anthropology largely from that angle, wanting to understand human cultures not as a means to help colonize or exploit them but as a means to help preserve them.* By 1879, she was a full lecturer in "Ancient America," a full protégé of Putnam, and a founding member of the AIA.

Within a decade, Fletcher held a lifetime fellowship at the Peabody Museum, and in 1906 she presented a proposal to expand the AIA's role in North America and strengthen its ties with its western chapters. One crucial step in her proposal was the creation of a Director of American Archaeology, whose job would include directing and coordinating all work undertaken by the various chapters. The committee accepted her proposal and gave the title of Director of American Archaeology to Hewett. This is how he was able to enact what was effectively a soft coup in 1907 that resulted in the creation of what would become the School of American Research as an entity entirely separate from the AIA.

◆ ◆ ◆

Through all this, Hewett was a busy man. In the years leading up to founding the school, Hewett worked closely with Lacey and Theodore Roosevelt between submitting his 1904 report and 1906, the ultimate result of which was 16 USC. 431-433, otherwise known as The Antiquities Act.

It's a remarkably short and rather vague piece of legislation. Its lofty purpose was to provide "Proper care and management of . . . historic landmarks, historic and prehistoric structures, and other objects of historic or scientific interest." Examinations were to be "undertaken for the benefit of reputable museums, universities, colleges, or other recognized scientific or educational institutions, with a view to increasing the knowledge of such objects." Major provisions of the Antiquities Act provided for penalizing those who damage or destroy objects of antiquity on federal land, and requirement of permits for excavation and removal of said objects. Looting was now officially a crime.

In addition to these elements, the Antiquities Act also carved a tiny bit of power over public lands from the legislative branch and

* Again: this was during the "vanishing race" intellectual period, so I think we can forgive her for that attitude.

gave it to the executive branch by allowing the president to create national monuments by proclamation to protect "objects of historic or scientific interest." That part would become a lit stick of dynamite.

This then trumpets the gradual, but probably inevitable, evolution in the American anthropological community from one of "the Indians are going extinct so we have to salvage and chronicle information about their cultures" to "the Indians aren't going anywhere so maybe we should try to salvage their material culture because it's really important for understanding their history." Efforts to "understand their history" were still firmly rooted in colonialistic philosophy—white people studying Indigenous people to figure out the developmental details of what they considered to be, in effect, really fascinating proto-humans.

This is when all that "living fossil" stuff became vogue, starting with the literary Romantics trying to convince everyone that Indigenous people were noble savages rather than simply savages and then synergizing with the nascent pseudosciences of race and phrenology. We could learn a lot about humanity's deep past by studying the cultures and histories of people who never evolved out of the Stone Age, the reasoned, so it's a good thing they weren't entirely wiped out after all!

But those colonialistic roots were also starting to stretch and creak. As early as 1921, an archaeologist with the lovely name Nels Nelson was regularly submitting formal, technical reports that included such florid prose as: "From earliest reports, the native life has been described as of 'exceedingly low type' . . . and their country inaccessible. There is an unfairness in this judgment, for the native mind fostered in this environment is filled with complex ideas (Navaho, etc.)." Nelson was an early and devoted proponent of involving Indigenous people in the study of their own material history, an idea that dated all the way back to Thomas Jefferson and Adolph Bandelier when they both took the bold step of asking local Indigenous people if they knew anything about it.

As the dominant attitude among American archaeological researchers shifted from viewing sites as treasure chests of potential museum-quality goodies to snapshots of historic information, excavation of sites also shifted from digging for treasure to digging for information. What they were digging for in those days was culture history, still broadly defined as the chronological sequence and spatial extent of material patterns in a given region.

Archaeologists set about trying to build all sorts of schema to explain what they were seeing in the archaeological record, the most far-reaching and enduring of which is probably the Pecos Sequence, introduced by A.V. Kidder at the first Pecos Archaeological Conference in 1927. It separated the material chronology of what would later be called the Ancestral Pueblo culture area into discrete periods and phases based on observable trends in the material culture, like how a hypothetical excavation of modern America would yield smartphones, then cordless phones, then rotary phones, then telegraph machines as one digs deeper and deeper. In the case of the Pecos Sequence, it went Paleoindian, Archaic, Basketmaker (II and III), and Pueblo (I through IV or V depending on the version).

Much of this was anchored in simple application of the concept of stratigraphy: older things are found farther down because the process of accumulation generally moves upward. Nels Nelson and Earl Morris had made their own observations about stratigraphic trends in their excavations, with Nelson tying his to the overlying Spanish colonial ceramics and whatnot. These observations are an example of "relative dating," which is simply the ordering of how things occurred based on their relative positions in the stratigraphy it doesn't give you actual dates. Morris did everyone an even bigger solid when he became obsessed with the fledgling science of dendrochronology or tree-ring dating, pioneered by A.E. Douglass at the University of Arizona in 1901. This and the later discovery of radiocarbon dating are examples of "absolute dating," which does provide actual dates, at least in theory.

These all converged in the Pecos Sequence, which categorized the material history of the Southwest into a neat series of chronological boxes. It was celebrated at the time as both a massive triumph and an inviolable catalog of the prehistory of the northern Southwest, providing a neat graphic schema of cultural phases and the date ranges associated with them.

The celebrations would last about thirty years.

◆ ◆ ◆

Archaeological schema like the Pecos Sequence were the result of an approach that started in Europe known as culture-historical archaeology, where data were used to reconstruct major steps in the cultural development of prehistoric peoples in different regions. Cultural-historical archaeologists believed that all cultural change resulted from just three factors: innovation, migration, and diffusion. Because American and European archaeology were still at least somewhat wedded at the time, this theoretical paradigm jumped the Atlantic Ocean without a great deal of fuss.

Culture-historical archaeologists were also fixedly concerned with the typological evolution of material culture, as well as the examination of interregional similarities and differences across the three distinct categories they established. Consequently, the establishment of chronology emerged as a central focus within their research endeavors—hence the Pecos Sequence. This would create subsequent pitfalls when people slowly but surely began to realize that, as the saying goes, pots aren't people.

The practice of culture-history reconstruction arguably reached its zenith in the US during the 1930s, when the Great Depression resulted in the deployment of major archaeological research projects as a component of public-works programs like the Works Progress Administration and the Civilian Conservation Corps. These were usually supervised by a board of archaeologists and administrators in Washington, DC and proposals were often evaluated on the basis not only of how important the archaeology might be but how many jobs the project might create.

In 1937, for example, a fellow named James Ford led an effort called the Louisiana Project that was intended—to quote Jeffrey Altschul—to "flesh out the culture history for the lower Mississippi River valley." He speculated that three distinct prehistoric cultures had developed in the region over time and proposed to test this theory by "peeling back key mound sites" in the region. His efforts were successful, resulting in a culture sequence for the lower Mississippi River region in much the same way Kidder and his colleagues had constructed one for the Southwest.

It was also in the mid-1930s that the next major piece of protective legislation was successfully enacted. The Historic Sites Act of 1935 was the first major effort to institutionalize historic preservation in the federal government, to protect the built environment and archaeological resources from destruction. "It is a national policy to preserve for public use historic sites, buildings, and objects of national significance for the inspiration and benefit of the people of the United States," as the bill states. It gave the National Park Service a prominent role in administering the federal historic preservation program. It directed the Secretary of the Interior to do the following:

- Make a survey of historic and archaeological sites, buildings, and objects to determine those of exceptional value for commemorating or illustrating the history of the United States;
- Restore, reconstruct, rehabilitate, preserve, and maintain historic or prehistoric properties of national significance;
- Develop related educational programs; and
- Erect and maintain commemorative markers.

After that, it took another twenty-five years before the next major piece of legislation was passed.

◆ ◆ ◆

With so little protective legislation for archaeological sites and materials on the books, the field continued to be dominated by research archaeologists—and, of course, looters. This was the state of the field when the Glen Canyon Dam Archaeological Salvage Project commenced, although it takes a bit of a run-up to understand that one.

Three months before Major Powell's death in 1902, the federal government created a reclamation program that lit the fuse on a century of dam- and canal-construction projects for which the government (read: taxpayers) footed most of the bills. These, in turn, precipitated homesteading and urban growth beyond Powell's worst nightmares, including large cities like Las Vegas being constructed in places where virtually every drop of water needs to be hauled in by trucks. Small farmers, whom Powell saw as the heart and destiny of the American West, were outcompeted by urban growth and the development of corporate mega-farms that could import water over hundreds or thousands of miles. But I'm getting ahead of myself.

Scouting for potential dam locations was a major focus of all the geographic mapping projects of the late 1800s and early 1900s, and a dam was planned at the narrowest chokepoint of Glen Canyon as early as 1924. It was one component of the grand vision encapsulated in the Colorado River Compact, signed in 1922 by six states—Colorado, New Mexico, Utah, Wyoming, California, and Nevada—to decide how best to utilize and manage the mighty but erratic Colorado River.

The Glen Canyon dam site ended up not being dammed in the 1920s, for reasons having partly to do with its remoteness and the nightmare logistics of hauling people and equipment there but mostly to do with California not wanting the "virtual faucets" of the Colorado to be built "in what amounted to hostile territory" in the upper basin, according to Martin. Instead, Hoover Dam went up downstream and created Lake Mead.

Meanwhile, developments continued on the cultural preservation front. The Committee for the Recovery of Archaeological Remains (CRAR) was established to provide a voice for American archaeologists who wished to express the opinion that "salvage" archaeology needed to be conducted to preserve archaeological remains before reservoir projects are completed. Its members included the irascible A.V. Kidder, along with pioneer Bears Ears archaeologist J.O. Brew, William S. Webb, and Frederick Johnson. The River Basin Survey Program began that same year to protect archaeological materials from destruction by dam construction and flooding, a symposium for which was published by Brew in 1947 and helped inform the Glen Canyon Project.

The NPS had official oversight of the project and directed University of Utah archaeology professor Jesse Jennings to run it however he saw fit in the role of principal investigator. Owing to the immense scale of the operation, and the fact that they were literally doing salvage archaeology ahead of the rising waters of Lake Powell, the fieldwork was split between the University of Utah and the Museum of Northern Arizona.

The Project officially ran from 1957 to 1963, although spinoffs like the Cedar Mesa Project that focused on the heart of what is now Bears Ears continued through the subsequent decades. More recently, with the dramatic drawdown of water in Lake Powell from what's turning out to be an endless drought in the Southwest, voices within and adjacent to the realm of professional archaeology have begun clamoring for a New Glen Canyon Project to inventory and inspect the conditions of archaeological sites gradually being exposed as water in the West goes bye-bye. My friend Erik Stanfield from the Navajo Nation Heritage and Historic Preservation Department joined NPS archaeologist Amy Schott and Museum of Northern Arizona archaeologist Kim Spurr on a leisurely boat trip to see if any sites from the original fieldwork were even discernible after sitting beneath the waves for so long, and a surprising number of them were.

◆ ◆ ◆

Coming along about halfway through the Glen Canyon Project, the Reservoir Salvage Act of 1960 was designed to help protect archaeological sites primarily from large reservoir projects and other public works constructed during the post-World War II era. It provided for the preservation of archaeological data that might otherwise be lost because of a federal construction project or a federally licensed or funded project. It also authorized Congress to provide funds to recover, preserve, and protect archaeological data.

"Salvage archaeology" projects for new reservoirs and highways contributed important data and led to what would later be known as contract archaeology—or, more commonly, cultural resource management. The Historic Sites Act of 1935 also set the stage for what came next. Thirty years later, the social and political context of the 1960s led to public activism that resulted in the passage of the National Historic Preservation Act (NHPA) of 1966. The passage of the NHPA is American archaeology's golden spike, in the sense of a geologic marker created by a global event that leads to lasting global changes. Not in the railroad sense.

In the early 1960s, American culture was largely about celebrating economic prosperity, materialism, youth, and generally all things new and shiny. Cheap gasoline allowed citizens to enjoy new highways, shopping malls, and housing developments in the suburbs. President JFK and his wife Jackie were a youthful presence in the White House. New trends and innovations included everything from the first heart transplant to Beatlemania to the first Super Bowl. Researchers even talked about a coming "new archaeology" that would become codified that same decade.

Big construction projects focused on urban renewal and construction of the interstate highway system. The federal government paid about 80 percent of the cost of urban renewal projects. Cities obtained new legal powers to condemn private property to clear out slums. Naturally, many historic buildings and neighborhoods, as well as prehistoric sites, were destroyed in the process.

The National Trust for Historic Preservation, the Society for American Archaeology, and other historic preservation organizations reacted against this wave of destruction. They developed an expanded concept of preservation, not limited to big events and famous people. At the same time, Lady Bird Johnson began her campaign to beautify America. The First Lady convened a White House Conference in 1965, which spawned a Special Committee on Historic Preservation. In 1966, the Committee—along with the National Trust and the US Conference of Mayors—published a book-length report called *With Heritage So Rich.* These efforts prompted the development and passage of the NHPA.

The statement of purpose of the NHPA is almost a page long but, a few key excerpts tee it up pretty well. "Historic properties significant to the Nation's heritage are being lost or substantially altered with increasing frequency. The preservation of this irreplaceable heritage is in the public interest so that its vital legacy of cultural, educational, aesthetic, inspirational, economic, and energy benefits will be maintained and enriched for future generations of Americans."

Realizing that sweeping legislation like this required a method of inventory, the NHPA called for creation of the National Register of Historic Places (NRHP) that could serve as a planning tool for cultural resource management. It was to be "composed of sites, buildings, structures, and objects significant to American history, architecture, archaeology, and culture." The word "significant" was—and, to a certain extent, remains—the fly in the ointment. Significant to *whom*, exactly?

The original intent was for the NRHP to be a publishable document of all the places deemed worthy of protection as "historic properties," in its official parlance, which seems rather ambitious. The latest version of the publication includes right around seventy thousand listings. Later revisions expanded the scope of NHPA to offer protection to material history determined by the managing agencies to be eligible for inclusion in the NRHP, not just those that are listed in it.

Then came the National Environmental Policy Act (or NEPA) in 1970. Its importance to the realm of historic preservation lies mostly in its defining consideration of culturally important places from an environmental perspective as non-renewable resources that should be preserved whenever possible. The Act also *strongly encouraged* all federal agencies to evaluate and consider alternatives to avoid or minimize the impact of their actions on the human environment, including cultural components thereof.

There's nothing in NEPA that's substantive or compels protection, but agencies are—again—strongly encouraged to adhere to best principles in accordance with NEPA so they don't get their pants sued off by watchdog groups. In that sense it's what legal eagles call a procedural law. It directs the process of analyzing environmental impacts without mandating any specific outcome or requiring project proponents to mitigate any identified impacts.

They keyword with NEPA is "disclosure." The primary function of NEPA is disclosure of potential effects and impacts from federal undertakings to the public, agencies, Tribes and other stakeholders, and project proponents in order to facilitate decisions that are compatible with everyone's needs and other, actual protective legislation—at least in theory. The spirit of the law is impressive in that it's designed to be a mandate for collaborative analysis, bringing people and laws together into one process, because of which it is probably—and not a little ironically—the most far-reaching protective legislation of all while not actually mandating any type of protection. Little wonder that it's been under attack since the day Nixon signed it into law.

This was followed by the Archaeological Resources Protection Act (or ARPA) in 1979. Like the Antiquities Act and the NHPA before it, ARPA resulted from a concerted effort by historic preservation organizations that were concerned about trends of increasing destruction and vandalism of archaeological sites. By the mid-1970s, it became apparent that it was difficult to successfully prosecute vandals for violations of the Antiquities Act. Not only was it difficult to enforce, but there were no substantive criminal or civil penalties to deter looters. Historic preservation advocates realized that we needed a more modern, stronger law to protect archaeological resources, as well as one that might finally offer a concrete legal definition for "significant prehistoric resources," "cultural aspects of our national heritage," "archaeological data," and other terms that were annoyingly vague in the earlier legislation.

Last on the list—for now—is the Native American Graves Protection and Repatriation Act (NAGPRA, pronounced how it looks) of 1990. It established the right of Indian tribes and Native Hawaiian organizations to claim ownership of human remains and associated objects that are held by federal agencies and museums that receive federal funds. The Act requires agencies to identify such holdings and to work with appropriate Native American groups toward their repatriation. In brief, NAGPRA:

- Provides detailed descriptions of protected materials including burial sites, human remains, funerary objects, sacred objects, and objects of cultural patrimony.
- Establishes rights of ownership for items discovered or excavated after November 1990.
- Identifies procedures for the inadvertent discovery and the intentional excavation and removal of human remains and associated objects.
- Defines penalties for illegal trafficking in protected remains and objects.
- Addresses procedures for inventories of remains in the possession of agencies and museums.
- Identifies procedures for the repatriation of materials to lineal descendants and tribes determined to be culturally affiliated.
- Establishes a Review Committee to address disputes.

Two other pieces of legislation that bear some relevance to the topic of archaeological preservation, albeit in an indirect rather than direct sense, are the American Indian Religious Freedom Act (AIRFA) of 1978 and Executive Order 13007 (usually just called "Indian Sacred Sites") of 1996.

Among other things, including acting as a shield against our ridiculous drug laws vis-à-vis traditional use of entheogens like peyote, the former protects Indigenous access to sacred objects and ceremonial places. Thanks to AIRFA, you can't build an enormous wall that separates a Native community from a place where they've gathered plants or performed other rituals since time immemorial.* The latter dictates that federal agencies shall accommodate access to and ceremonial use of Indian sacred sites, shall avoid adversely affecting the physical integrity of such sites, and shall maintain their confidentiality.

* Unless that wall happens to keep Brown people from crossing an invisible barrier to look for a job in the very country whose foreign policies destabilized the economy of their homeland in the first place. Then it's fine.

The First Amendment of the US Constitution, inked in 1791, states that Congress "shall make no law respecting an establishment of religion, or prohibiting the free exercise thereof," despite which Native Americans were still prohibited from practicing their religions and traditional ceremonies. For the most part, freedom of religion in the United States just means freedom to be Christian—a concept that was enforced in harsh and brutal ways during the Indian School era. Passage of AIRFA finally extended actual freedom of religion to the Indigenous community.

To a point, anyway. It doesn't count if their religion says a mountain that would make a lovely ski resort or a valley that would make a lovely open-pit copper mine are sacred.

Finally, one other ancillary or indirect tool for archaeological preservation that doesn't often appear in mainstream discussions of the topic is the concept of Traditional Cultural Properties, or TCPs. They were the subject of National Register Bulletin 38, published in 1990 and undergoing revision in 2024, and are broadly defined by topic expert Patricia L. Parker as "a property, a place, that is eligible for inclusion on the National Register of Historic Places because of its association with cultural practices and beliefs that are (1) rooted in the history of a community, and (2) are important to maintaining the continuity of that community's traditional beliefs and practices." Examples include plant- or other resource-gathering areas, ceremonial or festival gathering areas, places where something really important or interesting happened, shrines, springs, and so on. Basically, any discreet location that is of demonstrable long-standing importance to living communities in accordance with NHPA criteria.

That can, and often does, include archaeological sites. Obviously. I've visited sites in northern New Mexico that are hundreds of years old, look like "ruins" in the usual colloquial sense, and are closed from public access four times a year because they're still used for religious ceremonies.

◆ ◆ ◆

That procession of protective legislation sounds impressive when you read it chronologically, especially with regard to the immense personal efforts of people like Fletcher, Hewett, and others poured into it. But there's a problematic throughline that deserves special attention. They all focus their energies entirely on public lands or federally sponsored efforts. The protections mandated by NHPA, for example, apply only to federally managed properties and federally funded or permitted projects on non-federal properties. Period. If a development project isn't on federal land or doesn't include federal funding, our capstone archaeological preservation law doesn't apply.

Similarly, the language of ARPA makes it clear the Act applies entirely to "public lands and Indian lands." It doesn't apply to state or private lands. The Act also stipulates that people with access to protected information (e.g., permitted researchers like yours truly) who share that information with the public are in violation of the law, but it doesn't apply to private citizens, which is why there are so many guidebooks and websites selling the locations of archaeological sites on federal lands.

This is also true of the opening salvo of NAGPRA, which applies to "the ownership or control of Native American cultural items which are excavated or discovered on Federal or tribal lands." Again, the three major legislative tools designed in part to preserve and protect access to traditionally important places apply only when those places are on lands not owned by municipalities, the military, the state, or private citizens. And then only when protecting that access doesn't impede extraneous efforts to prevent access by other socially designated undesirables.

In other words, general looting or vandalizing of archaeological sites on federally managed lands is a crime, but doing so on private land doesn't violate anything. Graverobbing in particular is a NAGPRA violation if it takes place on federally managed lands, the consequences for which can be severe, but if it happens on state or private lands it's subject to local or regional ordinances instead—like the Utah Division of Indian Affairs Act or the Arizona Antiquities Act. To quote the State Burial Laws Project at the American University's Washington College of Law, "such laws vary widely from state-to-state, and thus there is no clear protocol" for how to deal with discovery or disturbance of Native American remains. Most states have some version of this, in any case, but figuring out exactly how, why, and when they apply can be tricky business.

Take the Lake County case in California. Severe drought in the recent past has resulted in shrinking lakes and lowered water levels, as well as abundant wildfires, all of which make it easier to find artifacts and sites. The implications of this scenario are not lost on looters. California's Native American Historic Resource Protection Act is supposed to address this sort of thing, but it was never enforced in Lake County prior to 2015, when local Tribes—looking at the above conditions and coming to the obvious conclusion—pressured local law enforcement to conduct training for how to identify and investigate such crimes. Shortly thereafter, by which I mean literally two days after the training, Lake County Deputy Sheriff Richard Kreutzer discovered numerous artifacts inside the van of a man he suspected of being high on meth and trespassing on private property.

Kreutzer provided the following quote to KQED: "In all honesty, I might have come across these types of things in other calls but didn't necessarily know what they were. Now thanks to this training . . . we are a little more aware of what we are looking at." That KQED article goes on to note how, according to the forensic archaeologist who led the training, archaeological crimes are "frequently connected to drug use, especially meth, with looters selling relics to buy drugs. Typically (looters) are going to be high on some type of drug like methamphetamine. They are going to be armed, and they know what they are doing is illegal, so it can create a very dangerous situation out there on the ground." Lake County has the highest per capita rate of drug-induced death in the entire state of California, by the way.

The sad fact is that most looting in the US is less an act of treasure-hunting than an act of desperation by addicts. They're not slick, clever villains like Juno Skinner in *True Lies* or Dr. René Belloq in *Raiders*. They're the person stealing your catalytic converter to swap for enough cash to cop their next fix.*

* Most of the time, anyway. Occasionally we'll get people who are just that obsessed with collecting antiquities. Anything can become an addiction if it presses the right neurological buttons.

In the case of Lake County, police were on the lookout for 41-year-old Brian Gene Smith over allegations that he had "left an inappropriate letter for a 14-year-old girl," according to the official police report. They found him behind a business building, high as a kite, with a van full of artifacts that included projectile points, ceramic bowls, and human bones—some of which had index cards explaining where they were taken. Snidely Whiplash this dude was not.

The even sadder fact, however—at least in the context of this book—is how little protective legislation there is for antiquities on private lands. The California Native American Historic Resource Protection Act covers just about any type of looting or vandalism and applies to both public and private land. But Arizona's A.R.S. § 41-865 only applies to human remains and mortuary items or features. The same goes for Utah's Indian Affairs Act, which applies to people who "knowingly sell, purchase, use for profit, or transport for sale or profit the remains of a Native American without rights of possession over the remains." In fact, as a rule, it is legal to collect non-mortuary artifacts on any private property in the United States provided you're either the legal landowner or have written permission from whomever that is.

Think about that for a moment. You pay money or do a trade or simply inherit a piece of paper saying that a chunk of the planet's surface belongs to you, and that means everything on that piece of the planet also belongs to you, excluding only human remains and—sometimes—the objects buried with them.

Exceptions to this primacy of private land are legion. Eminent domain, where the government can seize private property for public uses "essential to [the nation's] independent existence and perpetuity," applies to private land. So does the Endangered Species Act, which essentially grants property rights to endangered species living on the land. The Clean Air and Clean Water Acts also apply to private land if it contains a wetland connected to a navigable waterway and/or contains some building or operation belching noisome fumes into everybody's air. You also can't build a home on private property unless you fill out all the proper forms and pay all the proper graft, including—as I learned the hard way—many thousands of dollars to dig a septic system even if you plan to use a composting toilet. You also aren't allowed to use federally scheduled drugs on private land, or harbor people from other countries who don't have a visa, or store certain materials, or do a whole bunch of other stuff.

In fact, there is a lot of protective legislation that does apply to private land in this country, for the plain and obvious reason that water and air and animals and so on don't really care about property lines. But you're still free to plunder someone else's material history, just so long as you don't seek federal funding or permitting to do so.

◆ ◆ ◆

So, that's one problematic element of all this protective legislation. The federal versions only apply to federally funded actions and federally managed public lands, and the state and local versions vary manically from place to place. The other problem is that of deciding how to actually apply those laws, and who it is that gets to apply them.

In most of modern American archaeology, at least since the passage of NHPA, the first step is determining if a new project or policy change slated to occur on public land is likely to affect important sites. Then, archaeologists are deployed to conduct surveys and research to see if any important sites are even there. Then (assuming there are), polite suggestions are made to move or alter the plans to avoid or minimize impacts. If the plans can't be changed, the final stage is mitigation of damages—excavating and curating or repatriating materials—or, if the project goes ahead and destroys important sites without doing any mitigation, lawsuits are launched.

That's the process in a nutshell: determine likely effects, identify historic resources likely to be affected, assess potential impacts and recommend actions to avoid or minimize them, and then implement those actions. And, like most simplistic explanations, it glosses right over a myriad of complexities, ambiguities, and cultural or political landmines.

Moreover, there's really no set-in-stone chronology for when something even counts as historic. According to ARPA, an archaeological resource is anything at least a hundred years old, but according to NHPA that parameter is a mere fifty years—although that's more of a guideline than a rule. But since NHPA is the legislation that guides the overwhelming bulk of archaeological work in the United States, anything that dates to as recently as 1976 (as of this publication) must be regarded as historic and treated as potentially significant enough to warrant protection. That's one year after computers were invented.

This is why so many archie veterans snarl and foam when they see a discarded tin can. Americans in the, uh, Good Old Days loved to just toss their trash all over the place, including cans, which came to prominence as the primary means of manufactured food storage in the late 1800s and have only recently yielded that exalted status to plastic containers—some of which are now also considered historic under this rule. I have no idea how many rusty cans I've recorded with the same level of respectful documentation as ancient lithic tools, but I'd conservatively put it in the tens of thousands.

On the other hand, and I do frankly love this, those same salty old field technicians voraciously pick up litter on public lands in a sort of morbid solidarity with future archaeologists who might otherwise have to curate it. Hey, whatever works.

The source document for that subpart of 43 CFR 7, by the way, is 49 FR 1027, which dates to January 6, 1984. That's five years after ARPA was implemented and four years before it was amended, although the 1988 amendments simply focused more attention on management actions and directing of federal land managers to engage more with the public. This means the legal definition of archaeological resources under ARPA was determined half a decade *after* that legislation was created to help protect them. Imagine telling your kid they're not allowed to play with the chainsaw and then circling back a month later to tell them what a chainsaw is.

More telling than all that is the ARPA Preamble, which states that the "purpose of this Act is to secure, for the present and future benefit of the American people, the protection of archaeological resources and sites which are on public lands and Indian lands . . ."

So, again, it specifies the present and future benefit of the *American* people. Meanwhile, literally all my Indigenous friends and colleagues refer to themselves as either something ethnically specific—Hopi, Diné, Metís, Anishinaabe, Núuchi-u, etc.—or more broadly as simply Indigenous. What they pointedly never say is "American."

◆ ◆ ◆

On the other end of the complexity spectrum, the Antiquities Act is often criticized for being frustratingly ambiguous, but for these very reasons it happens to be my favorite among the major federal historic-protection documents. Here's what it says about creating national monuments:

> That the President of the United States is hereby authorized, in his discretion, to declare by public proclamation historic landmarks, historic and prehistoric structures, and other objects of historic or scientific interest that are situated upon the lands owned or controlled by the Government of the United States to be national monuments, and may reserve as a part thereof parcels of land, the limits of which in all cases shall be confined to the smallest area compatible with proper care and management of the objects to be protected: Provided, That when such objects are situated upon a tract covered by a bona fide unperfected claim or held in private ownership, the tract, or so much thereof as may be necessary for the proper care and management of the object, may be relinquished to the Government, and the Secretary of the Interior is hereby authorized to accept the relinquishment of such tracts in behalf of the Government of the United States.

That's it. That's Section 2 of the Antiquities Act in its entirety. Historic landmarks, historic and prehistoric structures, and other objects of historic or scientific interest located on public lands can be set aside from development by POTUS. Historic and prehistoric structures can be anything from Hearst Castle on down to a Basketmaker pithouse, and at no point does it specify what an "object" is or to whom something is of historic or scientific interest.

This kicks open the door to things like Bears Ears National Monument, where the Tribes involved in its creation insist the entire landscape is of extreme historic interest given its role in many of their respective histories. And that, in turn, prompted the Obama administration to use the phrase "cultural landscape" in the 2016 monument proclamation, marking the first time that phrase was ever used in a federal designation of this sort. The term was invoked again in the Biden administration's 2023 monument proclamation for Baaj Nwaavjo I'tah Kukveni—Ancestral Footprints of the Grand Canyon National Monument, which notes that at least twelve Tribes "describe the lands here as a cultural landscape to which their ancestors belong."

This is the sort of thing that can happen when you pass legislation enabling the protection of important stuff but don't stipulate to whom that importance must apply. Teddy may have been racist, even for his time, but the most important piece of legislation he passed in terms of conservation was vague enough that people of virtually any background can use it to make an argument for why something deserves protection. The wealthy white guys who comprised the conservation movement when it started had, intentionally or not, set a tool on the bench that potentially any other person or group could come along and use.

◆ ◆ ◆

To better understand how all this protective legislation began to manifest in the public's eye, consider how archaeology is the epitome of survivorship bias—the logical error of focusing on entities or variables that passed a selective process while overlooking those that did not. Probably the most infamous example of survivorship bias—and one that bears a lot more relevance to/for the study of material history—is that of Allied military aircraft in World War II.

Military analysts during the war conducted an analysis of planes that successfully returned from active combat after receiving minor or even serious damage. Many of them had taken the most serious damage to their wings, some of which looked like cheese graters by the time they touched down. Others had taken extensive damage to their tail or central fuselage. Based on these data, the US military commenced a plan to strengthen the armor in those areas where damage was statistically concentrated the most—until a professor from Columbia University named Abraham Wald politely pointed out how their analysis focused entirely on the planes that survived taking heavy damage. Which means the military analysts were all set to add additional armor to the parts of their aircraft where damage proved to be least fatal during the mission. The parts that caused planes to, for example, instantly disintegrate when they took a hit would have remained vulnerable because the planes that got hit in those parts were too disintegrated to be part of the analysis.

Long-term material preservation works the same way. The further back in the archaeological record one looks, the more one sees large stone tools and the bones of enormous animals but less and less of everything else. In the past, this led a lot of researchers to come to the same conclusion as the military analysts in that infamous aircraft anecdote: this is what we're seeing because it's the important stuff and it tells the whole story. This is how we got images of ancient people wearing basically no clothes and doing nothing with their time outside of hunting enormous beasts with hilariously front-heavy spears.

In fact, as with the returning military aircraft, what we're focusing on is the stuff that can survive the longest. Clothing, wooden shelters, most forms of jewelry, small animal bones or other food items unlikely to fossilize, and of course immaterial things like music and language aren't preserved for nearly as long as mammoth femurs or large stone weapons.

In terms of architecture, cliff dwellings last much longer than structures built in open areas because cliff dwellings are constructed inside lean-tos of living rock that protect them from the elements, at least when those elements don't include sections of the alcove ceiling crashing down. The number of surface sites in most of the Colorado

Plateau would absolutely dwarf the number of cliff dwellings if we could still see them all, but we often can't.

This is why early Southwest archaeologists slapped the label Cliff Dweller on entire periods of Indigenous material history, as if that was the only game in town at the time. Copious ink was spilled trying to figure out why, seemingly all of a sudden, everyone in places like the Four Corners moved from open areas into alcoves in canyon walls. Were they hiding from enemies? Were they trying to maximize farmland? Was it simply a trend that everyone jumped on?*

But not everyone moved into cliff dwellings in the later Ancestral Pueblo era. Because of course they didn't. To take just one example, the open-air Yellow Jacket Pueblo in southwestern Colorado was occupied at about the same time as the not-open-air Cliff Palace in Mesa Verde, but Yellow Jacket had more than five times as many people living in it. You won't see Yellow Jacket on the cover of any magazines, though. The unexcavated portions just look like big piles of rock.

For that matter, pyramids last for a really long time because a pyramid or cone is arguably the most stable shape for any structure to take on the planet's surface. It's the same shape flour makes when you pour it out, the same shape sand dunes make when they've got nothing better to do, and the same shape mountains assume after eons of erosion. This is why I always chuckle when I see pseudoarchaeology kooks wave their arms about how there must have been some mysterious worldwide culture that loved to build nigh-indestructible pyramids because we find them all over the world!

Sure, but have you looked at all the various cubical or cylindrical buildings built by the same people who built those pyramids that have since collapsed and eroded away? I'm guessing not. Chiefly because they've collapsed and eroded away.

The ramifications of this bias for archaeology and the wider realm of anthropology go way beyond early Western scholars concluding that, starting in about AD 1200, every single person in the northern Southwest moved into giant holes in the wall before

* Believe it or not, I met a guy in the town of Cortez who believed everyone in the ancient Mesa Verde region moved into cliff dwellings so the dinosaurs couldn't reach them. How they survived sharing open plains with dinosaurs long enough to figure this trick out was a question he couldn't confidently answer.

moving back out of them a few generations later to build mesa-top communities like the Hopi villages. Survivorship bias can also heavily skew Western perceptions of non-Western communities that managed to endure the horrors of colonialism.

This is one of the biggest problems with the "living fossils" approach of past and even modern ethnologists studying forager groups like the Aché or the Bedouins to understand how all people most likely lived in our collective deep history. They aren't looking at the vastly greater assemblage of Indigenous communities with widely varying cultural practices that didn't survive into the modern era, because they can't. Not without a time machine or a necromancer on call.

Those that did survive into modernity often retain cultural narratives and other forms of collective memory, so while they may not be embodied proxies for deep human history any more than I am an embodied proxy for ancient Italy, they have much to share nonetheless. Cultural narratives may change over time, but oftentimes the central premise or key observations remain intact, because collective memory can endure for far longer than most people would expect. This also speaks to how involvement of actual Indigenous people in the practice of archaeology on Indigenous material history is a good idea to say the very least.

Anthropologists working with Australian Aborigines have shown this to an almost ludicrous degree. One 2015 study, by Nick Reid and Patrick Nunn, showed preserved Aboriginal stories about locations along the Australian coastline that have been underwater for at least seven-thousand years. "It's important to note that it's not just one story that describes this process," says Nunn in a writeup on Science X. "There are many stories, all consistent in their narrative, across 21 diverse sites around Australia's coastline." I often think of this story when I hear quantitative archaeologists argue that you can't trust qualitative data like cultural narratives because human memories are too unreliable.

Near the modern town of Taos, New Mexico, is an archaeological site called Puye Pueblo, pronounced approximately *poo-jeh* in the dialect of the people of nearby Santa Clara Pueblo who manage the site as a National Historic Landmark. If you do a quick online search, you'll note that the site is called Puye Cliff Dwellings in almost every single instance, including its official website. What this conceals is the fact that while there are indeed cliff dwellings built into the walls of the Puye Mesa, there's also the remains of an enormous pueblo on top. So enormous, in fact, that it's recognized as the largest of all the archaeological settlements identified on the Pajarito Plateau, a place Adolph Bandelier and Edgar Lee Hewett wanted preserved in its entirety because of its dizzying array of archaeological splendors. Being top dog in a place like that is no mean feat.

Back in 1907, Hewett—then still acting in cooperation with the AIA—set about excavating the site. It was the first systematic excavation of a prehistoric pueblo in the Rio Grande Valley. It is also emblematic of Hewett as a tireless promoter of archaeology for the public, stating at the time that his intention with Puye was to "put on a big [work] force, clear out as much of it as possible . . . and make a show ruin of it." To that end, he worked closely with Santa Clara elders in his diggings, trying to learn as much as he could from them about their own history so he could build it into his interpretations. He also partially reconstructed a two-story community house in one corner of the mesa so that visitors could see what the rest of the rubble once looked like.

The community leaders at Santa Clara Pueblo greatly appreciated this effort, especially after Hewett assured them that turning the place into a tourist attraction would not result in its being acquired by the American Government the way Mesa Verde was a couple of years before.* Why they believed him in light of all the similar promises the American Government has broken with Indigenous communities is anybody's guess, but it remains true, and touring the site requires joining a guided tour by a Santa Clara individual.

I had a chance to visit the place in the early winter of 2023, and I can't recommend it enough. Because of the intense cold, my In-

* This simple statement glosses over a lot of very complicated history, by the way. The initial footprint of Mesa Verde National Park was deeded to the federal government by the Ute Mountain Utes after lengthy negotiations, most of them headed up by Virginia McClurg and Lucy Peabody. However, numerous subsequent expansions of the park for "management needs" were not done with Ute consent. It remains a tense situation to this day.

digenous guide and I had the entire place almost all to ourselves, so he felt comfortable dropping a lot of formality and just chatting about modern life at Santa Clara Pueblo. It was he who told me that although Hewett started out on great footing with the Tribe for all the reasons listed above, the relationship soon soured, and he was ultimately banned from working there after he broke a promise not to excavate any burials.

◆ ◆ ◆

What followed Hewett's work was a hodgepodge of legislation based largely on his own notion that at least some archaeological sites should be preserved for future researchers, the enjoyment of tourists with consent—and, where possible, involvement—by the Tribes. Preservation of material history for its own sake rather than as items to fill colonialistic trophy cases known as museums really began to blossom during this period, at least among archaeologists who weren't completely engulfed in the academic side of the discipline. They were still collecting and analyzing tchotchkes based on the culture-history notion that things and people are one and the same.

However, by the 1960s—at the same time federal protective legislation really started ramping up—culture-history approaches were largely exposed for their rather severe limitations. Chief among them was the fact that humans and their history are not as simple as rigid graphic schema would like them to be.

This is the problem into which we run whenever we try to reduce a continuum into a set of discrete quanta—or, if you will, try to pigeonhole a spectrum into separate bits. For the purpose of convention and to ease communal discourse we develop standardized conventions, so that there are four cardinal directions (N, S, E, W), eight chromatic notes (A–G), and six fundamental colors (three primary and three secondary). And then we have to add a whole host of modifiers, like "north-northwest," and the flat/sharp system, and the Munsell Color Guide that supposedly prevents people from describing soils as "kind of reddish-brown purple/tan with what looks like stripes of candy-apple mahogany." Because no symbol is ever perfectly representative of reality, and no continuum ever fits comfortably into a set of hard-edged boxes. The reality about direction, sound, and color is that their variability is literally infinite.

The ink was barely dry on the otherwise remarkably durable Pecos Sequence of Southwestern material history before people started twisting and contorting it into localized coruscations of often-untranslatable complexity to fit local material records. The Archaic Period was broken up into three or sometimes four major sub-periods, and then, depending upon the area, as many as a dozen or more phases and sub-phases.

To employ an old catechism and call the whole thing a "dog's breakfast" falls well short of the reality—at least we mostly know what a dog can and cannot swallow. When it comes to physical history, and especially the physical history of the predecessors of people very much unlike the majority of those doing the studying, researchers are often flying blind. Especially when Indigenous input became less and less common, owing to both the preponderance of racist attitudes in the early 1900s and the growing concern among Indigenous peoples that their cultural knowledge was not being used by white archaeologists so much as misused by them. Absent that line of input, a lot of attempts to explain or understand those culture-history developments was just wild guesswork.

It was recently discovered that a Sumerian artifact in the British Museum—an oblong-round object made of hardened clay with a fluted opening at one end—was the head of a fired-clay mace or heavy club and not, as they'd long believed, a vase. This speaks volumes.

To combat this obsession with things (literal things, in the case of artifacts, as well as the figurative things of imagined material cultures and phases), increasing numbers of researchers began turning instead to examining the processes that shaped human history. Never mind what particular group adopted agriculture in a given valley, for example, since we can never so much as ask them what they called themselves. Instead, we can ponder *why* whoever they were adopted agriculture there. And why then? What was it about the local environment, or the climate, or the nature of the cultivars themselves that made agriculture catch on? Did they learn it from their neighbors, or did their neighbors invade and bring it with them? How successful was it?

Meanwhile, outside the tight realm of purely academic research, the passage of NHPA also compelled land management agencies to inventory and manage an immense assemblage of archaeological materials and places, almost all of which is Indigenous. But neither NHPA nor any of the other legislative protection laws specify that managing agency personnel need to understand the archaeology they're tasked with managing—they just need to manage it. Highfalutin ideas about cultural evolution and process, and later bugbears like structuralism and post-processualism and behavioral ecology, were the realms of academics. Agencies, in the wording of the law itself, were tasked with protecting *significant* cultural resources, and therefore required that archaeologists define what that significance actually is.

In so doing, NHPA effectively split the domain of American archaeology into two separate, seemingly mutually exclusive practices: that of academic archaeology and that of resource management. The term "cultural resource management" (or CRM for short) hadn't entered anyone's lexicon yet, because it simply never appeared in any of the official documents covered so far—what appeared instead were terms like "historic resources" and "archaeological resources."

This was the start of CRM nonetheless, and it has retained the primacy of culture-history approaches to this very day, often while doing little more than doffing hat to the variety of theoretical approaches developed by academics in the following decades—starting with processualism and getting more creative thereafter.

It's also how the majority of us make a living.

◆ ◆ ◆

Preparation for fieldwork in those days mostly consisted of arriving in the field after taking a university course or two and being told "start digging here" or "go survey that area over there." Archaeological field schools, where archaeologists could go and spend a season learning the tricks of the trade from salty older archaeologists, didn't really become a thing until anthropological archaeology was established as a scientific-humanistic discipline, at which point universities began offering specialized training for college credit. Early professors like Hewett and Cummings would drag their students into the field to help on their projects, resulting in *de facto* field schools that were more like apprenticeships. Neil Judd, Earl Morris, and A.V. Kidder—to name just a few of American archaeology's most colorful characters—got their start this way.

Back when I was a bartender in New Orleans, and then New Mexico, and then Alaska, Vermont, Oregon, Colorado, Utah, and finally Flagstaff, Arizona, I was often asked how I'd managed to land such a fun job. Did I go to bartender school? Take an online certificate course? Apprentice with a salty old mixologist? And my answer was always: "I just spent a lot of time in bars watching how it was done." Maybe too much time.

But that's how I learned that the actual mixing of drinks isn't the most important part. You can always whip out a recipe list on your phone, most drinks are self-explanatory in any case (Jack and Coke, Seven and 7, etc.), and you're going to make so many standbys like margaritas that it'll become second nature in no time. Nor is managing the cash register or maintaining your station the most important part—those, too, become second nature pretty quickly.

Tending bar is more about managing people. Knowing how to detect the woman who's about to fall over or vomit, how to spot the guy who's about to get violent or try to take advantage of the falling-over woman, and—above all—knowing how to schmooze and perform for a diverse audience of strangers because that's how you earn tips. It's what prepared me to be an effective public speaker in the dovetailing realms of archaeology and conservation, and it's also the part they can't really teach you in bartender school. As my old and dearly departed friend Ryno used to say, quoting one of his favorite films, "You wasted $150,000 on an education you coulda got for $1.50 in late fees at the public library."

Similarly, the thing that best prepared me for the realities of working in archaeology was not my undergraduate program, which mostly focused on the history and development of the practice without any real practical training. Nor was it my graduate program, which mostly focused on theoretical research and preaching the gospel of behavioral ecology—with, again, no real practical training. Nor, for that matter, was it my field school in the University of Utah's Range Creek Field Station, where I learned how to do archaeology if it was still 1955.

The thing that prepared me the most was Dungeons and Dragons.

In field archaeology, you and a group of others are investigating a place you really don't know beforehand, oftentimes because it's literally buried beneath the ground. You research it as much as possible and prepare accordingly before you arrive. You have an overall strategy or goal in mind, and you go into huddles to plan each successive move based on what you find along the way. You encounter challenges like snow and mud and rattlesnakes and riled up humans, and you often have to think quickly and flexibly to deal with them. You take careful notes and draw careful maps of everything you encounter, because that's all going to help you figure out what it is you're dealing with and how that helps or hinders your pursuit of the overarching endpoint. And you need to do so before the glowing orb of funding runs out and/or the flailing tentacles of development destroy it all.

In role-playing games like D&D, you pretty much do the same thing. You and the rest of your campaign go forth and explore some place you don't or barely know with some overarching goal in mind, you encounter puzzles and monsters along the way, draw maps and take notes to help conceptualize the place, and you try to reach your goal before the dark lord assumes control of the kingdom—or it gets too late and your parents start sending furious texts.

When I was in field school in the late 00s, my good pal Glenn, who would go on to help me understand why Roman history and archaeology helps explain a lot about modern America, confided in me that he and some other soldiers played D&D when they were bored and listless during their deployments in Iraq. But he only told me about this where the other students couldn't hear. Games like D&D were still associated entirely with "nerds" in those days, and nerdiness wouldn't become trendy until a few years later.

Because my friend and I caught an earlier wave of something that would eventually become hip and trendy, we weren't overly excited to celebrate that fact until about the last decade or so. But it contributed immensely to our understanding of how archaeology works. We basically arrived at field school with preloaded mental software about the importance of taking meticulous notes, making carefully detailed drawings and maps, and generally trying to piece together a narrative in our imaginations using the sparse clues we encountered within often inflexible time and budget constraints.

This is not to cast formal education in a totally negative light. What we did learn in field school was how best to pack and carry field equipment, how often to apply sunscreen and bug spray, how to treat snakebites and other forms of harm, how to fix a flat tire on sand, how to shower in a creek, and how to ham it up when the folks from *Time Team America* show up to film an episode. We also heard a lot of great stories around the campfire at night, along with a lot of complaining about federal protective legislation—why it goes too far, why it doesn't go far enough, and how someone can be right about both of those things at the same time because they're old and they've earned it.

Anyone who's played a lot of D&D or other role-playing games will likely report something similar. The game—the project—is only part of the fun, and oftentimes it's not even the biggest part. The rest is the experience you all enjoy together. Lots of banter and hamming it up for each other. Lots of laughing and occasional arguing. Human stuff.

Because, in the end, it's all about *people*. Not things.

Or at least it's supposed to be. That's true of D&D for most folks who understand the game and its intentions, although you'll still get the "check out my crystal dice set—it's so much better than yours" types who think the humanistic element is a side item at best. This is also true of archaeology, but the divide in that case tends to be oceanic. Literally.

CHAPTER 5

INTERPRETERS AND IMPOSTERS

The most relevant distinction between European and American archaeology is that of people studying their own (or at least closely related) heritage and people studying someone else's. After all, whatever else you can say about the immense variety of Eurasian material culture, it is definitely Eurasian.

As simplistic as that might sound on its face, it's important for understanding the material record and how it gets portrayed. The Mesolithic Period in Ireland manifested quite differently from the Mesolithic Period in Japan, for example, with simple Bann flaked tools dominating the former by about ten thousand years ago and elaborate Jōmon pottery dominating the latter at about the same time. That's a hell of a difference in cultural trajectories. But the barriers between these areas were never as challenging as, say, the Atlantic or Pacific Oceans.

In fact, sustained contact among groups across greater Eurasia (including north Africa and the Indian subcontinent) has occurred with at least some regularity since the dawn of anatomically modern *Homo sapiens*, and most likely earlier than that. Despite emerging in Africa sometime in the early Pleistocene, fossils of *Homo erectus*—arguably the first fully "human" member of the hominid lineage—were initially discovered in Peking.

Long-distance trade played a major role in the sociocultural exchanges that took place between the major population centers in Europe and Asia during the latter stages of antiquity. Some of these trade routes went back centuries in time and followed any of several different possible routes, but by the beginning of the Common or

Anno Domini era civic and religious leaders, merchants and traders, and anyone else could cross the ancient Euro-Asian world from the Euro- bit to the Asian bit along safe and established routes—at least to a given value of *safe*. Silk from China came west into Europe, hence the so-called Silk Road. Spices made their way to wealthy European dishes primarily from South Asia, hence the Spice Road, along with what were then called the Spice (and now called the Malaku) Islands. Yet another route, known as the Incense Route, was controlled by the Arabs.

Although there were occasional encounters like that of Leif Erikson around a thousand years ago, sustained contact between greater Eurasia and the Americas wasn't really a thing until the 1500s. That's at least ten thousand years after people first migrated to the Americas, and it's probably more like twice that amount—long enough for some rather seismic differences to emerge.

Frantic efforts by early Euro-American scholars to square the history of Indigenous Americans with that of ancient Eurasia was largely inspired by the culture shock of encountering people whose culture was so radically different from theirs. For what I assume are reasons having to do with evolutionary neurology, encounters with people or things that are wildly different from one's baseline experience usually engender a desperate scramble to identify commonalities. Hippopotamus means "water horse" and porcupine means "spike pig," to take just two examples. Calling everything some version of pig was actually a bit of a trend for a while—porpoise means "pig fish" and aardvark means "earth pig." The German word for anteater means "nose bear" and their word for raccoon means "wash bear," which I gather comes from the fact that raccoons love to wash their food in water before eating it.

It gets better. When colonists sent an illustration and the preserved skin of a duck-billed platypus back to Europe in the 1800s, it was initially dismissed as a hoax. Hell, I've seen those animals up-close in zoos, and I'm still not convinced. After confirming that it does indeed exist, nineteenth-century scientists had a fun time trying to name this creature based on its hodgepodge of bits that seem borrowed from other animals. *Platypus anatinus*, meaning "flat-footed duck." Then *Ornithorhynchus paradoxus*, meaning "paradoxical bird-snout." And then *Ornithorhynchus anatinus*, meaning "bird-snouted flat-foot," which has stuck around until now and does short shrift to the fact that they also lay eggs and have venomous fangs on their hind legs.

This isn't just a European trend, by the way. Earliest accounts from the conquest of the Aztecs show them referring to Spanish horses using the Nahuatl word for "stag" because they'd never seen a horse before. Closer to home, the Diné called dogs łį̨į̨ prior to European contact, which meant simply "pet." But when Spanish horses were introduced to the Americas, they transferred the word łį̨į̨ to the horse—which became the new favorite "pet" among many Diné people—and started calling dogs łééchą̨ą̨'í, which literally translates to "shit pet." This isn't because they decided dogs are bad pets or anything, but because dogs tend to eat excrement, especially excrement from creatures whose digestive systems let a lot of perfectly serviceable nutrients slip through.

Grappling with the unknown by attempting to jam it into the known wherever the shapes are approximately the same is, in other words, fairly common practice—even today. Space-time is not a "fabric," for example, nor do atoms look like little solar systems. Those are just useful ways to envision how those things behave.

However, something else was at play in the minds of Europeans and early Euro-Americans at the time of contact, vestiges of which can also still be found lingering around today. Accepted history prior to the written word was covered by the Bible, and the Bible pretty clearly states that human civilization originated in the Middle East. There's mangers and magi and camels, after all, along with a marked absence of bird-snouted flat-foots or spike pigs.

Squaring this with the presence of millions of people and animals about whom Europeans had no previous inkling is how we got the Lost Tribes of Israel and other mythical ditherings, but it also underpinned what would end up being the biggest break between European and American archaeology: that of history and anthropology.

◆ ◆ ◆

At its simplest, history is an academic discipline that uses narrative to investigate, describe, and analyze what happened in the past, relying on both written and material records to craft that narrative and then getting into screaming matches with other historians over whose narrative is the best one according to this researcher or team of researchers. The process of reconstructing the past is no easy feat, and various efforts include equally various methods, but the end goal is the same: satisfying people's curiosity about the past. This thing happened, and then this thing happened, and here's the best possible explanation for why. This week, anyway. Next week we'll come along with different findings and methods and theories and whatnot, and the story will change.

This is why I keep emphasizing how history is a living thing. It's not alive in the sense of being conscious or moving around, you can't weigh it on a scale and see if it's been bulking up, but it evolves and changes through time as people explore and reconsider its elements. Understanding history is therefore less like understanding the past and more like understanding an unfolding and oft-changing story *about* the past.

The goal of anthropology, by contrast, is to understand people. Why do we do the things we do? Why do we look the way we look? It's a fascinating realm of inquiry, but the breadth of its scope includes pitfalls. Those like a tendency to believe in universals where they may not exist and a general trend of treating human beings as mere subjects of inquiry rather than as people. Its roots extend all the way back into the late Enlightenment Period, but it really took off as a discipline in the late nineteenth and early twentieth centuries following publication of Darwin's *Origin*.

Sociocultural anthropology emerged as a subset of the broader discipline by fits and starts. Scholars on both sides of the Atlantic gradually became convinced that progress and advancement were innate to the human species, with early cultural anthropologists like Edward Burnett Tyler arguing that social evolution accompanied increasing intelligence and Lewis Henry Morgan arguing that humans invariably morph from promiscuous brutes to erudite landowners. All that differs from one group to another is the timing.

Still, that wasn't the only game in town. An alternative to this strictly evolutionist model of anthropology established itself in the German-speaking countries. Its scientific roots were in geography and philology, and it was concerned with the study of cultural traditions and adaptations to local ecological constraints rather than with universal human histories. This more particularistic and historical approach made its way to the United States in the late 1800s with the German-trained scholar Franz Boas.

Boas was skeptical of evolutionist generalizations and advocated instead for a "diffusionist" approach that saw cultural developments and particulars changing unpredictably through time as a consequence of human migration or the migration of their goods and ideas. This approach became known as "historical particularism," and was impressively holistic thinking for the time.

From there, sociocultural anthropology—including the much older practice of ethnology, along with the relatively newer practice of ethnography or careful documentation of cultures—took off in its own direction starting in the 1920s. It was practiced as a subfield or adjacent field to sociology and linguistics rather than biology or archaeology, focusing most intently on social interactions. They were, in effect, comparative sociologists, studying different societies by comparing them with one another instead of focusing on just one and seeking to learn its ways.

They spent a great deal of that comparison-making on foraging and pastoralist groups that managed to survive colonialism. Ponderings on cultural evolution weren't in vogue among these scholars at the time, but one gets the definite impression that cultural types and behavioral trends as they categorized them could be arranged into a chronological series from primitive to sophisticated. They didn't say that part out loud, as a rule, but it was part of their thinking nonetheless.

Similar attempts to classify or categorize people into something like a scholarly database included the study of kinship groups and marriage patterns. Claude Lévi-Strauss presented a whole classification system for marriage systems from a variety of societies and cultures as he'd come to understand them in 1949, and it too had an orthogenic flavor even if his schema weren't explicitly presented that way. The key breakthrough that launched societies toward civilization, he seemed to think, was the introduction of the incest taboo, which obliged men to trade their sisters and daughters away to other men in exchange for wives of their own. From this, societies were constructed. At least in his estimation.

One can clearly see the nomothetic fanaticism of early science taking root even here. The search for general or universal truisms that can be applied to all of humanity beyond simply "we're all mammals" or "we all need to drink water" has driven a lot of otherwise very intelligent researchers to make some bold leaps—ones that often begin and end firmly in their own social teachings but somehow take in everybody else while they're airborne.

That was sociocultural anthropology as it developed in Europe, essentially a form of sociology that sought to answer questions about humanity at large by doing comparative studies of different lifeways. The focus was always on the social level. The story played out somewhat differently in the United States, and understanding why helps to explain the emergence of anthropological archaeology as the American model of practice.

◆ ◆ ◆

American archaeologists were—and are—almost entirely Euro-American people studying the material heritage of Native Americans, as I keep repeating, while early European archaeology originated out of Enlightenment antiquarianism that focused on local historical trends and The Classics. Anthropology, meanwhile, came about on different footing and was mostly utilized as a means to understand the people Europeans had colonized and/or those they were trying to beat in various wars. This was already taking place in the domain of physical or biological anthropology, in the hands and minds of people like Morton and Hrdlička, both of whom spent their entire careers looking very carefully at piles of skulls in order to determine just how inferior everyone else was to Europeans.

Anthropology wasn't something you practiced on your own

people, in other words—the very idea would be positively *gauche* to post-Enlightenment scholars. It's something you practiced on those weird foreign people in far-away places, like studying the habits of exotic animals. Since European archaeologists spent the bulk of their time studying the deep past of people whose presence they pretty well understood, or at least thought they did, there was no reason to explicitly link their research with the quantitative study of human animals in groups. Doing so struck them as fundamentally dehumanizing—mostly because it is—so they thought it was a practice best practiced on people from elsewhere.

This was in Franz Boas' heart at the St. Louis World Fair in 1904, when he proclaimed in a speech on the history of anthropology that the field comprises four subfields: physical, linguistic, ethnological or cultural, and archaeological.* Drilling down on archaeology in particular, Boas delivered the following summation: "Two great problems have occupied the attention of archaeologists—the origin and first appearance of the human race, and the historical sequence of races and types of cultures."

The cut and thrust of Boas' assertion lay largely in the fact that he was an ethnologist born and raised in what we now call Germany who became obsessed with studying non-Western cultures after spending some time as a geographer with the Inuit peoples of Baffin Island. Why ethnography and geography were conflated at that time and place is a messy question, but the synopsis is that geographers were in the vanguard of a trendy argument over whether the environment is the prime shaper of culture or if diffusion of ideas is more important. The results of his work on this question appeared in a monograph titled *The Central Eskimo*, published in 1888 by the American Bureau of Ethnology.

Boas railed against the idea that human societies evolve in a manner analogous to ontogenesis, where the blueprint for full-fledged organisms are coded into their basic stuff at creation. He preached instead the idea that human societies evolve in a manner

---

* Boas is often called the father of the four-field approach for this reason, although in fact he was largely interpolating ideas that were already floating around among European scholars intent on "classifying" non-European peoples.

more accurately analogous to Darwinian evolution, where what appear to be patterns or structures in human cultures are largely the outcome of diverse mechanisms driving cultural responses, including environmental factors and the migration of ideas or people with ideas. Hence the concept of historical particularism. The historical part would, presumably, be provided by archaeologists. That was our initial invitation into the fold, although it took us a while to respond to it.

Boas also trained a whole cadre of what would become some of the most celebrated ethnographers of the day. Included in the gang was Clark Wissler, who left the field of psychology to serve under Boas at the American Museum of Natural History in 1902. He would eventually be named Curator of Anthropology when the Archaeology and Ethnology departments were combined into one Anthropology department in 1907. Unfortunately for his legacy, he was also actively engaged in the eugenics movement of the early 1900s, which sought to purify the American populace with hereditary qualities deemed most desirable—a notion that was picked up with considerable gusto by the Nazis.

The upshot for our purposes is that the foundation of the four-field approach of anthropology in the United States was thereby established, although it would take a while for it to really catch on. Most archaeologists in the US during the early 1900s were still fundamentally treasure hunters, albeit treasure hunters with increasingly systematic and scientific methods of dealing with that treasure. Boas wasn't interested in reconstructing history, and neither were most other scholars at the time—but they were beginning to understand that reconstructing human history is a useful way to understand the human present.

Then, starting in the 1950s, a school of thought emerged in American sociocultural anthropology that many authors call the "culture-and-personality" perspective that drew on what were new movements in psychology—in particular the practices of psychoanalysis and Gestalt psychology. That latter approach is one I think most of us take for granted these days, and its emphasis was on the human tendency not to focus on details when trying to make sense of the world but instead to perceive them as parts of more complex systems. We do not, as it were, see the trees so much as the forest when we're forming our ideas about how the world works. A common example of how this works is the way most people put together jigsaw puzzles. We don't sit and marvel at every individual piece as its own separate entity, because that isn't the point of the process. The point is to think of the whole and try to slot the little pieces into it.

American anthropologists at the time consequently began trying to establish universal functionalist relationships in patterns that represented "cultures" rather than assuming everything is the function of one or another given "society." The goal was to compile all the cultural attributes one could collect into a metaphorical pile of leaves and then see what sorts of patterns or trends emerged from it. That, in turn, meant bringing evolutionary concepts right back into the fold after they'd been so roundly pushed out by Boas with his historical particularism and cultural relativism.

These new cultural evolutionists revitalized the notion that human development in general could be understood by such a means, but not because we are all inherently designed by God or Nature to progress in a preordained sequence of stages like the way larvae become butterflies. They argued instead that the environment was the primary driver of how we evolved or adapted over time, and the more complex our adaptations to those environmental constraints, the more civilized or advanced we became. Harnessing the power of local rocks to make cutting and smashing tools was, for example, way down the ladder from harnessing the power of local rocks to make smelted iron or nuclear fission.

Cultural practices were conceived as behavioral units of adaptation to environmental challenges, in other words, with the whole—the "culture" itself—being a mere epiphenomenon resulting from whole bunches of people working together to meet those challenges. Society, the unit of study for European sociocultural anthropologists, is the thing that happens when a whole bunch of people share a common culture. Great Basin researcher Julian Steward in particular argued that studying evolutionary processes in terms of environmental constraints could reveal a throughline that explains things like the origin of state-level societies and how technology evolves.

They were effectively on the path to stripping human agency right out of human societies, reducing the metaphorical forest to an ecosystem of evolutionary automation where the individual trees, as it were, don't actually matter apart from being data points comprising the whole. This was the stage at which the de-humanization of what is an otherwise humanistic field of inquiry got its start. We're not looking at people, we're looking at *patterns of behavior*, constrained by environmental factors acting upon organisms designed by natural selection to do whatever it takes to maximize the survival of their genes. Being a "person" doesn't fit anywhere into that model.

This was all to the great delight of archaeologists at the time, especially in the Great Basin, because you can't ask artifacts or bits of old human bone any potentially indelicate personal or cultural questions. What you can do is analyze them for behavioral patterns as if you were analyzing birds in a cage or fish in a tank. It was a seismic shift in the science, one that established the rift between Old and New World archaeologies.

◆ ◆ ◆

In the early 1960s, pioneering American archaeologist Lewis Binford came home from studying with Francois Bordes in Europe and published a foundational 1962 paper simply called *Archaeology as Anthropology*, in which he argues that archaeology needs to be explicitly linked to sociocultural anthropology or else it's basically useless. What's the point of examining an ancient mound or cliff dwelling if you don't understand anything about the cultures of those that created them? Archaeology needed to be paired with ethnography in the US because the people doing the investigating weren't from the same cultures as the people who did the stuff they were investigating.

Binford argued that the aim of anthropology is to "*explicate* and *explain* the total range of physical and cultural similarities and differences characteristic of the entire spatial-temporal span of man's existence," and that archaeology hasn't really done much to further the *explain* part of this goal. He was here echoing sentiments expressed by Willey and Phillips a few years before, who argued that "so little work has been done in American archaeology on the explanatory level that it is difficult to find a name for it."

Furthermore, since archaeological data were viewed particularistically—*a lá* Boas—explanations tended to be one-off affairs about specific instances rather than components of any sort of grander paradigm. According to Binford, "specific 'historical' explanations, if they can be demonstrated, simply explicate mechanisms of cultural process. They add nothing to the explanation of the processes of cultural change and evolution. If migrations can be shown to have taken place, then this explication presents an explanatory problem; what adaptive circumstances, evolutionary processes, induced the migration . . . ?"

This and related efforts led to what came to be known as the New Archaeology of the mid-1900s. The central goal was to make traditional archaeology more scientific, including the adoption of quantitative methods, behavioral models, and generally attempting to explain or interpret the archaeological record rather than assemble it into historical narratives. The dogmatic slogan was "process," and the resulting theoretical paradigm—briefly teased in the last chapter—was thus nicknamed "processualism."

Human cultures and societies are group-level responses to the problems of surviving in a given environment, after all, and nothing more than that in the eyes of the processualists. So, in the same way that Newtonian determinist Pierre-Simon de Laplace quipped that someone who knew the precise location and momentum of every atom in the universe could precisely calculate all the past and the present based on classical mechanics, an archaeologist who knows all the biological and environmental variables of a given period of human history could explain precisely why things shook out the way they did. It would simply be a matter of teasing apart the processes.

All of them.

Easy stuff, right?

This is where the iceberg of academic archaeology finally, momentously cracked into American and European halves. The earlier marriage of sociocultural anthropology (both ethnography and ethnology) with archaeology was glued with the topic of history, as both disciplines were interested in how local histories had resulted in the makeup of respective local cultures. In the US, a new marriage was glued with the topic of behavioral science, while most European archaeologists continued to regard their practice as reconstructing and examining history. The current four-field approach in American anthropology came about because of this synthesis rather than the original efforts of Boas, despite his efforts to lay the foundation more than half a century earlier.

◆ ◆ ◆

Because archaeology is fundamentally the reconstruction of past events using only the barest fragments of leftover evidence, fixation on the science of general humanity versus the history of specific humans was ultimately the biggest flashpoint that stoved the American/European rift. The scientific component of American archaeology having now been established, it took off with aplomb.

The notion of a science-history dichotomy is a fraught and frankly absurd one, but it's a notion that has proven remarkably hard to shake. Back in the 1940s, American researchers like Klyde Kluckhohn and Julian Steward reviled history as particularizing or ideographic, while science is more generalizing and nomothetic—i.e., science applies to more than just one instance. As recently as 2001, Binford and his colleagues vehemently argued for "archaeology as science" as a reason for the practice of archaeology to abandon the increasingly non-scientific aspects of anthropology, with its historical particulars and its relativism and humanism and other annoying non-quantitative stuff.

This marks the shift from the Descriptive Period of American archaeology to the Interpretive Period, when the field as a whole sought to go from simply describing everything they saw in terms of its physical traits and its place on a chronological timeline to interpreting it all in terms of human behavior. Using hard science to tease apart the processes that comprise cultural evolution was resoundingly popular in a field whose roots were deeply embedded in colonialism and treasure-hunting because it legitimized the practice.

The move wasn't compelled by insecurity, necessarily. The more one obsesses over hard quantitative data, however, the less one focuses on subjective or "soft" qualitative data, which can make the supposedly humanistic science of anthropology increasingly dehumanized. I had this point driven home to me in field school way back in 2008, when I looked at a petroglyph panel and openly mused that it could represent clan migrations. "Yeah, sure," sniped a visiting lecturer with a wry little chuckle. "Now try testing that hypothesis in a laboratory." When I mentioned that I could always just ask some Indigenous people what they thought, he laughed even harder.

I ran into similar sentiments as a graduate student about half a decade later, where it was often repeated that objective, quantitative data is paramount in scientific investigations of anthropology because human observations and testimonies are so easily biased. Sure, the Indigenous people living in this study area *say* that they are primarily hunters, but does their overall caloric intake reflect this fact? For that matter, aren't most cultural narratives just easily manipulated group interpretations of history with a smattering of creative thinking on top? "Culture is not an explanation," as summarized by Professor Jim O'Connell. "It is the thing to be explained."

Because of this, Great Basin researchers in general—up to relatively recently—continued down the path set by the processualists into deeper and deeper analysis of finer- and finer-grained processes. In doing so, they borrowed heavily from studies of behavioral evolution in other animals, which tend to break everything down into caloric input/output metrics and how they articulate with evolutionary fitness. If an organism finds a way to burn five units of energy in order to capture ten units of energy, netting a surplus of five units, it has a much greater chance of passing along its genes than an organism whose process isn't as efficient. Freakonomics for the animal world.

The result is a discipline called human behavioral ecology, an offshoot of E.O. Wilson's "sociobiology," which was still lauded as the end-all/be-all theory for explaining human behavior in the Great Basin when I was grad student there.

In simple terms, human evolutionary or behavioral ecology is the study of human behavior from an adaptive perspective, with a particular focus on how human behavior varies with ecological context. It involves breaking down and, to the extent possible, isolating patterns of behavior into structural-functional relationships that allow researchers to explicate that behavior in terms of its associated ecosystem rather than as isolated phenomena floating in space. The hunting strategies of North American wolves, for example, are well-adapted to the North American environment and the types of prey they're likely to find there, so they probably wouldn't work as well in Africa. The same can be said of human behavior, at least in theory.

Optimization is the key, and tools like optimal foraging models—which mathematically investigate the desirability of taking one prey item versus another in a given environment—are at the center. It makes more sense to gather a thousand calories of nuts and berries than it does to hunt for a thousand-calorie deer, for example, because hunting returns aren't guaranteed while the nuts and berries are just sitting there. And if your hunting grounds have both lots of deer and lots of rabbits in them, it makes sense to pass by the rabbits in favor of the deer because the deer yields a higher caloric return to the hunter.

Fair enough. If I have enough money to buy quality food, I'll pass right by the crappy stuff in the grocery store. Why would I eat instant ramen when I can afford lasagna? Where this reductionism runs into problems is when people behave in ways that aren't optimal, and especially in ways that run precisely counter to optimal. I, for example, *can* afford to eat lasagna, if only just barely. But I happen to like ramen noodles.

The aggregate nature of these models should wipe weirdo "outliers" like me out of the curvature of what is otherwise totally predictable behavior—again, in theory. But in many cases that still isn't true, especially when it comes to the set of resource procurement strategies we call hunting. Say your hunting grounds contain lots of rabbits but very few deer. If you've got a family at home waiting for you to return with food, and you pass by fifty rabbits in search of a deer that may or may not even be there, you aren't exactly making a wise choice vis-à-vis energy capture versus energy expenditure. And yet, hunters in hunter-gatherer societies apparently do that all the time. Why?

Enter costly signaling theory, an idea focused on prestige behavior that proposes animals will sometimes send "signals" about their fitness through costly biological or behavioral displays that seem wasteful and dangerous but attract the right kind of attention for that very reason. It was introduced by Amotz and Avishag Zahavi as the Handicap Principle of mate-selection in a 1975 paper and 1999 book arguing that animals like peacocks signal their fitness by being able to haul around enormous tail feathers that are a downright detriment to their survivability. The peacocks are, in effect, saying "I'm such a badass that I can afford these heavy accoutrements without breaking the bank."

So, according to this thinking, that's why hunters in hunter-gatherer societies routinely walk right past easily hunted rabbits in favor of rarer and harder-to-kill deer. They aren't doing it to maximize group fitness by bringing home important protein and lipids to help provision the entire group, they're doing it to maximize their own fitness by signaling how awesome they are. Probably because they're men.*

The core of this perspective is, in effect, that human beings are nothing more than wet robots designed by natural selection to be efficiency machines. And there is some appeal to that. In what may be millions of years of looking, depending upon where you draw the line between *ape* and *human*, nobody has ever found tangible and consistent evidence of the existence of a soul or spirit separate from observable human consciousness. Which *ipso facto* leaves only physical explanations, even if we haven't yet found those either.

This is why I've always had difficulty enjoying horror stories that

* This was a real hot button issue among ethnologists from the early 1990s until at least the early 2010s, largely based on the assumption that hunters are always men and gatherers are always women. We now know this is patently untrue.

included the supernatural. A horror story about a psychopath or a fungus that turns people into zombies is one thing. But a story in which the hapless victims encounter hard evidence of the existence of an immortal soul or an afterlife or magic or whatever—that would be the greatest thing that ever happened. Literally. *Ever.* I know if I found myself face-to-face with something I knew with absolute certainty was a ghost, my feeling would be one of overwhelming relief at finally knowing for sure that there's more to all this than . . . well, all this.

Anyway, none of this is to say that approximate cultural universals don't necessarily exist. Consider the midwinter holiday. Just about every known extant and historic society has one, and it makes perfect sense why that is. For most of the history of the human species, we lived in tight groups bound to the seasons by foraging or farming, the middle of winter is dark and cold, and we're all huddled together in caves or huts or whatever, and goddamnit some fatty food and loud music and bright colors and a gift-giving ritual might be just the thing to assuage murderous ennui. Christmas might have its own specific historical particulars but a general trend across human societies is nonetheless evident.

The problem lies in mistaking those statistical generalities for concrete rules about the human condition, when cultural variability and individual behavioral adaptability are still the most human of things. In 2009, foundational human behavioral ecologist Kim Hill beautifully expressed this conundrum. "When I began material for a synthetic overview of modern hunter-gatherers," he wrote, "I became bothered by a recurrent problem. Although behavioral ecological models clearly had the potential to explain many interesting patterns . . . the strongest predicter of almost any hunter-gatherer pattern, whether it be polygyny level, infanticide rates, warfare, food taboos, postmarital residence patterns, child-rearing practices, puberty rituals, or body piercings, was 'ethnolinguistic membership.'"

Culture counts, in other words. A lot. You can't just wish it away with complicated math or hijacked theoretical alternatives like "prestige behavior" when people don't do what your calculations tell you they should.

◆ ◆ ◆

All of which is to say that the only thing science is equipped to deal with is the quantitative and corporeal. It remains the most powerful tool ever devised for sussing out the nature of reality, but there's a problem here nonetheless, namely that scientific inquiry has thus far been totally unable to figure out what consciousness even is. Taking it on faith that consciousness is entirely the result of billions of synapses firing away in the brain makes sense as an operative assumption, but it's still an act of faith.

This is what philosophers call the "hard problem of consciousness," defined by the *Encyclopedia of Philosophy* as the problem of explaining why any physical state is conscious rather than unconscious. Why aren't we just billiard-balled around by physics without the added menace of, say, lying awake at night wondering why we aren't just billiard-balled around by physics?

How, in other words, do we know that we know? Ideas have been advanced, but the fact remains: we simply don't know for certain. It's possible we'll never know. Which makes modeling human behavior based on something as simple as the amount of energy it takes to heat one kilogram of water by one degree Celsius—the literal definition of a kilo- or nutritional calorie—a rather interesting approach.

Having said all that, rigid scientific theories like behavioral ecology aren't all bad. Very much the opposite, in fact. It's just a matter of how and where they're used.

One genuinely great thing about human behavioral ecology is that it's the only anthropological theory I know that explicitly treats human beings like animals instead of some exalted special creation that stands outside (and ostensibly above) the animal kingdom. It sets into scientific language the long-held belief that we can learn a lot about ourselves by studying other animals and comparing our behavior to theirs. In so doing, whether intentionally or not, such a process of thought elevates other animals toward a level of respect that is long overdue.

Wolves, for example, have societies that are almost as complex and intriguing as our own. There are leaders (more like parents than monarchs, although they can and do change roles from time to time), caregivers, hunters, fighters, lovers, affairs, *coups d'état*, wars, treaties, and who knows what else. The same goes for coyotes, and meerkats, and elephants, chimps, lions, baboons, and pretty much any other species of animal that lives communally.

Furthermore, one can follow that metaphorical rabbit hole far enough to wind up at an adjacent discipline called zoopharmacology, or the study of how animals use medicine. African elephants, for example, chew on the leaves of a particular tree from the *Boraginaceae* family to prevent birth or induce labor, a practice that was subsequently picked up by local Kenyan tribespeople—from whom Western scientists learned how to synthesize some of the earliest forms of oral birth control. Women from the WaTongwe tribe in Tanzania apparently learned from chimpanzees how the leaves of the African bitterleaf are effective for treating intestinal ailments. Parrots in the Manu River basin of Peru routinely eat clay for what turns out to be remarkably similar reasons to our own consumption of clays and activated charcoals: detoxification and battling hangovers (they also eat a lot of fruit that's been sitting on the ground fermenting).

Plus, it's not like animals don't also learn behaviors from us when it suits them. My favorite example of this is probably corvids, the bird family that includes ravens, crows, and magpies. There is a myriad of studies and reports of them manipulating humans into giving them food by mirroring human-like behavior, up to and including mimicry of human voices. This is something good to know before you go backpacking in New Hampshire as a teenage Boy Scout and wake up just before dawn to something invisible laughing maniacally at you from a nearby treetop.

Behavioral ecology also remains the most powerful theoretical tool I've encountered for generating predictions about the archaeological record, but it's a tool that only works well on its own when the data sets are very old and very large, like when researchers are curious about how we invented agriculture and examine the entire Pleistocene record to find out. As the focus narrows from "the full range of human evolution" to "those people who lived in that valley over there for a while," the volume of unignorable variables goes parabolic, and the bulk of those variables are cultural. Math sucks at predicting the whimsies of culture.

As for the deer-versus-rabbits puzzle that often serves as the linchpin for researchers arguing on behalf of costly signaling, I once posed the question to an Indigenous colleague while we were guiding a bunch of tourists around Bears Ears. His response, after chuckling and rolling his eyes, was: "Ever tried to make a wikiup from rabbit leather? Ever tried to use a rabbit bladder as a canteen? Ever tried to club an enemy with a rabbit femur? Ever tried to make a sharp tool from a rabbit antler?"

◆ ◆ ◆

To this day, albeit with waning zealotry, behavioral ecology continues to be the dominant theoretical model used by archaeologists in the Great Basin. Down in the Southwest, by which I mean just across the Colorado River, it's a whole different story.

For historical reasons, this situation is at least partly a result of what Bears Ears archaeologist Winston Hurst once described to me as The Iron Curtain of Jennings. By the 1970s, Jesse Jennings of the Glen Canyon Project—also in charge of the Anthropology Department at the University of Utah at that time—regarded the Southwest as "plowed ground." Everything there worth finding had already been found, reasoned he, so why keep looking?

The mentors of early Southwestern archaeologists J.O. Brew and A.V. Kidder made similar pronouncements about half a century earlier, with Hewett having evidently told the latter that Southwest archaeology was "a sucked orange." David Roberts was so amused by this he made it the title of the last chapter of his recreational archaeology primer *In Search of the Old Ones*. Kidder also made abundant jokes about it in his later years.

The animosity Jennings had toward the Southwest goes a considerable way toward explaining why his graduate students and their colleagues in the department set their own sights elsewhere. They continued the steady march set in motion by New Archaeology and the processualists toward quantitative, theory-driven behavior reconstruction, narrowing their focus tighter and tighter toward finer-grained analyses, and devising mathematical formulae to explain and support their results that are downright dizzying in complexity.

"Theoretical physics can prove that an elephant can hang from a cliff with its tail tied to a daisy," as the man said. So can theoretical behavior models.

The Great Basin was an ideal place to do this, because aside from Fremont farmers, the Indigenous cultures of the Basin never included any of the "complex, wild-assed, agency-driven Formative societies" (Hurst again) that we get in places like the greater Southwest and the Mississippi Valley. Science occurs as a process of minimizing or accounting for variables, after all, and forager economies quite simply involve far fewer variables than complicated agricultural and/or state-level ones do. Supposedly.

That's part of the story, anyway. Another part has to do with the fact that the Southwest is definitely "Indian Country." It says so in those exact words on a number of gas station roadmaps. There are reservations and plentiful Indigenous individuals residing in the Great Basin, but on nowhere near the scale or density one finds in the Southwest—especially in the Four Corners area. The Navajo Nation alone is larger than ten American states and contains about half a million residents.

Across the Curtain from the house that Jennings built, archaeological theory in the Southwest developed along a markedly different track. History reconstruction is one thing—there's nothing personal about X preceding Y if that's what the material record shows. But the idea of white researchers using fancy math and science to reconstruct the behavior and intentions present in their ancestors' daily lives strikes many Native Americans as problematic, if not nakedly offensive.

For this reason, many (although certainly not all) Southwest archaeologists eschewed behavior reconstruction, turned right around, and started marching back toward the early days of archaeology with nouveau forms of culture-history reconstruction. It's also in the Southwest where archaeologists are far more likely to collaborate with Indigenous people, as well as—increasingly—for Indigenous people to be the archaeologists.

◆ ◆ ◆

This quick little recap of the Southwest v. Great Basin procedure-and-theory drama is an illustrative heuristic for understanding one of the biggest problems in American archaeology as a whole: overly narrowed or siloed foci. Institution A specializes in the northern Southwest and ancestral foodways, while Institution B specializes in coastal maritime archaeology with an emphasis in structural-functionalism, Institution C thinks they're both out to lunch and insists Great Plains ethnoarchaeology is the way to go, and so on, all of which differs even more considerably from conditions overseas.

Among the most obvious problems arising from this mess is that of varying interpretations. Two sets of researchers coming from two very different academic schools of thought can look directly at the same historic material assemblage and see it as very different things. This happened in the Bears Ears area not long before I got my first actual job there, when researchers rediscovered and analyzed the alcove where Richard Wetherill first documented the Basketmaker ancestry of what were then called Cliff Dwellers in the region. One of them, a team from the Great Basin, looked at the immense array of skeletal material excavated there by Wetherill and concluded that it was the location of a massacre. The other one, a team from the northern Southwest, looked at the same array and concluded that it was the location of a cemetery.

In other words, because of their varying academic lenses, one team saw war and a bunch of people dying in one location as a result—and the other team saw people going about their normal lives and choosing to bury their dead in a centralized location rather than scattered all over the place. Which one is right? And does it actually matter?

Tribal reps would prefer the materials were reburied and people stopped asking those sorts of questions to begin with, of course, but since most of the remains predate the Pueblo era as defined in the Pecos Sequence they're legally regarded as *unaffiliated.* Keep that ticking timebomb in mind.

This, then, leads us all the way back to the opening salvo for this chapter: the biggest split between European and American archaeology is that of people studying their own (or at least closely related) material heritage and those studying someone else's. Europeans studying the deep history of Europe are mostly looking into their own ancestry, the result of which is their own culture, so there's really no need to invoke convoluted processual theories or book-length mathematical equations to connect the two. Archaeologists in the United States studying the deep history of the Americas are, by contrast, almost entirely white people studying non-white peoples' ancestry and trying to make distinctly Western "sense" out of it.

Even in Meso- and South America, because of distinct Spanish-Indigenous relations, most archaeologists are partly of Indigenous descent. The extent to which that makes them *de facto* Indigenous in matters of politics and social justice is contentious and debatable—according to Diné /Yankton Dakota author and activist Jacqueline Keeler, all that really means is their background is "one-half Indigenous and one-half six hundred years of proud colonizer"—but at least it's *partly* their own heritage they're investigating.

This is how you get situations where professors roll their eyes at the very idea of anything counting as knowledge if it can't be replicated in a lab and rolling them even harder when you suggest that Indigenous people might have some pretty solid ideas about their own deep history. Despite being a supposedly humanistic science, it runs dangerously close to being functionally inhumane when we care more about data than we do about people.

Imagine someone studying geese. They stare at the ground taking very careful measurements of the footprints and feathers geese have left behind. They read voluminous books and attend long, exhaustive lectures about geese. They buy, borrow, or steal goose skeletons and subject them to all manner of intensive scrutiny. They go on long adventures to find the abandoned nests and discarded shells of breeding pairs of geese and create complicated graphs correlating things like brood size and local climate conditions. They amass the greatest storehouse of information about geese ever assembled, publish widely and with applause, and are showered with accolades and degrees. And then, one day, a live goose lands on their front porch, and they go "What the fuck is that?"

◆ ◆ ◆

This also tees up the perennial and infuriating thorn of plain bad actors in American archaeology. The desire to protect trees, snails, and archaeological sites as at least somewhat equal components of the North American environment culminated in legislation like NEPA, which mandates that impacts to natural and cultural resources need to be considered whenever some big thing is going to affect public lands. This went hand-in-hand with the civil rights movement that was erupting at the same time. Saving culturally important places dovetailed nicely with the idea of enshrining respect for the rights and sovereignty of put-upon people whose cultures were intimately intertwined with those places, and Indigenous people started demanding elevated legislative protection to stymie the wanton destruction of their heritage. Hewett had been saying the same thing since at least 1904, but for the most part the Indigenous community never felt they had a voice in American politics before the 1960s. I'm sure I don't need to explain why.

Something similar is occurring right now in the form of both a new civil rights movement, spurred largely by the internet and aimed mostly at combating the rising threat of fascism and its evil tendrils like racism and transphobia; and a new environmental movement, also spurred largely by the internet and focusing its ire on the increasingly obvious effects of climate change. Indigenous figures like Deb Haaland are beginning to appear in the highest levels of white-dominated politics, while youthful figures like Greta Thunberg are making a big splash in public view for a topic often dominated by dry-as-bones climate scientists.

These efforts are making such an impact that the backlash is ferocious, brazen, and reckless beyond belief. That doesn't mean we're *winning*, but it's often a good sign when your opponents decide the only strategy left to them is to burn the whole stadium down. That's the time to turn your attention toward the stands, where the overwhelming bulk of actual human beings are, and compel them to rush the field.

I seriously cannot stress enough how important it is to foster more public scholarship. They were doing it in the 1700s with electrified children and nobody thought that was weird.

The problem in academic archaeology, as my friend Kelsey Hanson recently articulated, is that members of older generations with older ideas still hold too many strings. Nonprofit enterprises rely on donors to keep operating, and most of those donors are older avocational or enthusiast types who want their funding to result in shovels moving earth because *that's* archaeology.

Similarly, a lot of academic institutions and university departments are still in the grips of tenured professors who got those jobs in the 1980s, and it shows. Professional archaeological societies have a stubborn tendency to operate like for-profit corporations, doing whatever seems trendy to whatever audience they're trying to woo for support at that very moment, whether it's sincere or not. The presence of reactionary conservative types in academic anthropology and their place in things like professional societies is probably best compared-and-contrasted with a pair of controversies that erupted quite recently.

◆ ◆ ◆

At the time of writing this, the American Anthropological Association had just confirmed they reached a decision to remove the session "Let's Talk About Sex Baby: Why biological sex remains a necessary analytic category in anthropology" from their 2023 conference program. They cited as the basis for this choice the first ethical principle in AAA's Principles of Professional Responsibility, "Do no harm," before presenting a comprehensive breakdown on their website.

This got the usual jeers and jibes from an always small but always loud contingent of roaring mice on social media but was generally received favorably by the broader anthropological community. Most people simply agreed that it was a good idea and moved on. So, kudos to the AAA in that regard.

So much for the first controversy.

In addition to being invited to this meeting of the minds at the AAA conference, organizer Elizabeth Weiss was also co-presenter (with retired attorney James Springer) of a paper at the Society for American Archaeology's 2021 meeting titled, "Has Creationism Crept Back into Archaeology?" The title alone is intriguing, because religious creationism hasn't exactly left archaeology to begin with. There are biblical scholars combing the desert for evidence of Noah's Ark as we speak. Best of luck, lads—you'll need it.

In fact, their paper was about NAGPRA, the potent federal law designed to restrict scientific graverobbing and either assist or force repatriation of bones and burial items back to the Tribes. Their stance: since the law and its practice are based on the beliefs of Indigenous peoples, rather than anything amounting to quantitative science, NAGPRA is therefore guilty of placing faith ahead of science in exactly the same manner for which biblical literalists catch hell for preaching creationism in public schools.

Or, to quote the horse and its mouth directly, Weiss argued during the session that archaeologists "have let creationism into the heart of our discipline" because NAGPRA gives "control of research over to contemporary American Indian communities," who may request repatriation or refuse to participate in certain research because of "religious beliefs." I.e., we aren't supposed to teach our religion in schools, but we can allow their religion to dictate what we do with the bones of their ancestors.

Such hypocrisy! After all, in both cases, science is taking a backseat to belief. Right?

Wrong. Teaching biblical stories about the creation of the world that are in flat contradiction with all known physical evidence is considered problematic precisely because of the teaching part. People are allowed to believe whatever they want, but if you stand in front of a classroom full of young and malleable minds trying to drill that information into them, you're not actually a teacher so much as a preacher in teacher's clothing. The action in this instance is the imparting of belief in the guise of fact upon the minds of people being educated.

By contrast, the action NAGPRA seeks to minimize or eliminate is the curation and/or destructive analysis of Indigenous ancestral remains by non-Indigenous investigators, usually in support of some obscure research question that doesn't do anything except net the authors another notch on their academic bedposts. It's a law designed to protect actual, tangible things—including the physical remains of human beings—rather than to advance ideas or beliefs whose connection to tangible reality is tangential at best. And it's not even very good at stopping them.

Case in point: in 2017, a team of researchers published the results of a study of mitochondrial DNA (or mtDNA) from eight individuals buried together in Room 33 of Pueblo Bonito in Chaco Canyon. They'd been exhumed by archaeologists in the late 1800s and early 1900s, and since then were held in storage at the National Museum of Natural History in New York. The team was able to show that the individuals all descended from a woman who was laid to rest among them, as well as showing that the group's lineage spanned at least three hundred years.

However, according to an investigation by ProPublica, one anthropologist unaffiliated with the team urged them to reach out to the Tribes to discuss it with them first. They hadn't bothered because NAGPRA stipulates that affiliated groups must be contacted before any destructive analysis can occur, but if the remains are old enough to predate the earliest legally established cultural history of any extant groups the remains are considered "unaffiliated." They're still Indigenous, obviously, but they're not affiliated with any federally recognized group, which means nobody is allowed to speak for them in legal matters.

It's an absurd contingency, but unfortunately it makes sense from a legal perspective because cultural histories get really convoluted as one goes backward in time no matter where you are on the planet. In Ireland, for example, if you go back deep enough, you'll run into English, Roman, Germanic, and Viking presences—among much else—and vestiges of all of them are still present in modern Irish culture. Ditto the Southwest, where modern Navajo culture includes very deep-rooted Diné beliefs and practices, but also farming, weaving, and sheep herding that all came from contact and occasional intermarriage with Pueblo and Spanish peoples over time.

Still, when all is said and done, any skeletal material found in the Americas that dates to before 1492 is almost certainly Indigenous rather than European. I'm talking a confidence level way higher than 99 percent. So, the fact that any given individual may be tough to affiliate with a single or even multiple modern Tribes doesn't mean it's therefore a figment from the eternal void whose care lies solely with white people. They're still the remains of a Native American. But that's not how the National Museum sees it, and that's not how the team of researchers saw it either.

The AMNH decided that NAGPRA did not apply to their research in a statement approved by the study's fourteen authors, which determined that "the cultural complexity of the region made it impossible to establish a clear ancestor–descendant relationship with specific modern communities based on existing data." In a separate statement, according to *Scientific American*, the AMNH said "the research had considerable scientific merit with little impact on the artifacts and human remains," adding that it had contacted "potentially affiliated tribes" during the late 1990s but that "none had come forward to claim affiliation."

Loads of people cried foul, including my friend and occasional colleague Ruth Van Dyke who heads the archaeology department at Binghamton University—the very town where I was born and raised, ironically, despite my having met her when our research overlapped in the Southwest at about the time this all happened. Her stance was adamant: "Studies using ancient Indigenous DNA should not be done without tribal consultation" regardless of what the law says, and I agree. Again, slavery was legal until 1865 but that doesn't mean it was ever the right thing to do.

The paper came out, journalists went wild, and social media

parrots leaped all over it. "Girl Power" and "Moms Rule!" were common titles, along with lengthier ones like "Chaco Canyon's Matrilineal Dynasty" in *Archaeology Magazine* and "Did women control the bloodline in ancient Chaco Canyon?" in *Science*. It was a cause célèbre that hit media streams at the height of the #MeToo movement, one that showed how the mightiest society in ancient North America appears to have been ruled by a matrilineal dynasty.

None of this came as much of a surprise to Pueblo individuals, who trace their roots to Chaco Canyon and maintain cultures that are centered on matrilineal ties despite generations of Western governments insisting that they'll only deal with men. Theresa Pasqual, director of the Tribal Historic Preservation Office at Acoma Pueblo, put it rather bluntly to ProPublica: "We could have told you that."

I have no idea how much money was spent on that project, and I can't even begin to imagine how much is spent every year on curation costs for artifacts and mortuary remains excavated at archaeological sites in North America. Hours and hours of work were put into this research, probably amounting to weeks or months of cumulative effort. All so they could publish something Indigenous folks could have told them to their faces if they'd followed the *spirit* of NAGPRA rather than the letter of the law and simply asked them.

This anecdote underscores the most damnable aspect of Weiss's presentation at the SAA conference in 2021: the fact that she was allowed to present it at all. According to Métis/Papaschase scholar Kisha Supernant in an interview about the controversy with *Science*, "there are Indigenous members of the SAA, me included, and there's so little care given to how a paper like that might have harmed us. It was a very difficult experience to sit through that paper . . . when your very humanity and human rights are being questioned. People are entitled to hold these views. But whether or not they're given a platform is up [to the SAA]."

◆ ◆ ◆

Based on all this, one might expect someone like me to loathe and excoriate the SAA every chance I got, never show up to their meetings or pay their exorbitant membership fees, and generally have nothing to do with them. One would be wrong.

The reality is that organizations like the SAA are so big, contain so many multitudes as Walt Whitman would say, that damning the lot based on the egregious nonsense of a few would be comparable to outright prejudice. There are good people in the SAA, both in its membership and its governing board—people that I like and respect very much.

In fact, when the State of Utah filed a lawsuit against the Biden administration for restoring Bears Ears and Grand Staircase-Escalante National Monuments to their original pre-Trump boundaries, the SAA cordially asked me to serve as their expert witness in the countersuit. They didn't even offer me any money, just asked if I would do it pro bono on their behalf. And I did. Of course I did. You can't criticize an organization for its ills and then refuse to participate when they ask you to help them do better. That, too, would be hypocrisy.

That lawsuit was dismissed by Utah District Court Judge David Nuffer on the grounds that it was a frivolous and moronic waste of taxpayer money (my words); and that Congress, via the Antiquities Act, gave the president the authority to establish national monuments "at his discretion" (his words). He therefore concluded: "President Biden's judgment in drafting and issuing the Proclamations as he sees fit is not an action reviewable by a district court."

Naturally, the State of Utah appealed the ruling. If you aren't reading how that appeal went at this very moment, it's because the case was still languishing in the courts when this book went to press.

When I was a college kid tending bar to pay for the first in a series of degrees, I was told over and over about how archaeology has a tarnished history (true), how tough it is to find a job in this field (not true), and about how much it differs from European archaeology (more on that in a moment). Nobody warned me I might also get roped into massive lawsuits against sitting presidents.

◆ ◆ ◆

History, as I keep repeating, is a living thing. How we look at it, interpret it, and treat it differs in many ways from how we look at, think about, and treat actual living things—obviously. But it's still crucial to remember that history is something that lives in our collective conscience, teaching lessons and issuing warnings, evolving through time and varying interpretations, and always in danger of being killed by people who don't like what it has to say.

That last point is true pretty much everywhere, including in the Old World where pharaohs like Akhenaten and dictators like Hitler and Stalin made a habit of trying their damnedest to erase those bits of history they didn't want people remembering. Favored classical methods include destroying statues and other public regalia, editing photos, persecuting or outright murdering historians, and burning books. Favored modern methods include budgetary legislation that slashes agency funding and eradicates the Historic Preservation Fund.

It's especially true here in the United States, where the historians and the players on the historic stage often come from wildly differing societies. What leaders like Akhenaten, Hitler, Stalin, and who-knows-how-many others in Asia and Europe tried to erase from history was usually what they considered some embarrassing earlier version of their own culture. We do that, too, with attempts to erase our own history when we find out schools are teaching kids about things like slavery, genocide against Indigenous people, systemic racism, police violence, and much else. But there's also a lot more history in the land of the United States than just United States history, and all of it is vulnerable to attack.

This is where archaeology has long been a tool of oppression, stealing artifacts and human remains to display in colonialistic trophy cases we call museums. When an otherwise ignorant—and almost famously abusive—Flagstaff hipster-activist named Ana accused me of "stealing arrowheads for science" because I'm an archaeologist, her prejudice wasn't entirely unfounded. But it's also where archaeology can be a tool of empowerment and social justice. It's all a matter of understanding the relationship that's in play—that of Western science and almost entirely Indigenous material history—and earnestly trying to make that relationship a healthy one.

It's that or go do archaeology someplace where you're investigating your own cultural ancestry, which for most of us Americans would be someplace in Europe.

◆ ◆ ◆

So, what does archaeology in Europe actually look like? A lot of American texts make note of the fact that the two practices differ, mostly by focusing on the "Europeans are studying their own history while Americans are mostly studying the history of other people" bit and how that steered the American practice away from the domain of history into the domain of anthropology. Presenting that tidbit and then just leaving it there is, in a curiously meta way, tantamount to ethnocentrism on the part of a lot of American authors.

Prior to World War I, most European archaeologists were "adventurers first and scholars second," to quote Brian Fagan in his excellent little book *Archaeology and You*. There was a small handful of professional archaeologists around at the time, most of whom were backed by serious piles of family money and spent their time in places like Egypt and Turkey, digging up tombs or copying hieroglyphs or reconstructing collapsed Roman temples *a lá* Khaemweset thousands of years earlier.

It wasn't unusual for an archaeologist to spend an entire career focusing on a single site, because they weren't trying to answer broad questions about human history or evolution. They were trying to find all the cool stuff they could at whatever place they'd struck archaeological gold.

To take just one example, Arthur John Evans began excavating the site of Knossos on the island of Crete in 1900 and then stayed at it for over thirty years. Note how Crete is a fair stretch from Britain. In its earliest days, British archaeology focused largely on examining the fascinating material histories of the places they'd colonized—often sending most of the materials back to the British Museum where many of them remain today.

The ancient Sumerian city-state of Ur, known to the outer world mostly for its characteristic ziggurat or stepped-temple tower, is another good example of this. The first excavations there were conducted between 1853 and 1854 by J.G. Taylor, the British Vice-Consul at Basra, whose discovery of inscribed tablets and bricks led him to believe it was the home of biblical patriarch Abraham. Between then and 1918, it was visited and dug primarily by looters and curio-seekers, but after Britain took control of Mesopotamia in World War I, the British Museum commissioned archaeologists to investigate and protect the site from further looting. The earliest of these, H.R. Hall, spent a season digging the site using seventy Turkish prisoners as his field technicians. The site was more fully excavated between 1922 and 1934 by Sir Charles Leonard Wolley on behalf of the British Museum and—oddly enough—the University of Pennsylvania, who took the time to close the site properly after they were done rather than leave gaping holes in the ground as others had done in the past.

In a comparative sense, Ur is a lot like Chaco Canyon, where the first archaeologists to excavate there were non-professionals like Richard Wetherill along with who-even-knows how many casual collectors and looters. Passage of the Antiquities Act resulted in Wetherill's family getting kicked out of Chaco (he was dead by then) and replaced by professionally accredited archaeologists, who then proceeded to do basically the same thing Wetherill had done but with legal permission and oversight. In both cases, the professionals and non-professionals alike were from colonial nations investigating the deep history of the peoples of an area they'd conquered.

Where this really started to change was World War II and the dissolution of the colonial European empires, a process that had admittedly begun long before then but ramped up considerably after the war. Britain in particular reigned their focus in to more local efforts. A great case study in this is the site of Sutton Hoo, popularized in semi-fiction just a few years ago in the film *The Dig* that I personally dug quite a lot.

Sutton Hoo is the name of a burial site consisting of a wooden longboat that was interred sometime soon after AD 637. Within the boat, the interred individual was surrounded by weapons and bits of armor, gold coins, silver vessels and silver-mounted drinking horns, and a bunch of clothing. The body had long decayed into nothingness by the time the burial was exhumed, so identifying the individual is a bit problematic, but most experts think it was a member of the East Anglian ruling dynasty. According to the British Museum, four kings are considered possible candidates.

Antiquarians and looters had sliced into the site innumerable times starting deep in the Medieval Period, but they'd all focused their efforts on the wrong spot, accidentally preserving the real heart of the burial until it could be more carefully despoiled by experts later. Thus it was that Basil Brown, played by Ralph Fiennes in the film, was contracted to dig the site in 1934 by a bereaved widow named Edith Petty, who lived in a mansion on the same property. She'd gotten into spiritualism after her husband died, as people sometimes do, and this seems to have been her primary motivation.

The site was extensively excavated between the years 1938 and 1992, with Brown working there on behalf of the Ipswich Museum when the buried ship was first discovered. Cambridge University's Charles Phillips heard about the amazing find not long after, and after pulling some strings with the Ipswich Museum, the British Museum, the Science Museum, and the Office of Works, he succeeded in pushing Brown out and taking over the dig. This sort of thing used to happen a lot. Brown initially refused their orders to cease digging while they got their own ducks in a row, something archaeologist and author Martin Carver—who headed up the final excavation efforts in from 1983 to 1992—thinks may have saved the site from being looted in the meantime.

That's still a problem today, by the way, especially where I live. Most excavations that take place in or near the major metropolitan centers of Phoenix and Tucson are done to comply with the aforementioned cultural resource protection laws, which is undoubtedly better than doing so just to see what's there, although of course the Tribes would prefer their ancestors weren't disturbed at all. Unfortunately it's often a choice between contract archaeologists, who will repatriate anything the Tribes want while being as respectful as possible during the whole operation; and bulldozer operators, who will do either. These excavations are sometimes the size of entire city blocks and can take years to complete. Keeping the site, the materials within the site, and the excavation materials used to dig the site safe from thieves is a complicated and sometimes dangerous business.

For example, my friend Hunter worked on his first-ever excavation in south Phoenix less than a decade ago, and the company for whom he was working hired a security guard to sit out there and watch over the place between sundown and sunrise. The guard was shot by thieves hoping he was there to guard something valuable—although I gather he survived the attack. The same can't be said for two guards at Guatemalan archaeological sites who were killed at their posts in 1998, or the guard at a storehouse at Ankor Wot who was killed earlier in the 1990s by thieves wielding—get this—a rocket launcher. Stories like these make me wonder why the writers of the *Indiana Jones* franchise keep having to invent silly supernatural dangers.

Back at Sutton Hoo, something weirdly similar but thankfully less tragic occurred when the Ipswich Museum announced the discovery of the buried ship and its treasures a bit "prematurely," in the words of Carver. In response, Edith Petty hired a pair of policemen to stand guard at the spot 24/7 until the primary excavation was complete.

Controversy popped up yet again when a row ensued over where, exactly, the excavated materials were supposed to end up. The Ipswich Museum? The Science Museum? The British Museum? The Prehistoric Society? The materials were shuffled around between Sutton and London until an official inquest reached the conclusion that they'd been buried by people who didn't intend for them to be dug up in the future—fancy that—so they rightly belonged to the land and, by extension, whomever owned the land. Edith Petty said thanks and promptly donated them all to the British Museum.

Digging at the site resumed about twenty years after World War II, prompted by an observation by Rupert Bruce-Mitford from the British Museum's Department of British and Medieval Antiquities that there were still unanswered questions. Because there always are. Principal investigators hate the term "data potential has been exhausted" when they see it on field forms because that's literally never the case unless the entire site has been vaporized down to its atoms, and even then, you could potentially conduct isotope analyses on them.

The site then passed into the hands of Carver, who oversaw the final digging until 1992, publishing a book about the place in 2017. That book was the basis for most of my information here, as well as most of what appeared in the film.

◆ ◆ ◆

This is an excellent example of how British archaeology came to look in the waning days of colonialism. British experts sinking their shovels into British soil to explore British history. The argument over which institution gets to house and display the findings was a struggle between different British factions. And then it was decided that the site and its materials rightly belong to the woman who currently owns the land because they are part of that land—a woman who is also British.

This was underscored for me in a hilarious way when a companion of my friend Dakshina went on vacation in France a few years ago, visiting a few archaeological sites while he was there. Dakshina is originally from France herself and is currently there working on a graduate degree in Paris, but her friend and I both know her from the years she spent doing fieldwork in the American Southwest. During his visit to her home country, this fellow hit Dakshina up to ask the usual questions about how old the sites were, does anyone know what the stone carvings mean, etc. He then asked her, "So what do the Indigenous people have to say about these sites?"

Dakshina had to pause for a moment. "You mean the French people? You're in France."

It would be funny enough if that was the whole story, but apparently it took her a good fifteen minutes to get into this guy's head that European history is European. Yes, there were Gauls and Celts and Angles and Saxons and Goths and Visigoths and Romans and so on moving all over the place at various times, so much so that one of the Knights of the Round Table was a dark-skinned man from northern Africa (Sir Morien). But it's all still European history. There isn't a hard historical divide when people from radically different ways of life suddenly showed up like there is in post-colonial places like the Americas and Australia.

There is not, in other words, the "othering" one finds with early American archaeology, which has turned out to have a bit more staying power than I'd prefer. I learned even more about this talking to other friends who've been more directly involved in European archaeology.

Two of my best friends are a married pair of archaeologists named Kris and Glenn whom I introduced to one another when I was in grad school. Glenn is a friend and Marine vet whom I'd met at field school in 2008—the one who also loves D&D—who went on to get a master's degree from the University of Sheffield in England where he focused on the archaeology of Roman chariots. Kris was a plucky undergrad in a few of my graduate courses who went to the University of Glasgow in Scotland to focus on the archaeology of Viking horses. They got married the moment they were both settled back in the States.*

According to Kris, the practice of archaeology works so closely with history in the UK because "the descendants are usually the ones studying their own ancestors, right down to the local level." They can get a bit shirty if someone says something about someone else's ancestors, like if an English scholar publishes something about the Scots or the Irish and vice versa. Imagine that.

Her own research focused on sites in Iceland, as Kris has a special affinity for Icelandic horses, but actually working there wasn't a consideration for her. "In Iceland, the field is very small and is almost entirely native Icelanders who literally trace their ancestors back to

* Having been the matchmaker, I was supposed to officiate that wedding. My plan was to get ordained online through the Universal Life Church—putting me alongside other ULC Ministers like Benedict Cumberbatch, Ian McKellan, Stephen Colbert, Lady Gaga, and The Rock—and then bring along a layered cake to be cut with a Marshalltown trowel. Those plans were thwarted when Kris's Mormon family threatened to disown her.

the Sagas," she explained. "So, it is a matter of self-discovery. This does mean you'll occasionally get people sneaking propaganda into their research [the old problem of nationalism popping up again], but it's still not as 'othering' of other groups of people. For example, Norwegian archaeologists are more likely to discuss the context as to why the Viking Age happened, whereas UK archaeologists are more likely to discuss what the Viking Age did."

Makes sense. From the perspective of a Norwegian archaeologist, Viking culture is something that developed locally, so understanding the Vikings means understanding the local circumstances that brought them about. From the perspective of a British archaeologist, though, Viking culture is a thing that appeared on their shores in a very sudden and alarming way in AD 793, so understanding the Vikings means understanding the impact they had on British history.

Meanwhile, I have Glenn's extensive knowledge of Roman history and archaeology—in particular the history and archaeology of Roman colonization of Britain—to thank for helping me to understand how knowledge of the deep past is not only interesting but can also be extremely valuable for understanding the present.

Societies up and disappear all the time throughout human history, but cultures never fully go away except in extremely rare cases—like when a volcano wipes out an entire group before they've even made contact with anyone else. Otherwise, ideas and concepts spread between human groups across both space and time, like how genes spread between individuals or groups in a given animal species. This is the original definition of "meme," a transmittable unit of cultural knowledge, before it became shorthand for a drawing of a penguin who can't get laid.

This concept also flies in the face of all that "vanished" or "lost" civilization nonsense. The immense and seemingly very powerful civilization centered on Chaco Canyon from roughly AD 900 to 1200 included architectural structures the size of the Roman Colosseum, highly distinctive and intricate manufacturing traditions, and a vast network of roads and trade routes that extended deep into Mesoamerica and as far east as the Mississippi. It was nothing but crumbling remains when Euro-Americans found the place half a millennium later, as were the mighty cliff dwellings of Mesa Verde, but the descendants of the people who'd built and occupied them were—and are—still living right down the road. The ideas, beliefs, clan identities, artistic and architectural styles, and other cultural accoutrements remain in one form or another.

Steve Lekson—after conducting both archaeology and consultation with numerous Indigenous people for longer than I've been alive so far—thinks that the strong emphasis on egalitarianism in modern Pueblo communities is a direct response to the hierarchical politics of Chaco. They tried that whole state-level stratification thing and found that it sucked, so they intentionally went the other direction after it fell apart. Meanwhile, my friend and colleague Lyle Balenquah, a Hopi archaeologist and wilderness guide who spends his winters making and selling traditional Hopi jewelry, incorporates a lot of Chaco-style designs into his work in a manner he says is consistent with Hopi practices in general.

All of which is to say the extensive societal structure centered on Chaco Canyon may have broken apart as-such nearly a thousand years ago, but Chaco as a cultural complex never really went away. A lot of people and their ideas flowed into it at one chronological end, and a lot of people and their ideas flowed out of the other end. This is a big part of why a lot of Indigenous people consider archaeological sites to be living parts of their history rather than dead vestiges of it. It's not some religious notion of spirits still inhabiting them or anything, at least not entirely. It's because material history—and the lessons it has to teach—still have life as long as the people do.

The same is true of Rome.

The founding of Rome is shrouded in mystery, thanks largely to the city being thoroughly sacked by the Gauls in 390 BC, during which all the extant historical accounts were destroyed. When later Romans asked about their history, historians threw impressive Hail Mary passes comprising equal parts propaganda and myth. Rome was founded by Romulus, brother to Remus, whom he killed after the two were saved from drowning and raised by a wolf. They established a population center at the place where they nearly drowned, peopled it with all the outcasts and brigands and ne'er-do-wells the surrounding townships and tribes didn't want, and then exit Remus.

To address the problem of their founding population consisting exclusively of men, Romulus hatched a scheme to kidnap women from the surrounding communities, whom he then gaslit into believing it was their parents' fault for letting them get kidnapped. Said parents attacked the small society of kidnappers, as you might imagine they would, but Romulus and his legion repelled them all. All, that is, except the Sabines, with whom they forged an alliance after the women convinced both sides to stop all the bickering over little old them.

The extent to which any of that is true is, to put it mildly, debatable. However, from an anthropological point of view, it is all-but worth the weight of truth because it speaks to the culture of what would become Rome. It was founded in defiance. It was founded on brutality, and entirely by men. It was populated with women only by force. That this was embraced as official history when leaders of the subsequent Republic of Rome were queried by their citizens tells you quite a lot about their traditions and values. Men owning everything and making all the major decisions was the norm. Minting coins with the heads of civic leaders on them so everyone carried reminders in their pockets was the norm. Colonizing other groups because you're the superior culture and you're really doing them a huge favor whether they want you to or not—that, too, was the norm.

The Roman Empire officially "ended" on September 4 of AD 476. That was the western or core portion, which had by then gotten intractably entangled with nefarious doings in Egypt and the Middle East. The eastern portion, known as the Byzantine Empire (or simply Byzantium) and centered upon the capital city of Constantinople, survived the breaking apart of the eastern provinces and endured for almost a thousand more years until the Ottomans snuffed it out in 1453. The Colonial Period with which we're more familiar, during which European nations—primarily the Spanish, French, and English—spread throughout the world on a mission of total conquest, commenced just under forty years later.

The tactics these colonists used were largely Roman tactics, including a bloodthirsty ferocity that even the Aztecs found shocking. The trade policies they enacted were Roman policies, particularly regarding the ownership and social status of slaves. Women had no political power, and when the colonists encountered societies where women did have an equal voice in decision-making (e.g., most Indigenous groups in the American Southwest) they did all they could to subvert or dismantle it. Since Christianity had become the official religion of the Romans in AD 313, any relationship that wasn't strictly monogamous heterosexual baby-manufacturing was either tabooed or outlawed—and that, too, made its way to these shores. Roman architecture is prominent throughout what became the capital city, Roman numerals were plastered all over the place, Roman symbols like the fasces (from which the term *fascism* derives) ended up on dimes and the speaker's podium in the House of Representatives, there's eagle symbolism all over the place, and so on.

Thomas Jefferson in particular, the "King of Hypocrites" according to journalist and podcaster Robert Evans, was infatuated with the writings of Cato the Elder. Cato was a Roman soldier, senator, and historian who was famous for being an ultraconservative firebrand. He wrote and preached about idealized citizen-farmers, despite himself never spending even a moment behind a plow, and the workaround for this non sequitur was slavery. His appeal for a man like Jefferson is, therefore, pretty self-evident.

Cato held very definite positions on how slaves should be kept and managed, including the notion that pitting them against one another would help prevent them from unifying against their master—the old "divide and conquer" routine. Jefferson gobbled up Cato's teachings and biographies of the man by Roman historians like Plutarch, believing that the independent American colonies should also be full of citizen-farmers with slaves to do the actual farming, all while paying lip service to abolitionists about the evils of slavery. Even his plantation, Monticello or "little mountain" in old Italian, was modeled on Roman villas, and to this day it's the only private residence in the United States to be designated a UNESCO World Heritage Site.

In other words, Rome never disappeared. Not entirely. Because history simply doesn't work like that. The empire and its bedrock principles of commerce *über alles*, might-makes-right militarism, patriarchal hegemony, enforced heteronormativity, and religious mythology dictating political legislation expanded westward from its humble beginnings as a ragtag gang of Mediterranean thugs; paused at the Atlantic coast long enough to develop oceanic seafaring technology (while dealing with a few domestic troubles along the way—like the total collapse of their centralized political system); and then simply kept on going.

What arrived here two millennia after the founding of Rome looked, acted, and talked differently from any imperial Roman citizen, of course. But not by much. At least to a given value of "much."

Glenn sees it this way, I see it this way, and apparently so did science-fiction legend Philip K. Dick, whose million-word journal *Exegesis* included a more interesting take on the idea that the Roman Empire never really ended. According to biographer Kyle Arnold, Dick learned from "psychic visions" how history was intentionally stopped in the first century AD, when materialism and despotism reached their respective peaks, and the world had remained enslaved to worldly possessions ever since. He also thought Richard Nixon should be impeached not because he was an unusually corrupt American president, but because he was a typically corrupt Roman emperor.

Dick was not really sound of mind by then but, still, he makes a few good points.

Archaeologists don't use psychic visions to inform their hypotheses. Not usually, anyway. But historians are—for understandable reasons—commonly criticized as mere storytellers by more hard-nosed scientific types. They often insist that any information not backed up by independently verifiable quantitative data should be treated as little better than propaganda and myth, just like the official "history" of Rome after the Gauls burned all their history books.

Fair enough, I suppose. But the official history adopted by Rome was only adopted by them because it fit with their worldview, and that in turn sheds considerable light on what that worldview was—especially as it related to things like women and violence. The stories we choose to believe reveal quite a lot about us, and that makes them worth listening to. Especially when the burning of history books is still a very real danger.

That said, Glenn's own understanding of Rome was also from a British perspective, because he was studying the archaeology of Romans and their chariots at British sites. He had to read a ton of Roman history and archaeology monographs by people from all over the place, naturally—including no small number of Italians. But, again, he was in Europe at a European institution examining the material history of Europe, even if a great number of Britons today don't actually consider themselves European.

◆ ◆ ◆

That's a brief snapshot of a few of the differences between European and American archaeology. As far as technicalities are concerned, differences in theory and practice are steadily becoming homogenized around the globe thanks in large part to the internet and its *de facto* standardizing behavior. You want your article about paleoclimates and adaptations to them to be read by as many people as possible, after all—especially people who live in countries that are simultaneously doing the most to hasten climate change and oppress any research in that direction.

Due to this modern trend toward global homogenization, archaeological practice is concomitantly becoming exportable. Dozens of my former co-workers in the private sector went to Saudi Arabia to work an archaeological inventory contract between 2022 and 2024, for example, and my Navajo-wegian friend Jamie once spent a year as a field tech (industry jargon for field technician or non-supervisory fieldworker) in Australia while weighing the merits of an Aussie boyfriend, to list a few examples.

Minor differences persist, of course, and they are numerous. Methods of excavation, for example, are often constrained by arbitrary units of measure in the US ("we dug down 50cm through three distinct layers of strata") and more often constrained by units of known history in places like the UK ("we dug through the Elizabethan era and down to the Roman colonial period"). But even those differences are largely dwindling.

The chief difference remains that of European archaeology being a branch of history, which is focused on constructing narratives about the past; and American archaeology being a subfield of anthropology, which is focused on parsing the behavioral developments of humanity as a whole. All because the bulk of European archaeology consists of Europeans investigating Europeans, while the bulk of American archaeology consists of Americans investigating Others.

But investigation is only one major goal of the operative process of archaeology. Starting with the late-1800s conservation movement and the Antiquities Act, and gradually snowballing from there, are the separate but overlapping goals of management and preservation of that material history. This involves herding such disparate cats as federal agencies, the American public, corporate development firms, conservationists and their various clubs, environmentalists, and the outdoor recreation industry—to say nothing of the researchers and descendant communities anchored at the very heart of the matter.

It can get a bit messy.

CHAPTER 6

MANAGERS AND MYTHMAKERS

Drilling down on the dual-pronged topic of preservation and management, most archaeological salvage operations in the mid-1900s were conducted under the direction of major institutions. The legendary Glen Canyon Project, for example, was funded by the federal agencies and run by the University of Utah and the Museum of Northern Arizona, with Professor Jennings of the former institution calling most of the shots. When the project commenced in the 1950s, the only pieces of protective legislation on the books were the Antiquities Act and the Historic Sites Act, both of which were important early steps but basically paper tigers in their own rights. Passage of the Reservoir Salvage Act of 1960 and the landmark National Historic Protection Act of 1966 started getting things on their current track, although they were largely toothless as well.

There was another, smaller piece of legislation passed not long after those two that set the ball rolling toward something more substantial: the Archaeological and Historic Preservation Act of 1974. It was created in response to concerns that the Reservoir Salvage Act concerned only work conducted by federal agencies, namely the Army Corps of Engineers and the Bureau of Reclamation—the fanatical dam-builders.

In effect, the law requires that if the activities of any federal agency connected with a construction program or "federally licensed project, activity, or program may cause irreparable loss or destruction of significant scientific, prehistorical, historical, or archaeology data" (according to Section 3(a)) then a study is needed. It provides the Secretary of the Interior with the authority to assist any agency or effort meeting the requirements of AHPA if the project is likely to damage the things listed above, undertake studies of the project or projects themselves, consult about ownership and curation issues, and compile a report for Congress.

Considering everything I've laid out already, two problems should immediately pop out. First, "federally licensed project, activity, or program that may cause irreparable loss or destruction of significant scientific, prehistorical, historical, or archaeology data" is not defined in the legislation. At all. Second, isn't all that already covered by the National Historic Preservation Act?

The short answer is "yes," and after a whole bunch of intervening legislative monkeyshines the AHPA wound up becoming basically moot. It's an updated version of the Reservoir Salvage Act that manifested out of concerns that archaeologists and federal agencies weren't taking the NHPA seriously enough, but then they *did* start taking NHPA more seriously and today it's considered the principle guiding legislation.

So, the AHPA itself was a flash in the pan that wound up effectively dissolved. But the concerns mentioned above which led to its creation signify the concerns growing within the broader American archaeological community about the damaging effects construction projects had on anything people find to be culturally important. In the brief time the law was alive it helped breathe fire into adjacent legislation which would probably still be toothless to this day without it.

The term "cultural resources" emerged from these discussions, coined in 1971 or 1972 according to archaeology historian Don Fowler, and "cultural resource management" officially entered the broader consciousness of American archaeologists in 1974 with Bill Lipe and A.J. Lindsay's publication *Proceedings of the 1974 Cultural Resource Management Conference, Denver.* Prolific CRM specialist and author Thomas King contests this, observing that the first use of "CRM" came in the airport bar following the Denver conference, while a number of the participants were waiting on their delayed flights. In any case, archaeologists in the Southwest popularized the term "Cultural Resource Management" beginning in the early 1970s.

The term itself is tough to define, but since it was apparently NPS employees who cooked it up, I'm obliged to offer their definition as canonical. In their documentation, cultural resources consist of the "physical evidence of past human activity" manifested as a "site, object, landscape, structure; or a site, structure, landscape, object, or natural feature of significance to a group of people traditionally associated with it." Not a whole lot of certainty in the wording—it means approximately places and things that have specific histories that make them important to people associated with that history.

Thomas King does a somewhat better job of defining cultural resources in his encyclopedic *Cultural Resource Laws and Practice* as "those aspects of the environment—both physical and intangible, both natural and built—that have cultural value of some kind to a group of people." That can mean a community, a family, a neighborhood, a clan, a club, members of a vocation or professional society, members of a religious organization, a tribe, a state, or an entire nation. Whatever group has a demonstrable interest in the topic, really—hence NHPA stipulating "interested parties" under its subsection on consultation.

That, in a nutshell, is the origin of CRM as a concept in the United States.* The mass of protective legislation heading into the mid-1970s required federal agencies to make sure any major projects taking place on federal lands either avoided or mitigated damages to those bits of material history determined to be significant by consulting parties like Indigenous tribes. Easy enough—there's only a little over half a billion acres of land under the aegis of federal agencies.

Granted, that's down from an initial total of eighteen billion acres back in the mid-1800s before approximately two-thirds of it

* Terminology time again. In recent years, a lot of talk about "cultural resource" management has shifted to "cultural heritage" or simply "heritage" management instead, chiefly because the word "resources" implies that these things are meant to be used. I know of at least one awful guy in southeastern Utah who uses this as his excuse to make and sell treasure maps to archaeological sites. Cultural heritage refers to the tangible and intangible assets a group or society has inherited from past generations, so it's really just a more respectful term for cultural resources, both of which include material history as a component.

was transferred to the private sector or set aside as national parks. That still leaves the Bureau of Land Management and the US Forest Service, the two agencies tasked with managing our "multiple use" lands (NPS lands and designated wilderness areas are considered off-limits to developers by default), in charge of an area about the size of Iran. If that comparison doesn't carry the weight that it should, it's also an area equivalent to nearly four Texases.

Of the two, it's the Bureau of Land Management or BLM that has to deal with this legislation the most because it manages great swaths of land brought under its direction by default, while the Forest Service is tasked with managing areas that were specified by people like Gifford Pinchot pointing to a map and saying, "manage that bit there as a National Forest." Underneath BLM lands, especially in places like the Great Basin, is a lot of oil and gas—and boy howdy did we want more and more of those in the mid-1900s United States. Car ownership underwent a bit of a frenzy in the 1950s, engendering an entire "car culture" that's often a focal point of nostalgia content today. About 73 percent of Americans owned a car by 1951, and the total hit about 85 percent by the mid-1970s.

Couple this with the Cold War and our eagerness to show up the Soviets with our weapons prowess, and the call to get environmental "clearances" for roads, well pads, derricks, pipelines, missile silos, and other forms of modernity started sounding more like a roar. On the agency side, full understanding and implementation of legislation like NEPA and NHPA was rising at about the same curvature. A lot of BLM districts were hiring archaeologists for the first time in the agency's history because of all this. According to former California state archaeologist Russel L. Kaldenberg, in 1972 the BLM had no professional cultural resources staff to conduct surveys for specific purposes, review submitted proposals or reports, or—really—do anything else to manage cultural resources on public lands.

The first BLM archaeologist, a fellow named Rick Hanks, was hired that year and started work in 1973. That's forty-four years after Jesse Nusbaum became the first NPS archaeologist at Mesa Verde.

The Department of the Interior didn't even delegate authority to issue permits for archaeological work until after they'd hired some of their own archaeologists in the 1970s. The department issued all those permits itself starting in 1929, and delegated authority to the NPS in 1967 after the agency reorganized to enable implementation of the NHPA. It wasn't until 1984—a few years after ARPA was passed and supplanted the Antiquities Act as the chief permitting apparatus for archaeological investigations on public lands—that the BLM was given permission to issue permits to archaeologists for limited testing, survey conducting, excavating on the lands they managed, or some combination of the three. This was a problem for developers. They had investors, they had quarterly profit targets to hit, and they had bulldozers at the ready. What they did not have in abundance was patience.

The BLM and USFS assured those developers that they would carry out all the necessary inventories to greenlight their projects, but the waiting time could often be measured in years rather than in days, weeks, or months. This was simply not tolerable for those looking to drill or mine on public lands, as the whimsies of the increasingly globalized economy suggested that a competitor could overtake their share of the market and/or demand could simply evaporate without a lot of warning.

As critical as I often am of these sorts of firms, it's a fair point. Those are legally defined public resources, after all, and people need them for things like driving from home to work or even having a home or work to begin with. Doing an end-run around environmental protection laws is always an option, if you're completely heartless and okay with occasionally being sued, but a better solution is to find a more efficient means of addressing those issues.

In the beginning of the CRM era, this was often accomplished by local universities and their students, who were always looking for handy field schooling opportunities anyway. The agencies, owning up to the fact that they really didn't have the capacity to deal with all these projects, started outsourcing more and more of it to universities.

When people in the public sector realize they could be doing what they're already doing for a lot more money in the private sector, that's precisely what they often do, Archaeology being no exception. Thus, many agency- and institution-affiliated archaeologists started going into business as private environmental consultants during this period—a trend that would only increase in time.

◆ ◆ ◆

The next major archaeological salvage project in the Southwest to have impacts throughout the domain of CRM after the mighty Glen Canyon Project was the Dolores Project Cultural Resources Mitigation Program, an unnecessarily long title for what most people simply call the Dolores Project. It began on June 6, 1978, when the Bureau of Reclamation signed a contract for the University of Colorado, Boulder, with David Breternitz as senior principal investigator and Washington State University as primary subcontractor.

This would be the last of the major archaeological salvage projects conducted on public lands that was contracted to an institution. By at least 1976, there were enough private CRM consulting firms—including moonlighting professors and their staff—to create a realm of open competition, with consultants battling each other for access to gigs. The full NHPA Section 106 process still includes project oversight, report and "significance" determination, and consultation with SHPOs and the Tribes by agency personnel. The part of the process that involves actually looking at things on the ground was increasingly chopped out and contracted to the private sector, a trend that hasn't slowed down since.

Following the Dolores Project was the Animas-La Plata Water Project, which ran from 2002 to 2009 in southwestern Colorado and was run by for-profit company SWCA Environmental Consultants under contract with the Ute Mountain Ute Tribe using Bureau of Reclamation funds. The next major one after that was the Navajo-Gallup Water Supply Project, the largest public archaeology contract in American history to the present, which was run by for-profit company PaleoWest (now Chronicle Heritage) on behalf of the Bureau of Reclamation starting in 2011.*

* There may be another big one lurking in the near future as for-profit utility company SRP ruminates with local and federal agencies about enlarging Bartlett Dam to meet Phoenix's increasing water demands, because for reasons I simply cannot fathom people continue moving to Phoenix.

At this point, according to an *American Cultural Resources Association* report from 2019, there are about thirteen-hundred CRM firms nationwide with a combined total of some ten thousand employees. It's become a billion-dollar industry—and, like most billion-dollar industries, it's gradually becoming dominated by a small number of mega corporations set on gobbling up all their little regional competitors.

◆ ◆ ◆

Such is "public archaeology" in terms of archaeology conducted on public lands, but there's another form of "public archaeology" that takes a somewhat different shape: that of popular media.

I've already touched on the impact H. Rider Haggard's *King Solomon's Mines* had on subsequent literature about dashing adventurers, lost civilizations, and pursuit of treasure as a means of making a living from history. Haggard didn't invent any of these ideas—he simply tapped into an existing drive in a very successful and targets way. Exploring for the sake of seeing what's out there is arguably how Homo erectus first made it from Africa to most of Eurasia, and historic Western literature included "adventurers" of one sort or another in the likes of Gilgamesh, Odysseus, and King Arthur long before 1885.

Lost cities or civilizations have seemingly always been an intriguing idea as well—one that was playfully employed by Plato when he used Atlantis to teach political lessons, and then barbarically employed by the Spanish when they used the legend of El Dorado to plunge like a fiery sword into the American Southwest. And hunting for historic treasure to pay one's bills is something a lot of people were doing in Egypt almost the moment the Old Kingdom tombs were closed.

Most historians nonetheless agree that Haggard was the first Western writer to combine those elements into one cohesive genre for which we don't really have an official title. He's often credited with minting the "lost worlds" genre of fiction, and that's how you'll find him cited all over the internet, but it wasn't lost worlds that he invented. What he really invented was Allan Quatermain, the daring adventurer who laughs at social conventions while navigating mysterious lands and negotiating harsh dangers in search of those lost worlds and their bounteous booty.

That's what everyone wanted to be. They envied the character. Quatermain's actual discoveries and fabulous wealth were ancillary, almost incidental, to the ego-tickling notion of being held in the same regard that *he* was—with special emphasis on the word he. Just look at the fiction it inspired.

In 1888, just a few years after Haggard's book came out, Rudyard Kipling—the man who gave us both *The Jungle Book* and *The White Man's Burden*—published a story called "The Man Who Would Be King" in a couple of anthologies. It centers on a self-insert caricature of Kipling as a British journalist working in India when he meets a pair of haggard (pun intended) adventurers and subsequently chronicles their efforts to install themselves as kings in the mysterious region of Kafiristan. They succeed, mostly by using their rifles to convince the silly natives that they're gods in human form, and all is well until one of them decides to marry a local girl. She freaks out at the prospect of marrying a god and bites him when he tries to kiss her, causing him to bleed, causing the natives to realize they aren't gods after all.

Sir Arthur Conan Doyle's 1912 novel *The Lost World* follows the exploits of Edward Malone, a young journalist who looks for a dangerous assignment specifically to impress a girl he likes named Gladys, who insists that she's only interested in brave men of action. He winds up in a place filled with dinosaurs, "ape-men," and local natives, before narrowly escaping back to England with what turns out to be a fortune in diamonds—only to discover that Gladys had changed her mind and married a boring clerk instead. The book ends with him deciding dinosaurs and "ape-men" might nonetheless be preferable to the company of fickle women.

Are you noting a theme yet?

A few years later, Edgar Rice Burroughs' 1918 book *The Land That Time Forgot* follows Bowen J. Tyler as he steals a German U-boat and pilots it to a land occupied by primitive humans and dinosaurs. At one point they take an actual Neanderthal as a prisoner. At another, Tyler must rescue a damsel in distress—the other survivor of the torpedoed passenger vessel that kicks the whole fiasco off—which leads to a series of fights with other primitive humans intended to be symbolic stand-ins for the evolutionary stages of human races. Tyler almost dies trying to rescue the hapless and apparently totally incompetent woman yet again before the two are reunited and build a love nest together.

Apart from the obvious running theme of lost worlds and derring-do, these and other examples also paint a vivid picture of how growing numbers of men felt about women in Western culture during this time, particularly in the United States. Zane Grey became the mouthpiece for many of them starting in 1922 with *The Vanishing American*, which actually does a fair job of presenting the horrors of colonization and cultural extinction being foisted on Native Americans up to and during the World War I era. The downside is it also characterized the American West as "a haven from modernity's gender roles and a site where the masculine imperative to adventure and *control of female sexuality* could be enacted," according to historian Thomas J. Harvey (my italics). There's no room for women's lib in the realm of adventurous men, apparently, and this aspect of the genre would also endure—from Grey to Abbey and beyond.

Not to keep beating the same drums, but the Roman populace taking as given that the Rape of the Sabines was a perfectly believable and acceptable tale about the founding of a major city-state seems eerily echoed here. Phillip K. Dick would be proud, and for all I know may well have been.

Meanwhile, excitement over the possibility of being heralded as a real-life Allan Quatermain was also helped in no small way by the exploits of a few actual adventurers in the years immediately following *King Solomon's Mines*, particularly those of Hiram Bingham III and Percy Fawcett. Their actual hijinks were nearly as exciting as Quatermain's fictional ones.

Bingham came first, although the two lived and worked during approximately the same period. He was born in Hawaii in 1875, long before it became a state, to a pair of missionaries who were there to bring the good word and probably the flu to Indigenous Hawaiians. He was a crafty but not especially successful businessman who married into the Tiffany jewelry fortune in 1900 and then divorced back out of it in 1937, after fathering seven sons with wife Alfreda Mitchell. He was also an academic, trained at Phillips University, UC Berkeley, and then Harvard before eventually taking a position as lecturer in South American history at Yale in 1907.

Bingham was a great fan of fanfare and spectacle, and sought early on to find some way to establish himself in the history books as an explorer of Quatermain level. He got his chance after serving as a delegate on the first Pan American Scientific Congress in Santiago, Chile, which stopped over in Peru on his way home. Based on stories and investigations of other sites during that stopover, Bingham became obsessed with the possibility of finding unexplored Inca cities, and organized the Yale Peruvian Expedition in 1911 to do just that. He and his team were led to Machu Picchu by local guides, arguably the only people in the region who still knew the place existed, and falsely declared it the lost capital of the Incas, the last redoubt where Incan revolutionaries had hidden before being routed and stamped out by Francisco Álvarez de Toledo.

Ironically, those stalwart adventurers had already found the last redoubt of Incan revolutionaries earlier in their expedition, a place called Vilcabamba (or *Espíritu Pampa* at the time). Being an inveterate devotee of fanfare and spectacle, however, Bingham didn't think the crumbling remains of Vilcabamba were glamorous enough to be the fabled city he was seeking—a hilariously similar case to that of Heinrich Schliemann irreparably damaging the site of ancient Troy half a century earlier because he thought it was too drab to be the real deal. I keep imagining some future archaeologist coming across the dismal swampy sprawl of Washington, DC and thinking "There is no way this mass of filth was the capital of a global empire" before concluding the real capital must have been Las Vegas.

Percy Fawcett, meanwhile, was the son of a Royal Geographical Society member and military man from England. He attended school alongside Sir Arthur Conan Doyle, and his older brother

Edward ended up as an author of books on philosophy and fictional adventure novels, so it's arguable that his life and legacy helped shape their fiction to some extent. Fawcett joined the Society in 1901 as a surveyor and mapmaker working in places like North Africa, where he met and befriended Haggard two decades after the author had published *King Solomon's Mines.*

Fawcett wound up deployed to South America on several excursions to survey and map the empty spots on colonial maps, including the sources of both the Rio Verde and the Heath River. It was on one such occasion that he first became interested in finding a place he'd come to call the "lost city" of Z (pronounced Zed in his British patois). Extensive research on documented history from the area seemed to support his contention, and today we know that there were indeed extensive civilizations in the Amazon over a considerable period. Whole networks of cities keep emerging from the jungle thanks to advances in LiDAR and other technology, another of which was discovered in Ecuador in 2024.

So, Fawcett and his sources weren't wrong. Sort of. There are indeed cities in the jungles of South America that could, for all intents and purposes, be considered "lost" to the people who were alive in his time as well as ours. Researchers now suspect these large civilizations flourished for hundreds of years building intricate networks of roads, neighborhoods, gardens, and communal architecture that rivaled those of the Mayan city-states that arose to the north centuries later.

Some were built and occupied by what are now called the Upano people in Ecuador between about 500 BC through sometime between AD 300 and 600, according to archaeologists Stéphen Rostain at France's National Center for Scientific Research and Fernando Mejía at the Pontifical Catholic University of Ecuador. Others are associated with the Casarabe Culture, which included monumental platforms and pyramids in Bolivia between about AD 500 and 1400, according to anthropologist Michael Heckenberger at the University of Florida and archaeologist Heiko Prümers of the German

Archaeological Institute.*

The fate of all these civilizations remains a mystery, but the latter appear to have left the Amazon Basin sometime just prior to 1400, so there's a good chance the megadroughts of the fourteenth century inspired them to move elsewhere.

Furthermore, ancient ceramics can be found mixed into the soil in a great number of places in the Amazon rainforest forming what's now called *terra preta*, an anthropogenic soil that appears to have been made on purpose by ancient farmers and is ridiculously fertile. You can see Fawcett freaking out over it in the movie adaptation of his biography, but his search for actual cities took far longer than he'd hoped. News of Bingham's successful "discovery" of Machu Picchu in 1911 seemed to irk Fawcett, and he became even more animated in his frantic search to find Z, but then World War I went and happened.

By the early 1920s, he was fully convinced that an advanced civilization had existed in the Amazon before being swallowed by the jungle, and he immediately returned to his obsession after returning from several years in the war. I can only imagine how his wife felt about that. He attempted to find it on his own in 1920 but had to turn back after becoming gravely ill and shooting his pack animal. He set out on a better-equipped expedition four years later with funding from a handful of London financiers and his eldest son Jack at his side.

They were never seen again.

Bingham's exploits found their way into several documentaries, including a 2000 episode of *Treasure Seekers* titled "Lost Cities of the Inca" where both he and Francisco Álvarez de Toledo are paired up for a nicely comprehensive look at Western investigations in Peru. Fawcett, meanwhile, has the distinction of being the star of a book by David Grann called *The Lost City of Z: A Tale of Deadly Obsession in the Amazon*, which in turn inspired a pretty decent 2016 movie adap-

* Note how French, Ecuadorian, American, and German archaeologists are all represented in just these two examples. Whereas colonialism resulted in situations like that in the past, globalization is the reason these days. It gets easier every year to do archaeology abroad. Something worth keeping in mind.

tation, but I don't expect that film to have the same inspiring impact that *King Solomon's Mines* did in the 1880s or *Raiders of the Lost Ark* did almost exactly a century later. Not with how the story ends.

◆ ◆ ◆

Raiders and the one—and only one—quality Indiana Jones movie that followed it had such a profound cultural impact that scholars of media today actually refer to the Indiana Jones Effect as an established behavioral phenomenon. Jones and his antics inspired countless students who watched them as wide-eyed children and went on to contribute great things to the fields of American and biblical archaeology.

Advertising the field of archaeology via whips and fedoras was, in other words, a great success. Maybe even too much of one. According to Dr. Jeff Rose in a 2023 article for *Times Higher Education*, one major result of this was the success of the franchise "flooding the market with aspiring archaeologists" when there wasn't enough work for them

How the tables have turned. Today, the field of CRM is experiencing a labor crisis—and not the one I was taught to expect. Back in Flagstaff, when I was tending bar at a country club to pay for my first in what eventually became a stack of archaeology degrees, the comment I most often heard was "Yeah, good luck in the job market!"

That was in 2012, the same year *U.S. News* ran an article with the catchy title "5 College Degrees that Aren't Worth the Cost." The dual topic of Anthropology-and-Archaeology made the list, along with Social Work, Elementary Education, Drama and Theater Arts, and Family and Consumer Studies. Their reasoning:

> According to Georgetown's statistics, it doesn't pay well starting out as Indiana Jones. New graduates from degrees in anthropology and archaeology start earning at around $28,000 . . . Unemployment for recent grads is very high at 10.5 percent.

Fast-forward eleven years, and we find an article in the Energy and Environment subsection of *Politico* with the equally catchy title "An archaeologist shortage could stifle the climate law." The leading sentence notes how a "nationwide shortage of archeologists could hamstring President Joe Biden's clean energy agenda." I don't think the author realized American voters would hamstring it even harder the following year.

This precipitates the obvious follow-up question: How? How the hell did we go from "don't do archaeology cuz you won't find a job" to "please do archaeology cuz we've got more jobs than we can possibly staff" in a mere decade?

By far the biggest reason I've seen is the one about payrates. *U.S. News* reported in 2012 that new graduates make around $28,000. That jumps up to about $47,000 "after a few years of experience," according to their research. In fact, the average starting wage for a field tech at that time was $15.28 per hour, or about $30,000 a year—which still isn't great, but my guess is their data was skewed a tad by all the cultural and linguistic anthropologists shoveling snow to make ends meet. Still, the average rent for a decent place in the US was about $800 a month in 2012, or just under 30 percent of a $30,000 annual salary, which is about what classic models say you should spend on housing.

At present, most labor-stats research puts the average archaeologist salary in the US at about $60,000 with an over/under of between $57,000 and $70,000, and I don't know where they're getting their info because that is incorrect. Wildly so. As of 2024, most private firms and federal agencies alike start their entry-level techs at about $18 an hour, or roughly $35,000 a year. That's not a tall leap from where payrates were a decade ago.

Costs of living, meanwhile, have leapt like a kangaroo on a trampoline. One of my federal agency colleagues bemoaned this fact in a meeting of the Arizona Archaeological Council in early 2023, saying how the agencies aren't attracting enough talent because federal (that is: General Scale or GS) payrates haven't risen enough. Every year, Congress decides whether to raise the GS pay scale, and if so by how much. They typically increase it by 1 to 3 percent every year, with occasional freezes or accelerations based on economic trends. As a result, the starting wage for an entry-level tech—which, in the feds, is the GS-05 pay level—was $31,087 per year in 2012. In 2023, it was $36,673 per year. That's a total increase of about 16 percent in eleven years. During that same stretch of time, nationwide rents increased by an average of over 40 percent, and nationwide house values increased by an average of just under 150 percent.

Private sector employers tend to offer better wages, if only to entice people away from the public sector. They'll often start at about $17 an hour as of 2023, followed by a battery of raises into the low $20s over the next several years to make one feel really appreciated. It's a dirty psychological trick. What they've really done is underfund the position upon commencement and then pile on the raises to bring it up to what they've actually budgeted as the starting wage—usually around $22 per hour for a full-time tech or low-level crew chief, equivalent to about $42,000 a year. That's enough to stay just ahead of the agencies without spending too much on labor. It's also enough to afford a tiny hovel in a high-crime neighborhood if you don't mind going halvesies with someone more gainfully employed.

Such was the scenario up until 2024, when the United States of America became what can only be called a *de facto* fascist dictatorship ruled over by an oligarch from South Africa and a reality television star best-known for slapping his name on many of the worst scams in recent history. One of this dynamic duo's first acts in office was to freeze or cancel all federal payments and purge as many federal positions as possible, leading to the immediate cancelation of millions of dollars' worth of work and the illegal termination of tens of thousands of workers for crimes like being newly hired, being disabled, or simply not white being enough.

Many of those illegally fired were veterans, and the majority of veterans voted for that very same leadership, making the whole situation eerily similar to the Night of Long Knives—an event in the rise of German fascism where Hitler purged many of the people who helped him come to power but didn't quite fit the Nazi chic, including a terrifying and openly gay street fighter named Ernst

Röhm. Supporting fascists in the hopes that they care about their supporters is always a very dangerous gambit.

The repercussions of that and whatever came afterward while this book was in the printing shop will likely be felt for generations, so there's really no guessing at this point what they might be, apart from the rest of the world largely deciding they're done with the US and its bullshit. Can't say I blame them.

Relative to this book and its themes, the most immediate repercussion was an absolute collapse in the morale and overall mental health of the federal workforce, including archaeologists. The work still needs to be done, because the current regime hasn't (as of drafting this) been any more successful at getting rid of NHPA than their predecessors, but the agencies were already understaffed and underfunded *before* all this chaos—and then even that got blowtorched. Three guesses where all that work is headed instead.

◆ ◆ ◆

The simple fact is that while archaeological work is mandated by law, at least for now, and while there's currently an overabundance of archaeology jobs begging to be filled archaeology simply doesn't pay enough. Not unless you're willing to slum it for a decade or more to reach the level that I've reached: able to afford a comfy apartment for myself and two cats in a neighborhood whose crime rate is only medium-high.

For this reason, efforts to unionize have ramped up across the discipline in recent years, culminating with the—as of now—first vote to unionize by the archaeological staff at the Salt Lake City office of SWCA Environmental Consultants. They did so by partnering with the Teamsters, since there's currently no such thing as a Union of Field Scientists in this country, and I gather that it's working just fine so far.

There's also unionized offices in the federal agencies, what are known internally as "bargaining units," something I don't think many civilians even know is a thing. Federal employees in those offices who opt into the union can count on them for legal defense against amoral fuckery—including employees who work in heritage management. In early 2025, when Donald Trump illegally deputized Elon Musk to head up the illegally created Department Of [*sic.*] Government Efficiency and illegally direct the Office of Personnel Management to illegally order the agencies to illegally purge their probationary employees,* the American Federation of Government Employees mobilized with guns blazing.

Apart from legal representation against corporate thugs, another obvious benefit of unionizing is that it usually precipitates higher wages. The trouble there, as critics are quick to point out, is that it gives non-union outfits an opportunity to underbid union ones when it comes to contract opportunities. How this plays out in the private sector is probably self-evident: higher pay means higher revenue demand to cover that pay, which means asking more from the client. A competitor who pays their employees in table scraps and Monopoly money can easily underbid them. There should be some sort of controls built into a system like that to prevent the downward spiral back toward literal slavery as businesses seek to underbid each other, but that would be profoundly un-American so of course there aren't.

In the public sector, federal agencies solicit requests for proposals, or RFPs, whenever they have a gig they can't work themselves that's likely to cost more than just a couple grand. Revegetating after a forest fire, say, or maybe de-vegetating whenever America's grazing lobby succeeds in convincing lawmakers that cows are more important than healthy forests—which is more often than you'd think. In the words of a smartass geologist with whom I currently work, cattle grazing is effectively a "hereditary aristocracy on federal lands."

Imagine you're the manager of an apartment building. One of your tenants pays not only sub-market rent, but in fact pays so little

* Again: hundreds, if not thousands of the people caught up in the purge were veterans' preference hires who openly supported Trump, making the whole thing remarkably reminiscent of the time Hitler thanked Röhm and his brownshirts for their unwavering support by having them all killed. The difference is many of the veterans were then forcibly rehired by order of the courts, and I don't think any of them were killed—at least not at the time I'm writing this.

that you lose money to overhead costs and have to subsidize the difference by robbing people every April 15th. And they and their "pets" absolutely trash the place, including priceless and irreplaceable antiques—sometimes before you even realize they were there in the first place. And they get to choose who inherits the unit from them when they die. And they openly hate and criticize you all the while they're freeloading off you. And you're forbidden by law from kicking them out. All because Americans have this unshakeable obsession with the myth of the Old West cowboy as a noble defender of masculinity rather than what they really were: impoverished laborers eating dust on horseback for the benefit of millionaires.

Because of this, it's not at all unusual for lobbyists to convince politicians to convince federal agencies thats it's in the best interests of the American people to, for instance, scrape away vast swaths of drought-adapted desert flora so they can plant grass with high water demands in order to feed the cows we imported from Eurasia. In addition to this being a very stupid task, it's also an enormous one for which the agencies don't have the personnel to conduct environmental inventory—so they contract it out. It's not unusual for the feds to fly solicitations for pedestrian survey on thousands or even tens of thousands of acres ahead of some project on public lands, and it's private CRM firms that compete to get the heritage portion of these enormous contracts.

Federal law also mandates that agencies are always supposed to go with the lowest-cost qualified bidder, in order to get the best deal taxpayers can buy. That's important.

A company that pays its workers a lower wage can afford to make lower bids on federal contracts. Companies that pay better wages need larger revenue streams to cover that cost, which makes them easier to outbid. This means that if only a few outfits in the CRM world voted to unionize, there's a fair chance they'll vote themselves right out of a job. It's a rare case of all-or-nothing rather than nuance being the rule, and company owners are not unaware of this.

◆ ◆ ◆

All that is how it works as of drafting this book, at a time when there are at least a handful of archaeologists and other field specialists working within the federal agencies to take up the bulk of smaller projects. It's only the really big ones that get contracted out to the private sector where an increasingly small number of increasingly large corporations compete over those contracts by seeing who can get away with screwing their employees the hardest. By the time this book hits shelves there might not be any subject matter experts left in the agencies to do any of that work, which would move every bit of it into the unregulated shark tank of the private sector—a place where exactly one office of one company has managed to successfully unionize.

So, all I can say to my fellow shovel bums seeking to unionize is best of luck. And I really mean that. It's a noble goal, but it's a tricky one in an industry where work goes to the lowest bidder.

Nor do big CRM firms react to such unionization efforts any better than Delta Airlines, who went as far as hanging a bunch of posters in employee gathering places that proclaimed: "Union dues cost around $700 a year. A new video game system with the latest hits sounds like fun. Put your money towards that instead of paying dues to the union." Yes, that really happened.

Granted, that situation is still better than it was in the 1920s, when companies would literally hire armies of mercenaries to go to war with striking union members (see: The Battle of Blair Mountain), but it strikes me as a lot more insulting. I'd rather face a machine gun nest than a Cool Bro CEO sitting backwards on a chair explaining how it's, like, hella sweet to buy a new PlayStation instead of paying dues to a union who might cut into his profits on my behalf.

Predictably, then, the initial response to unionization efforts was hostility. Alex Press covered this topic in an article for *Jacobin* in which she interviewed my friend and former coworker Freeman Stevenson, a fascinating fellow who's fond of Taylor Swift and kittens (he gave me my cat, Toulouse) and, incidentally, joined a Kurdish militia to fight as a mercenary against ISIS in Syria. That seems wildly contradictory, but my war hero grandfather was the same way—a jovial man who loved nothing more than a wiggly puppy or a slapstick comedy and never lost a second's sleep over all the fascists he turned into piles of gnarled gristle during World War II.

Anyway, in addition to noting how archaeology techs in the Salt Lake City office of SWCA successfully voted to unionize with Teamsters Local 222, the article reports how acts of retaliation had already occurred before the vote took place. To take one example, a key organizer in SWCA's Pittsburgh office named Evan Flannery was fired for "unclear reasons" just before they were going to submit their union authorization cards. He submitted an Unfair Labor Practice charge in response.

As for why unionization for archaeologists is overdue, Freeman says it best. "We're overeducated and underpaid blue-collar workers." He goes on to mention how he and his colleagues once "surveyed an entire mountain range for a mine. You ever see transmission lines cutting across mountains and wonder how those got there? Well, we walked the entire route, hundreds of miles, up and over, looking for things. It's a passion job, but it's definitely hard work."

◆ ◆ ◆

I was on one of those transmission line projects with him. On one especially memorable week-long field session, enshrined forever in our memories as Session 7, we encountered a total of twelve rattlesnakes, had one of our crew chiefs get harassed by an armed trespasser, had that same crew chief and an accompanying tech nearly crushed beneath a rolling ATV, had the road on one end of the project area collapse due to flash flooding, had a young tech get chased by an angry badger, and had my own crew get chased down a steep hill by a landslide—and then chased down another hill by an angry mountain lion that was probably defending her den. All that in a single week while otherwise slogging up and down steep slopes in the summer heat for about ten miles per day before retiring to a seedy roadside motel. And, again, most of us were making about what a talented barista makes.

Other sessions on that same project were deeper in the backcountry, which requires camping, something I love to do when I'm not dragging myself through a burn area getting covered with ash for eight days approximately eighty miles from the nearest shower. Another friend and former coworker named Lisa Stenten once showed me a pair of boots she'd used that entire eight-month field season while her corporate bosses hemmed and hawed over whether they should give field workers a yearly boot stipend, and I swear the soles were as flat and smooth as racing tires.

The company notched record profits that year.

Granted, oil workers and wildland firefighters also routinely spend weeks at a time living in tents or crappy motels and dealing with heinous physical conditions. But those jobs don't require exorbitantly expensive college degrees, generally pay a lot better, and include hazard pay to boot.

At least there's work, for now, and loads of it at that. Back when *Raiders* premiered and got an entire generation of people wondering if treasure hunting really is a worthwhile career choice, only a fraction of them made it as far as realizing archaeology isn't actually about treasure hunting. Fewer still stuck with it after running aground on that disappointing truth, and only a fraction of those were willing to endure tribulations like the ones mentioned above and stick with the discipline beyond a few field sessions. But they are among our finest—there's no denying that.

◆ ◆ ◆

That's the upside of popularizing archaeology in mainstream culture. The downside is depressingly down. Much like how mainstream Western culture's fixation with archaeologists as "adventurers" has no clear starting point but can at least be blamed on *King Solomon's Mines* as a prime mover, the primest mover of current mainstream pseudoarchaeology is probably Erich von Däniken. He wasn't the first, by any means—but he was the first in terms of causing an appreciable splash. His 1968 book *Chariots of the Gods* posited that, among other things, the human species resulted not from evolution but from a combination of genetic material from ancient apes and extraterrestrial beings.

He expounds on many lines of evidence showing pictorial depictions of ancient peoples interacting with space aliens, including an array of petroglyphs that very clearly depict anything but that, and ultimately ends on plain old racism. In his 1980 book *Signs of the Gods?* he asked:

> Were the extraterrestrials able to opt between different races from the beginning? Did they endow different human groups with different abilities to survive in different climatic and geographical conditions? . . . Was the black race a failure and did the extraterrestrials change the genetic code by gene surgery and then programme a white or a yellow race? . . . Once this basic question is accepted, we cannot and should not avoid the explosive sequel: is there a chosen race?

Nazi propagandists would have loved this guy if they hadn't met their fitting end nearly half a century beforehand.

This is a throughline that deserves way more attention than it often gets. Ken Feder, emeritus professor of archaeology at Central Connecticut State University and author of the excellent *Frauds, Myths, and Mysteries* series of books, compiled the stats in von Däniken's writing where he claims that ancient achievements are simply so great that local people must have needed help from learned outsiders from as far away as Alpha Centauri. Lo and behold, 96 percent of them are in places with non-white histories. You'll find this is true of the bulk of pseudoarchaeology.

Statistics aren't everything, of course—and correlation does not always imply causation. The extent to which pseudoarchaeological horseshit is remarkably correlated with the archaeology of non-white peoples merits contemplation, and I don't know what the p-value or ANOVA results are for that correlation, but I also don't care. The *res ipsa loquitur* is so powerful here that it would be much more challenging to prove there isn't a causal correlation between offensive hogwash and the material history of peoples of color.

It's racism, in other words. The root of all this type of asinine speculation is racism. Just like it was in the 1800s when people looked at the mighty temples of the Mayan homeland and concluded they must have been constructed by mysteriously vanished white people.

In related news, *Ancient Aliens* premiered on the History Channel in 2010, and by 2024 had a total of 240 episodes of insulting and racist schlock under its belt. Its success spawned at least one spin-off, *In Search of Ancient Aliens*, which is also part of the History Channel's catalog—along with *Search for the Lost Giants*. What's more, recreational reading of pseudoarchaeology appears to trump recreational reading of actual archaeology. The fourth best-selling book in the category of archaeology books in 2014 was *The Ancient Giants of North America*, and the number one spot for the prehistory category that same year was Graham Hancock's *Fingerprints of the Gods: The Evidence of Earth's Lost Civilization*, followed pretty closely by Frank Joseph's *Before Atlantis: 20 Million Years of Human and Pre-Human Cultures*. Because the demonstrably not-real civilization of Atlantis simply will not go away.

Hancock would follow up 1995's *Fingerprints* with a 2019 book called *America Before: The Key to Earth's Lost Civilization*, in which he doubles down on his theory about a world-spanning civilization that was wiped out—like, completely wiped out, without a single trace to be found anywhere—by a global cataclysm that ended the last Ice Age. Both are *New York Times* bestsellers, and they even yielded a deal with Netflix to premier a documentary series called *Ancient Apocalypse* "where British writer Graham Hancock presents his pseudoarchaeological theories about the alleged existence of an advanced civilization active during the last ice age" to quote the delightfully sassy Wikipedia page.

The fact that Hancock's son Sean is senior manager of unscripted originals at Netflix undoubtedly had something to do with this, although Netflix also brought us the hilariously inaccurate *Roman Empire* and *Queen Cleopatra* docudramas, so we can safely assume they would have greenlit *Ancient Apocalypse* even without the catalyst of blatant nepotism. This is a shame because their docudramas about the pirate kingdom of Nassau and the rise of the Samurai in Japan were both remarkably accurate, even if the former left a lot of history out to streamline the narrative.

In my own realm of experience, my otherwise kind and conscientious friend Jamie hooked me up with a film crew that was recording the pilot for a new show about the exciting realities of archaeology. They'd reached out to her because she's known for being very charismatic and articulate on screen, in addition to being an archaeologist with half-Indigenous lineage, but she politely declined and recommended they reach out to me instead. Warning bells in my head went unheeded.

We met at a bar in Cortez, Colorado where I was living at the time. The director, a wiry Australian fellow, immediately made a wry comment about how I wasn't wearing a wide-brimmed "Indiana Jones hat" like I was in the photo my friend had sent them—to which I responded as politely as possible that I'm not in the habit of wearing my field clothes into a bar unless I'm returning from the field at that very moment. I sat across from the show host, a handsome young guy with piercing blue eyes and a friendly smile, and we exchanged pleasantries.

Beers were placed in front of us. The host told me a bit about himself, how he was also a professional archaeologist who took the gig because it seemed fun and he needed the money and explained the concept of the show. He, as host, goes around the country visiting sites and speaking to local experts on-camera about some of the most enduring mysteries of the ancient Americas, which is the exact format of *Time Team* but with the added twist that they specifically go looking for the juiciest mysteries. Louder warning bells went still unheeded.

Quiet was called for, the camera started recording, and I was immediately pelted with questions about widespread cannibalism in the ancient Southwest and all the reported alien sightings at Skinwalker Ranch. I heard the bells at last.

The pilot never got picked up, and as far as I can tell that's mostly because a competing production company over at—*sigh*—the History Channel got to Skinwalker Ranch first. Their show aired a little over a year after I was filmed for the pilot of the failed one. Still, part of me likes to daydream that the show never aired because my twenty-minute speech excoriating these villainous twats for capitalizing on ignorance and racism really got through to them. It didn't, of course—but it makes for a nice daydream.

◆ ◆ ◆

All this is to say that bullshit springs eternal in public perceptions of archaeology, and it's not especially difficult to understand why. Back in the days of Bandelier and Wetherill and pioneering patriarchs and matriarchs like A.V. Kidder and Earl and Ann Morris, addressing the needs of a culture whose primary fixations are ownership and spectacle consisted straightforwardly of showing them all the exciting goodies dug out of other peoples' graves. Hence the fictional likes of Allan Quatermain and Indiana Jones.

As the discipline has evolved, however, that smash-and-grab model of archaeology has slowly but steadily shifted toward one of preserving material history and respecting the descendent communities with which it's associated. In 2023, revised guidance on NAGPRA caused a respectable handful of museums and agency visitor centers to—literally—throw sheets over public exhibits that might be considered disrespectful to the Tribes.

But people still want to see cool things, and people are still curious about history. What fills that need for many folks are the very social media algorithms that have also played major roles in election meddling, violent divisiveness, and at least one genocide—specifically in Myanmar. Without getting too deep into the weeds: the proximate purpose of social media is to provide people with a place to share things with other people, while the ultimate purpose is to make money for the company and its investors, mostly through ad sales. The higher your view count, the more you can charge advertisers to post on your platform, and decades of research by behavioral scientists of all stripes strongly support a causal correlation between interaction and rage. People who are content, or bored, or emotionally checked out don't often wave their arms and shout about it, but we certainly do when we're angry.

Facebook made full use of this by tweaking their algorithm to give the angry emoji much more "weight" in their predictive newsfeed than the like, care, or heart emojis, with predictable results. Other social media platforms like YouTube, Tik Tok, and Instagram all weight the "success" of a video or post based on the interactions it receives—even if those interactions are mostly or entirely negative. It doesn't matter. The interaction quotient shows how many people are staring at it and sharing it with others, which translates to concomitant dollar value for advertisers.

Netflix and other major streaming platforms didn't fail to notice this, either. Quality is nice when you can afford it, but cheaply made controversy can often yield even greater financial windfalls if you get enough people screaming about it.

Two people I respect a great deal, mainstream critic Gabi Belle and my dear friend Jonathan Bailey, both "love" *Ancient Aliens* the way that a lot of people "love" those godawful 1980s horror films. They're hilarious if you watch them as pure entertainment. It's like watching a stage magician reach into a hat, pull out a wad of dryer lint, and scream "It's a rabbit!" at the quizzically riveted audience.

I've never watched an episode all the way through, but I've watched or listened to them give extremely colorful commentary on some of their own favorite episodes, and I can't help but chuckle thinking about those performances even now. But that's still interaction, of a sort. When we interact with that garbage by making fun of it, we notch its interaction count just a tiny bit higher every time, and that helps to ensure it will reach a few more people—any number of whom are uninformed and/or racist enough to actually believe it.

All of this sounds profoundly negative and infuriating, but a silver lining is there. People in this country are still curious about history and still overly fixated on looking at cool stuff they wish they could own, but archaeology doesn't really provide that the way it used to. And that's a very good thing.

Nature abhors a vacuum, so when grifters and other scum smell an opening to soak suckers for investment returns they'll invariably rush in. That vacuum exists entirely because we've come so far from the days of archaeologists and museums proudly displaying burial goods and literal skeletons ripped out of places like

Chaco Canyon for the public's amusement. What's lacking now is a robust body of sincere efforts by researchers to reach the public with equally effective and compelling messaging that also happens to be factual.

In a 1982 article with the cheeky title "Will the Real Archaeology Please Stand Up?", former Fort Lewis College professor W. James Judge plainly stated it like this: "We need to make archaeology accessible, intelligent, and comprehensible." It's the three variable modeling problem all over again. Academics are plenty swell at being intelligent. Being accessible and comprehensible, on the other hand . . .

So, for the present, what I consider positive and encouraging developments in American archaeology have unfortunately opened a gap for heinous swine to step in and fling hyperbolic nonsense around like monkeys in a zoo. It's certainly fun to watch, but the downside is a popular conception of professional archaeology that continues to drift pretty far afield from reality.

We walk a lot, and we write a lot, and we spend increasing amounts of time collaborating with, working alongside, or even working on behalf of the descendant communities whose material heritage forms such a major component of the American environment. We seek more and more often to manage and protect that heritage rather than steal or exploit it, and to show kindness, sympathy, and respect to marginalized peoples whose heritage was forcibly wrenched from their hands.

Mostly, though, we walk a lot.

◆ ◆ ◆

My first survey in the private or corporate sector took place near St. George in southern Utah during a winter warm streak. In addition to seeing lots of rocks and rusty cans, I also got to see a young teenage boy stumble out of the dust looking like he'd just escaped a serial killer. My crew chief clocked my expression and quickly grabbed my attention before I could run over to the kid to offer aid.

"Hoods in the woods," he said. "Wilderness therapy for troubled teens. They grab these kids right out of their beds and drag them into the wilderness for a form of rehab boot camp. Sometimes it helps the kids get over addictions or whatever. Oftentimes they're abused. A few of them die. He looks like he escaped from one and he's headed back to town."

This struck me as one of those things you hear about Victorian England or the cult hysteria of the 1800s, not a multi-million-dollar industry still in operation. It really is incredible how little we care about human life in this country when someone finds a way to turn a profit from misery. How this is even legal blows my mind, although there's also a simple logic underlying that fact. It makes money. A lot of money. And a lot of money greases a lot of wheels, especially in Utah, where conservative lawmakers see "discipline bad kids" and "we've got a check with your name on it" in the same memo and collapse into paroxysms of glee.

Heading into that winter, I got my first taste of similar sauce within my chosen adulthood profession. A big chunk of BLM land was being considered for a land swap with the city, a fairly common practice where different agencies or municipalities can exchange bits of land with each other for various reasons. All the state land parcels within Bears Ears National Monument were swapped to the state of Utah in exchange for equal acreage of BLM land someplace else, for example. And when the Gila Bend Indian Reservation in southern Arizona got repeatedly flooded after creation of the Gillespie Dam, despite assurances from the federal government that exactly that wouldn't happen, the authorities copped to their error and let the Tohono O'odham Nation pick out replacement parcels of equivalent size elsewhere in the state—which is how they were able to build a casino just outside of Glendale.

In our case, it was a gorgeous expanse of red rock wilderness that was intended to become a park. However, since a change of both ownership and management constitutes a situation likely to affect the environment, consultation was required. The company I was working for submitted the lowest qualified bid, and we were deployed into the backcountry in the middle of winter to survey the area.

We hauled our equipment, food, and camping gear by backpack

into a misty haze, using handheld Garmin GPS units to navigate because we couldn't see where we were going. The mist didn't let up and the temperature steadily dropped, but we felt like bona fide adventurers—that's how they get you—so nobody complained. At first.

The complaints started near the end of the second day. Everything we owned was soaked. A team of horses arrived that night to bring us extra water, having been contracted beforehand, and one of the fell beasts laid down and starting flailing around on its back like a giant cat right in the center of the only archaeological site we'd found. The cowboys were still laughing about that when they led the horses back out just before dusk.

The next day it poured. That special kind of winter rain you occasionally get in the high desert that somehow feels wetter than it should. Still we stayed. Our crew chief kept radioing back to corporate HQ that conditions were unpleasant bordering on deadly and kept being told the budget was too tight for us to retreat and return for an additional session. Only when the freezing rain gave way to snow did the project manager finally consent to us bailing on the session, because when it snows you can't see what's on the ground.

◆ ◆ ◆

I worked in the private sector for a total of eight consecutive years. Which is sort of a marvel in my usually chaotic seasonal roustabout work life.

In that time I was chased by the previously mentioned landslide and mountain lion in Session 7, shot at by unhinged sovereign citizen types, nearly froze to death, nearly cooked to death, had to step around live bombs in a testing range, had unpleasant run-ins with rattlesnakes and scorpions and one very pissed-off badger, watched my fellow employees succumb to alcoholism and in one case die in the field from a heart attack, and heard others' horror stories that make all this seem benign in comparison.

One crew in the Pheonix area rounded a bend in a canyon to find themselves in a backcountry meth operation and barely escaped with their lives. In another instance, a woman was fired in the field for drinking too much during work hours and responded to this by pulling a gun on her crew chief. I also know of at least ten individuals who've been utterly traumatized at the cheap motels where CRM companies routinely house their employees to keep project costs low—everything from bedbugs to muggings to attempted rape. Gotta keep those costs down in order to be competitive.

Still, even corporate inhumanity can sometimes be twisted and tweaked to at least make life more enjoyable for those on the bottom rungs. I made this work for me on two magical occasions, both of which were also in southern Utah, the more memorable of which is cemented for the ages in Morgan Sjogren's book *Path of Light: A Walk Through Colliding Legacies of Glen Canyon.* The chapter title, named for the place where we spent several weeks together working on our respective book projects, was Camp Snowball.

On a map, it's the Comb Wash Campground in Bears Ears National Monument, one of extremely few developed campgrounds in the entire monument. That often strikes people unawares, especially when they travel there based on hearing about the place through social or formal media without doing any other type of research. It's not a national park—it's a national monument, and a remarkably undeveloped one at that. Hopefully it stays that way.

I was there on behalf of a major for-profit firm for whom I worked for about five years following eight years as a seasonal employee with the agencies. I was doing solo work for the reasons outlined above, and no sooner had I arrived than the area received one of the largest single-episode snow dumps in recent memory. Morgan arrived right about then to visit, and the two of us ended up "trapped" in all the snow, which was deep enough in and around our campsite that we had to dig tunnels between my tent, her Jeep, the picnic table where we cooked our food, and the pit toilets.

The thing is, we weren't really trapped. Far from it. But that was the mentality we cultivated to mythologize our predicament. Every morning I would wake up, note how the snow had melted a smidge but was still comfortably higher than my knees, and drive the work truck up to the top of a nearby incline where I had cell service. "Can't work today—still too much snow" would be my outgoing message.

"Roger that, stay safe down there" would come the reply from Salt Lake City.

Then I would drive the truck back to camp, rally up with Morgan to melt snow for coffee and manufacture some creative breakfast out of our dwindling communal food supply, then plan the day's excursion. We felt like royalty. Cars would occasionally pass on the nearby highway that ran between Blanding and Natural Bridges National Monument, but we were the only ones we saw stomping through the snow for the rare and wonderful chance to see alcoves and cliff dwellings hung with chandeliers of ice. It was incredible. When author David Roberts was writing his book *The Bears Ears: A Human History of America's Most Endangered Wilderness*, which hit shelves half a year after my own Bears Ears book, he asked me for a quote about the greatest time I ever spent in that area—and it was this one.

The other instance took place on a relatively obscure mesa located closer to the Grand Canyon. The firm for whom I was working at the time was contracted to inventory all the archaeology within a hundred-foot radius of the many spiderwebbing dirt roads atop the mesa to determine which, if any, should be closed. It's a pretty place with a lot of lovely archaeology, even if most of it was and continues to be looted by the locals. We were there to catalog that as well.

Months of fieldwork yielded an impressive assortment of sites, including petroglyphs and room blocks that hadn't previously been recorded, and in general it was an interesting project in a gorgeous place with a fun crew. Then the contracting agency tore into the report—not enough photos, maps with minor inaccuracies, previously known sites not detected, etc. They loved the report overall, they just pointed out a tall stack of things that needed to be fixed before it was acceptable.

Easy enough for them to say, but the budget—always tight on federal projects in order to beat out the competition—wasn't scoped for an extra session. A full eight-day field session involving one crew chief and three techs, with travel time and per diem and all that, usually runs between $25,000 and $30,000 at present rates in the regions where I work.* Not the end of the world for a firm worth tens of millions, but the way you become a firm worth tens of millions is by squeezing every penny. I could tell they were sweating it.

I smelled a truffle in the filth. What if they only sent one person instead of a crew? Someone fully permitted and trained to address all the outstanding needs on their own? They'd get away with spending about a quarter of what they were afraid of spending.

That is how I once again secured myself a "workcation," getting paid to do something I love doing all by myself in a breathtaking place, at my own pace, in my own style. I shored up all the gaps in the data, the final report passed muster, and I was hailed as a hero for spending a little under two weeks living out of a Tacoma and doing what I probably would have done for free if it wasn't my job.

This is how I became known as the company rescue dog. The guy they would send on sketchy solo gigs because they knew I wouldn't complain or get myself killed. I stayed at that for several more years having mostly amazing experiences before the pandemic threw everything into chaos, at the end of which I emerged with an office job. Que será, será.

◆ ◆ ◆

While management and preservation of cultural resources on public lands can be messy, in addition to often being really fun, it's worth reiterating that it carries with it the ever-present bugbear of Western people foisting Western perspectives onto non-Western cultural histories. Even the boundaries we draw can be radically different, given how mainstream Americans' ideas of important places are almost always built environments—cemeteries, monuments, churches and cathedrals, and so on—while Indigenous ideas of important places are far more often locations on the land.

What, for example, is the radius of that importance? In the case of an American cemetery or church, it's the wall or fence that

* If that sounds absurd, it's because the business model of consultants is to sell labor. If you make twenty bucks an hour, say, the company charges its clients something closer to sixty an hour for the use of you. Twenty goes to you; the rest goes to overhead and profits.

surrounds the place—beyond which just about any activity is fair game. But what is the boundary extent when no physical boundary exists? How do we determine where to draw the line? Who gets to do the determining?

CHAPTER 7

PRESERVATIONISTS AND POLITICOS

Once upon a time, according to Hopi archaeologist Lyle Balenquah, some federal agency folks were having a consultation meeting with members of the Hopi Tribe and posed the question of which places, exactly, they consider important enough to warrant legislative protections. They put a map on the wall and said, "Okay, show us what is sacred."

The cultural preservation advisors and other Hopi individuals had trouble with this, and immediately fell into unproductive discussion. "This bit here is especially important to the greasewood clan, while this bit over here is where one of the most cherished stories takes place, and meanwhile over here . . ."

The federal agency consultants grew increasingly frustrated, as did the Hopi attendees, until finally one of the men went into his office and came back out with a photograph of the Earth taken from space. He held up the photo and said, "This is the place that Hopis consider sacred."

This is why Lyle and many other Indigenous scholars and citizens consider "sacred" to be a problematic word. It's a Western concept, just like "culture" and "history" and quite a lot else that gets foisted onto non-Western people and their stuff. Language can be exceedingly tricky and limiting in that way, and the concept of sacredness or even just importance is especially tricky and limiting because those concepts are rooted in a culture that tends to think in terms of delineation rather than in terms of context. A church is sacred, for example—separate and distinct from the neighborhood it's in. You can tell because it says so on the property deed for tax-exemption purposes.

Whereas in most Indigenous philosophies, context is everything. According to Zuni scholar and conservationist Jim Enote, "These are sacred places, not sacred sites. A site to me is a point on a map, and it would be too easy to say, 'We'll protect this spring, or we'll protect this rock shrine.' When actually it is the context of a place that makes those areas sacred and worthy of protection." Inclusion of this sort of perspective in archaeology and heritage management is absolutely crucial. It's also one to which we're only recently beginning to adjust.

◆ ◆ ◆

Except for a few colorful anecdotes and asides, Indigenous people have thus far been conspicuously absent from the story of American archaeology outside of being its objects of study—and, more recently, legally mandated consulting parties. This exclusion has persisted despite being the people whose heritage comprises almost the entirety of archaeological focus in the United States.

The one big exception to this was ethnoarchaeology, a quantitative analytical method that nonetheless involves working very closely with Indigenous groups and taking careful notes while doing so—a practice Jesse Walter Fewkes was advocating for all the way back in 1900.

This was and remains hampered by overtly Western nomothetic approaches to non-Western cultures, often relying way too much on ethnographic analogy or the assumption that everyone does things the way "we" (relative to the observer) do them because that's what seems most logical to us. Everyone prepares and cooks food in a dedicated kitchen, everyone buries their dead underground, everyone eats three meals a day, everyone keeps dogs as pets and turkeys as food rather than the other way around, and so on. Obviously. Because that's how we do it. Even though all these and countless more examples have turned out to be vastly different across various places and societies.

Similarly, it's possible that the Fremont and Ancestral Pueblo peoples of the Great Basin and Colorado Plateau regions were using granaries for all the same reasons as the Bedouin peoples of northern Africa, for instance, but since they were very different people living in very different parts of the world it's also quite possible that they weren't. Maybe the Bedouin built theirs in high ledges to protect against thieves while the Fremont did so because they liked to eat lunch with a view?

Still, it can be an entertaining fallacy. I once had a middle-aged guy on a guided tour of an archaeological site ask what ancient Native Americans used for toilet paper and got to enjoy watching his face as I explained that toilet paper wasn't invented until the 1850s. That it is, in fact, the worst way to clean your exit wound due to its abrasiveness and the toll it takes on the environment, and that it's quite unpopular in most countries where advertisers and lobbyists don't dictate—respectively—cultural norms and government policies. He didn't ask a lot of questions after that.

Meanwhile, historic preservation laws started piling up not long after Fewkes' efforts, and with the civil rights movements of the mid-1900s, the Indigenous community began having more of a voice in American politics. Native Americans began to assert greater levels of control over their own cultural affairs, as well as how their heritage is treated on at least public lands in the United States. They also began vociferously protesting archaeological research, especially with regards to excavation of burials.

Native scholars like Vine Deloria Jr. began publishing invectives against American anthropology and its treatment of Native Americans as data points rather than human beings in the 1960s. He particularly raged at "the position that the scholarly community has enjoyed for the past century; e.g., that only scholars have the credentials to define and explain American Indians and that their word should be regarded as definitive and conclusive." Although archaeologists of every kind have hired Indigenous locals for menial tasks like guiding, hauling equipment, and digging square holes since at least the mid-1800s, it wasn't until the passage of NHPA and the rise of CRM as the dominant form of American archaeology that Native Americans began having more and more of a consequential role in the practice. According to Bill Lipe, upwards of 30 percent of field technicians working on the Animas-La Plata project in the late 2000s were local Indigenous people, depending on the location and crew.

This became even more true with the amendments to Section 106 of the NHPA that went into effect in 1992, which requires that Native American "values" be considered in the management and preservation of archaeological sites and materials. They also codified that TCPs may be considered eligible for the National Register of Historic Places and, thus, afforded the same level of consideration regardless if they are technically archaeological sites or not. Ritual pilgrimage sites, sacred locations, places where foods and medicines are traditionally collected, and other such locales can be considered TCPs so long as they aren't on private land.

Those amendments also empowered Tribes to implement their own historic preservation programs for their respective lands along the same lines as the SHPOs, which is how we got the Navajo Nation Heritage and Historic Preservation Department, the Hopi Cultural Preservation Office, the Gila River Indian Community Tribal Historic Preservation Office, and so on.

◆ ◆ ◆

Direct participation in archaeological activities by Native Americans has also continued to increase over time, to the point where at least 10 percent of the employees at my last private-sector CRM job were Indigenous, and in many cases individuals from within the Tribes are incorporating their own CRM companies to do contract archaeology on their ancestral lands. My friend Aaron O'Brien is working for one of those companies as I write this, a firm called Dinehtahdoo Consultants, which is owned and managed entirely by Diné folks but is nonetheless happy to hire white ones who know their stuff and can behave respectfully.

All this marked a major departure from a lot of academic institutions, which continued down the path of ever more refined and detailed scientific methods and models for interpreting Indigenous heritage—often, as in the case of Great Basin researchers, with less and less input from actual Indigenous people in the pursuit of impossibly objective quantitative data. In recent years the academic community, or parts of it anyway, have also begun steering their own trajectories toward collaborative research and applied or preservationist paradigms over the old model of academics for Academics.

A synergized result of these developments in both the business and academics worlds is increasing cases in which archaeologists and Indigenous communities don't just "consult" with each other but collaborate as equals. This is the paramount way that American archaeology as a discipline can be used to help Indigenous people rather than capitalize on their heritage to build what are not exactly lucrative careers, but careers nonetheless. It should go without saying that colonialism was devastating to Indigenous peoples, and in many cases led to being incidentally or forcefully severed from their landscapes and cultural histories. Reconnecting those severed ties is something archaeological methods and practices are uniquely set up to do.

Take, for example, the Bureau of Indian Affairs (BIA) and the Kodiak Area Native Association (KANA), which began partnering in the early 1990s with a field school that lasts two months and is centered on teaching archaeological methods to Indigenous youths. Almost half of a thirteen-hundred-year-old village was excavated in the course of the field school, "despite bear problems and some of the worst weather on record" in the words of S. Neal Crozier. The project was hailed as a victory not only in terms of education, but as an early model for how similar programs could help toward the goal of cultural resource management and protection through cooperation with Native organizations rather than through merely checking a box saying you sent them a copy of the report for their approval.

That last part is crucial. Collaboration is something that starts on day one, while consultation is something that often happens at the very end and is usually regarded as tokenization at best or, at worst, an annoying procedural afterthought.

Passage of the American Indian Religious Freedom Act in 1978 also facilitated a surge in Native American individuals and groups demanding access to locations of significance in their history and culture. The Department of the Interior Appropriation Acts of 1990 and 1991 had a synergizing effect on this, as they included appropriations for Historic Preservation Fund grants to the Tribes. One result of this played out in Wyoming in the late 1980s when the Bighorn National Forest floated plans to build an access road to Medicine Wheel National Historic Landmark in response to a dramatic increase in tourism.

The centerpiece, the Medicine Wheel itself, is a large circular alignment of boulders with "spokes" leading from a central hub that dates to at least seven thousand years ago. Native leaders opposed the road because they thought it would disturb or destroy the "spiritual integrity of the Medicine Wheel," according to Wyoming SHPO liaison Fred Chapman. To that end, a group of Northern Arapaho elders went around the Forest Service and attempted to work directly with the Wyoming SHPO to better understand how federal laws could be used to protect sacred sites and traditional use areas. The gambit worked, and the Wyoming SHPO wound up creating a Native American Affairs Program to continue helping the Arapaho and other Tribes work toward protecting places of great importance to them.

Because of this, the road to Medicine Wheel was never constructed. It's accessibly by a two-mile walk from a parking lot managed by the Bighorn National Forest, who've also made considerable efforts between 1991 and now to inform visitors about the immense cultural importance of the place and how to behave around it (stay on the path, keep dogs on leashes, don't take photos if there happens to be a ceremony taking place, etc.).

More recent is the case of University of Georgia researchers Jennifer Birch and Victor Thompson, and their work with the Muscogee and Huron-Wendat Nations. In a 2024 paper, the authors note how, as traditionally written, "culture-histories are not histories, but packages of material traits bundled into geographic and chronological phases that reflect narrow dimensions of the lives and histories of past peoples. Worse," they continue, "such cultural-chronological phases allow archaeologists to disassociate and associate groups as they will. For example, there are many cases where archaeologists argue that strong descendant ties cannot be made because of the uncertainty of the chronological record." (See the Chaco mtDNA study recapped earlier.)

They go on to show how using culture-historical taxa and artifact-based chronologies should only be used as a starting point, and a combination of radiometric assessments with Indigenous input and interpretation can result in much more meaningful histories.

All this leads us back to the position that Indigenous cultures are, by nature, more deeply rooted in American lands than aren European cultures like the Spanish, French, English, and eventually American cultures that came later. Study and preservation of material heritage as a means to help these groups rather than simply "understand" them represents a means by which American archaeology can at least help to address, if not actually undo, some of the damaging legacies of colonialism.

◆ ◆ ◆

At present, the best case study in the interactions between American archaeologists, Indigenous groups, conservationists, and politicians is that of Bears Ears National Monument in southeastern Utah. The earliest call for elevated legislative protection in southeast Utah dates to the end of the nineteenth century, when Edgar Lee Hewett referred to it as the Bluff District in a report to the GLO that would partly inform his 1904 doctoral dissertation. He pressed the GLO for preservation of "the historic and prehistoric ruins of the Southwest" from despoilers, among whom he counted people like the Wetherills. A doctor named T. Mitchell Prudden, a close friend of Richard Wetherill who often frequented their ranch to excitedly dig and explore, nonetheless made the very same argument in a 1903 publication that ends with the following statement:

> It is to be hoped that steps may soon be taken to protect these relics of a most instructive phase of primitive

> culture, and that authorized and intelligent research may be encouraged to enter a field still full of the promise of most interesting discovery.

The 1906 passage of the Antiquities Act was at least partly predicated on the rampant looting and vandalism Hewett and Prudden saw in the Bears Ears area, even if the former counted amateur excavators like the Wetherills part of the problem while the latter saw them as an order of magnitude better than the average pothunter.

Regardless, southeast Utah didn't receive what they considered due with passage of the Act. Mesa Verde National Park was created by an act of Congress following all the work Virginia McClurg and Lucy Peabody poured into it, part of the incredible Pajarito Plateau was preserved as Gila Cliff Dwellings National Monument, and Chaco Canyon was preserved as Chaco Canyon National Monument, prompting Richard Wetherill to relinquish his claims there—to Hewett's great delight. El Morro in New Mexico; the cliff dwellings of Tonto, Navajo, and the ridiculously named Montezuma Castle in Arizona; and Natural Bridges just to the west of the Bears Ears formations were all made into national monuments before the end of Teddy Roosevelt's term in office. But not the immensity of archaeology comprising greater Bears Ears.

A.V. Kidder was working in the same area at about the same time, under the direction of Hewett, and expressed some grumpiness over the situation. In a 1910 report on his field activities, he noted how many of the burials in the area "have been much pillaged by 'pot-hunters,' relic-seekers, and other vandals who, digging carelessly, have broken fully as much as they have recovered, and who have also entirely destroyed the skeletal remains." Byron Cummings, then still dean at the University of Utah, griped in an article in the *Salt Lake Herald* that same year about the "spoliation of prehistoric ruins in Utah and the devastation of ancient cliff dwellings of their trophies of ante-civilized tribes" and at least managed to get government officials to notice his worries.

In 1935, the Department of the Interior floated for consideration an Escalante National Monument that included almost all of what is now Bears Ears. It was to serve as an exciting pass-through corridor for tourists on the way to a proposed Wayne Wonderland National Park in Wayne County, which makes it sound more like a place filled with Ferris wheels than one filled with interesting rock formations. Wayne Wonderland did indeed get created a few years later—renamed Capitol Reef, thankfully—but the Escalante proposal was shelved during World War II and never really came back to life.

◆ ◆ ◆

While all these white folks were trying to establish elevated protections for the area, local Indigenous individuals and communities maintained their ancestral connections to the place as best they could. The ancestors of the modern Pueblo communities had depopulated the area by the late thirteenth century, but Hopi Yellowware pottery—made exclusively on the Hopi mesas starting in the 1400s and unique for being fired with coal rather than wood—found scattered throughout it indicated that they never stopped going there for practical or ritual purposes. Ute and Diné families were largely driven off the areas that make up the heart of the place, but neither were driven very far, and they and Southern Paiute residents continued using the area for both traditional purposes and for newly adopted purposes like sheep herding.

Then came the 1960s and the civil rights movement, when marginalized people across the country decided they'd finally had it with not having a voice in American politics and started demanding one. This played out in the Bears Ears area in 1968, when presidential candidate Robert Kennedy—a huge supporter of Indigenous rights and sovereignty, if his campaign promises are anything to go by—met with members of the Tribes in Bluff. There they all but begged him to do something to help protect the immensity of heritage being destroyed by looters and vandals in the Bears Ears area. This was part of Kennedy's campaign promise to improve the lives of Native Americans throughout the country, and Bluff was one of many stops on his campaign tour, so it's likely he intended to at least try to make good on those promises. Unfortunately, he was shot before the election took place, so we'll never know.

Several smaller legislative units were created after that, including Grand Gulch Primitive Area in 1971, which ended grazing in the primary canyon system of Cedar Mesa. Upon establishment of the Primitive Area, seven full-time rangers were hired to patrol the area, including Lynell Schalk—the first-ever female BLM backcountry ranger—and Fred Blackburn, who would go on to become a prominent Bears Ears historian and conservation advocate. By the time of the 2015 effort to create a national monument there, budget cuts had reduced that to just two full-time rangers, and by "full-time" I mean full-time seasonal. They were both employed while on furlough for a big part of the year, and they also both retired a few years ago.

A few years after the Primitive Area designation, Bill Lipe would be tasked by the BLM to conduct an additional inventory of visitor impacts and vandalism in Grand Gulch. This was the first vandalism study conducted within the greater Bears Ears area and wouldn't be followed up upon until almost fifty years later under avocational archaeologist, journalist, and conservationist Jerry Spangler, who ran an article in 1995 in *The Deseret News* in which he complained that visitors were "loving the place to death." That was one year before David Roberts published *In Search of the Old Ones*, when all that loving-to-death stuff jumped up a few notches.

In 1989, the BLM proposed a 400,000-acre National Conservation Area for the Cedar Mesa-Grand Gulch area. Although this proposal didn't go anywhere, Grand Gulch, Road Canyon, Fish Creek, and Mule Canyon Wilderness Study Areas were named in the final Utah State Wilderness Study Report two years later. Wilderness Study Areas don't offer the same sort of long-term protection as a national monument or congressionally designated wilderness area, but they were at least stopgaps for a time.

Twenty years later, former Utah Senator Rob Bennett asked Native people in San Juan County if they had any interest in how public lands were managed. White Mesa Ute and Utah Diné grassroots people responded that their connections are so deep that they had been afraid to speak out for fear of what might still be taken away.

The ancestral lands of Bears Ears are outside reservation boundaries and hold special historical and spiritual significance for regional Native people. Nonprofit group Utah Diné Bikéyah grew from local Utah Diné elders' and leaders' caring and concern for this area, and the nonprofit set about collecting stories and testimonies from many of them in what became a growing push for a Diné Bikéyah National Monument. Soon enough, other Tribes from around the region joined in the fight, and the effort was renamed to Bears Ears National Monument to be more inclusive, since the word for the place in all the various Indigenous languages thereabout translates approximately to "the ears of a bear."

Sensing where all this was going, Utah legislators Bob Bishop, Mike Lee, and Jason Chaffetz sought to nip the conservation proposal in the bud with their alternative, the Utah Public Lands Initiative or PLI for short. It was an impressive effort in its own right and included a lot of interviews and public town hall meetings with stakeholders that included members of the Tribes, conservationists, scientists, local landowners, ranchers, and pretty much anyone else who thought they might have a say in the matter. This effort went on for several years and gave many people hope that it would offer the protective legislation they wanted all along.

But it wouldn't. Not even close.

As the process dragged on, it became clearer and clearer that the PLI was just business as usual, and the final version included the typical shadiness, sweetheart deals, and catering to development and grazing lobbyists that characterize Utah public lands policy *in toto*. It also included a proviso rider saying the Antiquities Act no longer applied in the state of Utah. It was dead on arrival in Congress, as everyone knew it would be, but the Tribes wisely got out of that flaming clown car by late 2014. Jason Chaffetz took an early retirement from public service and become a Fox News correspondent, where his obligatory disingenuousness wouldn't cost him any votes. Rob Bishop took a timelier retirement to become a lobbyist for the mining industry. And, as of this writing, Mike Lee remained in Congress to expand his efforts to sell of all the public lands in the country beyond the border of Utah—and to harass Minnesota governor Tim Walz for being upset when a Minnesota legislator and her husband were assassinated by a MAGA terrorist.

Back in the spring of 2015, a handful of Tribal representatives convened a series of meetings in Towaoc, Colorado, within the Ute Mountain Ute Reservation. The results of the meetings were unprecedented. What ultimately emerged was the Bears Ears Inter-Tribal Coalition, a consortium composed of Hopi, Diné, Zuni, Ute Mountain Ute, and Uintah-Ouray Ute representatives. The Coalition submitted their "Proposal to President Barack Obama for Creation of Bears Ears National Monument" on October 15, 2015 outlining the need for protection of nearly two million acres of southeastern Utah. Friends of Cedar Mesa and other conservation groups abandoned their own proposals and joined in the fray, as did conservationist individuals and no small number of archaeologists, including myself.

Bears Ears National Monument was designed by the Obama administration on December 28, 2016, making it the first successful Indigenous-led national monument effort in the history of the United States. It set a dangerous precedent in the eyes of people who would do well to remember "who conquered who," in the words of local blogger Monte Wells. When the Trump administration used the Antiquities Act to slash the monument boundary by 85 percent a year later, San Juan County Commissioner Phil Lyman used the same word at a celebration of the slash in the town of Monticello, according to the *Salt Lake Tribune*. At least three times in Lyman's speech, he alluded to an out-of-context line from Thomas Jefferson about the day when our "children wake up homeless on the continent their fathers conquered."

I first started poking around in the heart of Bears Ears as a wide-eyed hiker in 2006, then did a bunch of research there for various university degrees, worked in Glen Canyon National Recreation Area for five years, worked for the Manti-La Sal National Forest for three years, and then oversaw a massive CRM project there for a private company on behalf of the BLM. Because of all this, I was asked to play an increasingly larger role in the conservation push, starting with testimony for the initial Indigenous-led effort and the eventual legal defense against its reduction—and culminating in my editing an issue of Archaeology Southwest Magazine, after asking local expert Ben Bellorado to help me as co-editor, as well as a book called *Behind the Bears Ears: Exploring the Cultural and Natural Histories of a Sacred Landscape.*

Then the election of Joe Biden in 2020 came with the appointment of Deb Haaland as Secretary of the Interior, making her the first-ever Indigenous woman to hold the title, and that basically meant a death sentence for the Trump era monument reductions. The Biden administration re-designated Bears Ears National Monument back to its full extent (actually just a tad bigger) in October of 2021, once again using the Antiquities Act as their enabling legislation.

Naturally enough, the state of Utah almost immediately filed a lawsuit seeking to block it, which is when the SAA asked me to act as an expert witness for the defense. The suit was dismissed in August 2023 by US District Court Judge David Nuffer, who wrote that the Antiquities Act grants discretionary authority to the US president when it comes to national monument designations. This is arguably a good thing until one remembers that presidents come in all sorts of different shapes and colors—orange, for example.

I bowed out of the Bears Ears National Monument battle after that, for a variety of reasons I won't unpack in their fullness here but having mainly to do with an overabundance of ego and officiousness that piled up there in recent years. New management turned out to be just as bad as old management—better in some ways, admittedly, but also a lot worse in others. Tourists and vandals continued to trash the place while its managers continued to paint conservationists and other well-intentioned actors as the real villains. And so on.

Business as usual, in other words.

But it was still a victory. The newly minted resource management plan included a ton of input from the Tribes, including a specified list of archaeological sites to be developed for tourists in order to provide them with satisfying experiences while simultaneously nudging them away from more culturally sensitive ones. This is the sort of decision agencies used to make on their own, with "consultation" often occurring late or even after the decision was made, so that level of collaboration is truly impressive.

On top of all that, the attention, goodwill, and monetary donations generated by the conservation battle continue to have positive effects, especially with regards to the Bears Ears Partnership. Their education center now boasts a sweet outdoor forum for public talks and shows, and the rotating displays and books and so on within the place are great. They've even taken a major management role in the Canyon Country Discovery Center up in Monticello, folding their public education programs together under an effective aegis.

The place was mostly in good hands, in other words, and there was precious little I could do anymore without stepping on their fingers. So I stepped away, recentered focus on my adopted home state of Arizona, and attempted to relax back into what passes for a normal life when one has chosen a career in management of very old things. This lasted all of maybe half a year before my phone started blowing up.

Because of the 2021 restoration of the monument boundary before a ruling on our lawsuit could be issued, the question of legal interpretation of the Antiquities Act remains unsettled in the higher courts. And the opposition is not unaware of this. Swords are being sharpened again. The monument is almost certain to be reduced again. Slippery politicians are proposing worthless and insulting "compromise" bills like the PLI again. Every rational person is ignoring them again. And very big, very expensive lawsuits will absolutely start flying again.

It is often said that the best way to make money during a gold rush is by selling shovels. The political equivalent of this is practicing law.

◆ ◆ ◆

All this is to say that archaeology is not divorced from politics in the United States. Never has been; never will be.

It was to archaeologists that government officials and pearl-clutching bleeding hearts alike turned to justify or assuage the guilt over genocidal colonialism. The initial trend was to regard Native Americans as subhuman savages. Then they were upgraded to actual humans who were nonetheless recent arrivals that supplanted an earlier and most likely white (if not extraterrestrial) advanced civilization responsible for all those impressive mounds and temples. Then, following the discoveries of Folsom and Clovis, it was grudgingly admitted that they've been here for a very long time but are nonetheless doomed to extinction by the natural laws of evolution. And so on.

That and more came from the work and testimony of archaeological researchers, especially those that were keen to drive the practice away from reconstruction of historical particulars toward construction of behavioral generalities. Under these auspices, Native Americans and their heritage morphed from moribund objects of curiosity to impressively backward subjects of study for the human condition, living fossils and doomed throwbacks all in one, whose literal skeletons were legally regarded as "osteological objects" rather than human remains until the early 1990s.

Preservation entered this arena starting way back in the late 1800s with Goodman Pueblo, a large Ancestral Pueblo village site in southwestern Colorado that became the first archaeological site protected by the federal government in 1889. What followed was all the legislation covered in the previous chapter. For the most part, remember, this wasn't really done out of respect for Indigenous peoples or anything like an effort to help them maintain their connections to the land. It was done to preserve material history for later study, and to keep the really cool stuff around so tourists could enjoy it and the tourism industry could profit from it.

Indigenous voices were initially included in the preservation aspect of American archaeology by the likes of Hewett in the early 1900s but were then largely absent or ignored until the civil rights era and the American Indian Movement half a century later. The right to vote wasn't legally enshrined for Native Americans until the Voting Rights Act of 1965, but then in 2013 the Supreme Court's ruling in *Shelby County v. Holder* eliminated the Justice Department's authority to block changes to voting laws in states with a history of discrimination. By 2019, according to federal commission investigations, at least twenty-three states had enacted "newly restrictive statewide voter laws" that included blatant efforts to disenfranchise Indigenous voters.*

As a result of all this, archaeologically informed legal protection of their heritage by the American government is not something for which most Indigenous people harbor much faith—especially when lawmakers seem hellbent on making their voices have zero sway in any legal matters. This doesn't leave many avenues open to them for involvement in active preservation of their own material history. Archaeology offers at least a few.

To that end, outside—but adjacent to—the growing and splintering professional realms are two other domains of archaeology that warrant considerable comment: recreational archaeology and conservation archaeology. These have their own respective histories, plotlines, and major players, but both converge on the topic of means outside the legal system for Indigenous peoples and their allies to take active roles in heritage management. Before reaching that goal, however, there are a number of unpleasant human hurdles to surmount.

◆ ◆ ◆

Recreational archaeology is the best term I've yet hit upon to describe the loose subculture of people who are intensely enthusiastic about visiting archaeological sites the way others get really fixated on birds or trees or trains or historic bridges. They expend great stores of energy huffing and puffing up canyon walls and along scary ridgelines just to see an especially lovely pictograph or masonry structure, take a few photos, and then scramble away again—often already planning the next such adventure. They aren't professionals,

* I'm using the past tense in that sentence because I'm citing an article from 2019, but those efforts continue unabashed to this day. Legislation requiring a passport or government-issued ID card that exactly matches one's voter registration was the latest one at the time I was writing this, despite how it would target legal citizens who happen to be recent immigrants, Indigenous people, or women who've changed their maiden name—and despite how it's also plainly unconstitutional for Congress to set voter eligibility requirements.

at least not in this capacity, but they aren't looters either. They're enthusiasts.

Birdwatchers have an entire history and culture that's all-but legendary, and in fact it was his obsession with birdwatching that played a large part in Teddy Roosevelt's impetus toward conservationism, so they make for the best basis of comparison for non-devotees who don't know what I'm talking about. Birdwatchers will come to a screeching halt on a busy highway and madly weave through traffic waving their binoculars or camera with a 600x zoom lens screaming about how they'd never seen a blue-winged ghost hawk in the wild before. They don't tag the bird, or geolocate it within a database, or blast it out of the sky the way naturalists used to—at least not for the most part. Birdwatchers just watch. They enjoy.

Occasionally, their enjoyment spurs them toward trying to save or protect the subjects of their fixation. Loads of nonprofits have been started this way, not by professionals but by avocational or recreational connoisseurs who don't give a damn if academics label them radicals because they aren't academics to begin with.

The recreational or *afficionado* archaeology scene is a lot like that. Not scientists, at least not when they're out visiting and photographing and just generally oo'ing and ahh'ing, but not looters or vandals either. My own start in the realm of Southwest archaeology started out this way, when a roommate of mine in Zion National Park took me to visit a backcountry rock shelter with a few pictographs and some painted pottery on the ground. I'd never seen anything like it.

My roommate didn't know it at the time, but what he'd reignited in me was the Goth teenager who spent probably very unhealthy amounts of time exploring old moss-covered cemeteries in the woods of New England, along with abandoned houses, an abandoned hospital, and the stately and menacing remains of an abandoned mausoleum. There wasn't much else to do for distraction in upstate New York, or so I thought as a depressive teen. I was really into Edgar Allan Poe and thought all things crumbling and forlorn were mesmerizing, and also that upstate New York was a dreary expanse filled with puritanical hypocrites and cows. It wasn't until

I went home to visit my dying mother after living in the Southwest for two decades that I realized the place is arrestingly lush and gorgeous, the people are mostly fine, and holy shit are the cows happy and healthy compared to the ones we've got eating cactus and dust in great number out west.

By the time I decided that I was still young enough to turn that pastime into a career, just over two years after that first trip with my roommate, I had probably hiked a cumulative distance at least comparable to that of the Appalachian Trail—and all in pursuit of some cliff dwelling or petroglyph panel or other photogenic archaeological thing. It's a mostly selfish pursuit, done for the sport and the beauty while not actually contributing to the study or preservation of the things being visited, but it's also a harmless pursuit. Mostly harmless, anyway.

So, what's the difference between members of this subculture and the world of full-fledged pothunters and vandals? The proximate answer is that weekend archaeology aficionados aren't taking or destroying anything, which is true enough, but the ultimate answer isn't so simple.

In my earlier days, when I was still but a student of archaeology and was therefore still almost fully immersed in the recreational archaeology scene, a lady friend and I sat up one entire evening with a bottle of wine and Google Earth Pro figuring out the locations of dozens of extremely sensitive backcountry sites based on the tiniest slivers of background landscape in photos people had posted on adventure blogs.

A few years later, after swimming deeper into the world of actual archaeology, I contacted most of those same people and pleaded with them to please take the images down or at least monkey around with the backgrounds a little. Some did; some did not. The point is that it wasn't too difficult for me to find where a lot of their images were taken, and I was half-drunk on cabernet and distracted by a lovely companion who was quickly getting bored of the enterprise. How difficult would it be for a focused and dedicated full-time villain?

I know a hiking guide who once led a client to a perfectly preserved pair of yucca sandals. The client dutifully took only close-up shots of the artifacts, showing no background imagery of any kind, and made sure that their camera wasn't recording GPS breadcrumbs. He then posted the image—along with the rest of the images from that trip—online. Then some nefarious nerd figured out the locations of landscape photos taken before and after the close-up photo of the sandals, looked at the time stamps on both and ran some calculations to determine walking speed between them, and then applied the hypothesized walking speed to the time stamp on the photo of the sandals to figure out how far that photo was physically located from the other two. The bastard got it exactly right and proceeded to brag about his accomplishment all over the internet.

Where these worlds collided for me was in what many have called the "heart" of Bears Ears National Monument: Cedar Mesa. The Grand Gulch Primitive Area is a portion of Cedar Mesa—one might call it the main portion—which is a highly desiccated plateau of uplifted sandstone located inside the "V" formed where the San Juan and Colorado Rivers meet. That "V" and the surrounding area as far north as Moab makes up San Juan County, one of the most environmentally heterogeneous places in North America, with snow-capped peaks, lowly swamps, desert, scrub, sagebrush plains, riparian New England-like forests, and what feel at times like jungles in the bottoms of some of the deeper canyons. Everything but coastline and tundra can be found there, more or less, and if you consider the shore of Lake Powell to be "sort-of coastline" then the only major ecozone still missing is the one with polar bears. Most of that is currently within Bears Ears National Monument.

The area practically overflows with archaeology, particularly "photogenic" archaeology like cliff dwellings. This fact is well-known enough nowadays to be threadbare, if not ingratiating, but when I first learned about the place a decade and a half ago it most certainly was not. I read about Cedar Mesa in David Roberts' *In Search of the Old Ones*, an almost biblical tome among recreational archaeologists, while working as a seasonal restaurant manager at The Grand Canyon Lodge the summer after I left Zion. I wasn't of the generation of archaeologists inspired to pursue it as a career by

Indiana Jones and his onscreen antics, but I was there in time for people like Roberts to write about how traipsing off into the wild thorny yonder to see something very old is a fine way to spend a weekend.

Much has changed since then. Cedar Mesa is now part of a controversial national monument, for a start—at least for now—but much has also changed in the recreational archaeology scene. Stories like the ones about Google Earth and the guy who Sherlocked the location of those sandals from time stamps became all too common between the early 2000s and the late 2010s. Along with this, more and more afficionados have realized they were more like enablers.

My friends and I still spend a lot of our weekends this way, even those of us who spend the rest of the week doing professional archaeology, because that kind of love is hard to poison. We rarely share what we find with the outside world anymore, though. Too many prying eyes. Too few ethics. And a few real monsters.

The lack of even avocational levels of education, research acumen, or professional accountability means this subset of the greater archaeological domain is particularly susceptible to infiltration by cranks, kooks, and lowlifes. The worst of which often tend to be "photographers," a term I here put in quotations marks because that's not really what they are. As my dear friend and colleague Jonathan Bailey loves to point out, most of photography takes place before the shutter is clicked—getting the right angle, catching or setting up intriguing lighting, and so on. Professional photographers working in this space also adhere to standards and responsibilities geared toward helping to protect archaeological sites rather than just exploit them. Then there's the opposite of that.

A little over a decade ago, a notoriously unethical French photographer named Alan, who specializes in heavily Photoshopped photography, stalked Bailey—then still a teenager—to his house to try to extort the location of an obscure pictograph panel. This would be disturbing enough in its own right, but again, this guy is French. Once or twice a year, he flies to the States and rents a 4Runner so he can go around to all the sites whose locations he gleaned from the internet, take his heavily doctored photographs, and sell them to outlets like *American Archaeology Magazine* (no relation). Part of one of those journeys involved a lengthy side trip to a tiny town in remote Utah to attempt to harass a teenager into giving up the location of one of those sites.

In my own experience, the epitome of this specialness is probably a character named Bill who splits his free time between photographing culturally sensitive archaeological sites for internet points (he's in his sixties, by the way) and posting right-wing rhetoric on Facebook. He once chased me across several social media platforms just to troll me for being critical of Nazis (again: sixties). I attracted the ire of another of these clowns at about the same time, and in a similar manner, when I cracked a joke about genocidal war criminal Henry Kissinger finally dying and found myself being excoriated by an older guy who spends his free time visiting extremely remote and culturally sensitive archaeological sites so he can make videos about them on YouTube.

All these and similar cases serve as useful reminders that archaeology is a very broad topic that attracts a very broad array of personalities, including the awful and the ignorant. Trolls like the ones mentioned above are extremely rare in the recreational subculture adjacent to that discipline, thankfully, although a common saying—common among Goth kids, anyway—comes to mind when contemplating statistics like those: If a million people visit a gravestone and only one of them pushes it over, it still breaks.

◆ ◆ ◆

Mingling with this scene is that of material reconstruction afficionados, also known rather gratingly as primitive technology enthusiasts. These are people who often don't have formal archaeological training, beyond reading a few papers or attending a few lectures to get a better understanding of how folks in the past knapped arrowheads or wove baskets or whatever, and they're also mostly harmless. In fact, some of them are exemplary people, giving back to the Indigenous community from whose technology they're borrowing (when they aren't Indigenous people themselves) and just generally being as respectful as possible. I know quite a lot of these folks.

Unfortunately, as another popular adage goes, it's the squeakiest wheels that get all the attention. And the wobbly wheels in the primitive technology scene are awfully damned squeaky, to put it mildly, not to mention prone to misappropriating others' heritage to further their own ends.

This most often manifests as members of a dominant culture adopting elements of a traditionally marginalized or colonized culture without permission, acknowledgement, or exchange of any sort. This is how you get Native American-inspired "sweat lodges" in Sedona that are made from non-breathable plastics and pretty routinely kill people, versions of Indian yoga (which is technically a form of meditation) that cost more than a car payment so adherents can feel all stretchy and smug, and an international lacrosse league that didn't invite the Haudenosaunee team to play in the 2022 World Games because they don't come from a sovereign nation—this despite the fact that their ancestors quite literally invented the game.*

In the realm of archaeology, this manifests most obviously in the so-called primitive technology scene. A lot of these people sell reconstructed artifacts, training seminars, and books without even a nod in the direction of the people whose cultural heritage they're exploiting. A few of them even spend the rest of their time openly supporting further marginalization of the very people from whom they're stealing.

One pivotal example of that last type of character was a retired primitive reconstructionist I knew who held a special grudge against anyone who dared speak out against oppression and mistreatment of marginalized peoples of any sort. Indians need to stop complaining so much, trans people shouldn't be allowed to exist, Black Lives Mat-

* This story has a happy ending, at least to a given value of "happy." The team from Ireland chose to bow out so the Haudenosaunee Nationals could play in their place. Nor was that move itself entirely without precedent. In 1847, during the height of Ireland's Great Famine (brought to them courtesy of the British government), the Choctaw Nation managed to set aside their own suffering (brought to them courtesy of the American government) to raise and send money to the starving Irish. Today there's a statue of nine giant feathers surrounding an empty bowl in County Cork in remembrance.

ter is a terrorist organization—that sort of thing. Not surprisingly, this often manifested as rambling social media missives. He became even worse when a battle with cancer confined him to his bed with nothing to do but rage on Facebook all day in long, asinine diatribes about how diversity and civil service are modern plagues for which the only remedy is a Fascism Cocktail.

At one point, his bilious bigotry prompted one of his own friends to respond, "We liked you better when you were dying." This was met with a torrent of outrage by other friends and colleagues who, for some reason, never provided any commensurate outrage when he expressed murderous hatred toward trans, immigrant, and other marginalized folks. He went to his deathbed cursing diversity initiatives for destroying our country.

All this from a white man who made much of his living by creating and selling precisely accurate Native American artifacts. Again, that alone is something plenty of other non-Indigenous people do in a respectful and collaborative way, and I shall not disparage the entire historical reconstructionism scene because of a few bad apples. But those apples are really bad. In this and similar cases, it's effectively theft with hateful rhetoric and calls for harm toward those being stolen from as a sort of bonus action. Blackbeard would be impressed.

Apart from such practices, cultural misappropriation and archaeology most often overlap in the form of *faux* Native American spiritualism—or, as some of my Indigenous friends like to put it, "plastic medicine." It's annoying as hell for archaeologists to investigate an ancient Indigenous site and discover that some knucklehead left behind candles and crystals they ordered online so they could ask someone else's ancestors for a new car, so I can scarcely imagine how actual descendent community members feel about it.

Examples abound, and I've mentioned a few in other writings, but serendipity springs eternal when it comes to things like this—and a perfect example materialized while I was drafting this very chapter. A woman in my on-again/off-again hometown of Flagstaff managed to set her minivan and the entranceway of a store on fire when she left a burning bundle of sage inside the vehicle while she went shopping. That's about as perfect a metaphor as I could wish for.

All these ne'er-do-wells represent what I like to call Pirates of the Colorado, considering the proximity of so much of their shenanigans to that invaluable lifeblood of the northern Southwest and its natural and cultural splendors. Looters and vandals loot and vandalize—they're just like human wrecking balls. The people I'm deriding here strike me as somehow even more insidious because they wrap themselves in the cloak of loving and appreciating the "treasures" of the archaeological record while in fact doing nothing but selfishly utilizing—and, in cases like climbing into fragile structures to get that sweet Instagram-worthy shot, actively despoiling—them, rather like the shakily ethical archaeologists of old.

What's more, a small but dogged portion of them spend their downtime actively campaigning against any efforts or individuals seeking to protect those places and/or make the world a better place for the grossly put-upon Indigenous people who consider them sacred—as in the noisome clown I just spotlighted. They hurt the resources, in other words, and then turn the rest of their efforts toward hurting the associated descendant communities and their allies. They take and take and take and then go out of their way to hurt the people who care the most about what they're taking.

So, pirates—but like *real* pirates. Not the Disney kind.

The worst part is that it's all legal—which, I suppose, makes them more like privateers than pirates but never mind all that. Laws like ARPA include stiff penalties for professional and avocational archaeologists who have permitted access to protected information, like the locations of sensitive backcountry sites. If I was to share that sort of information, for example, I would definitely lose my job and could very well wind up in prison. But unaffiliated, unpermitted, and profoundly unethical civilians are allowed to share it as freely as they like. The only potential consequences they face are seething wrath and chastisement from people with an actual moral compass, and those things never deter pigheaded behavior.

◆ ◆ ◆

Still, these lowlifes aside, the non-professional archaeological community in general is a decent bunch—a consortium of respectful rascals. You can usually count on them to support progressive causes and eschew distasteful research about as reliably as you can count on professional archaeologists being unmarried in our fifties or passing out in a port-a-potty at the annual Pecos Conference. Not always, in other words, but often—and more and more frequently as younger generations rise through the ranks.

Circling back at last, recreational archaeology also offers a great opportunity for Indigenous people to educate the public in a way that's interactive and fun, in addition to bolstering management and preservation goals. I opened this chapter with a quote from Hopi archaeologist Lyle Balenquah, and in fact he spends most of his free time as a wilderness guide. In that capacity he often works for Louis Williams, owner and proprietor of Ancient Wayves River and Hiking Adventures—one of a small but rapidly growing number of Indigenous-owned wilderness guiding companies and the only one permitted to operate in Bears Ears National Monument. I've also worked with Navajo guides like Brandi Atene while pitching in for Canyonlands Field Institute, and I've known or consulted with at least a dozen others.

Outdoor recreation is near the top of the heap whenever most people think of privileged activities, and for rather obvious reasons. Women have to watch out for creeps and monsters, non-hetero folks have to watch out for same, and people of color have to watch out for racists and, to quote a young Black woman I used to date, often feel "uninvited" in the outdoor recreation culture to boot. For these and related reasons, the American hiking scene is overwhelmingly white, male, hetero, and wealthy.

Then again, so is the American voting scene, and it's becoming blessedly clear that a lot of those same folks are willing to pay big bucks to have honest-to-gosh Native Americans drag them through the wilderness while talking about their ancestors' history with the place. It might only help in a small way, at least for the moment, but it certainly does help!

◆ ◆ ◆

Then there is the other major domain outside—but adjacent to—the ever-expanding and bifurcating realms of professionalism: conservation archaeology. This is exactly what it sounds like.

Curiously enough, The preservation ethos in professional archaeology came about as a result of the historic preservation championed by the likes of the Mount Vernon Ladies' Association, which purchased and protected George Washington's estate in 1853; the efforts of Boston philanthropist Mary Hemenway to push for protection of Casa Grande, which occurred in 1892; the efforts of McClurg and Peabody to protect Mesa Verde, which Congress finally did in 1906; and others besides. There were lots of women in the early historic preservationist movement, for the ironically sexist reason that they weren't expected—or, indeed, even allowed—to have jobs and were thus free to spend time reading and caring about things. So, again, privilege had much to do with this—but they set a great precedent, nonetheless.

From there the principles of archaeological preservation became a matter of national policy, starting with the Antiquities Act and running through to NAGPRA, which continues to be amended and updated to this very day. An update to the legislation implemented in January of 2024 by the Biden administration requires institutions to acquire permission from lineal descendants and affiliated Tribes or Native Hawaiian groups for the display of human remains and other items of sacred or historical significance (there's that word again).

The first institution to publicly acknowledge this was the Field Museum in Chicago, revealing in a statement that some displays in the Robert R. McCormick Halls of the Ancient Americas and the Alsdorf Hall of Northwest Coast and Arctic Peoples were now obscured from public view. "Pending consultation with the represented communities," their notice read, "we have covered all cases that we believe contain cultural items that could be subject to these regulations."

The biggest paradigm shift leading up to all this was Bill Lipe's

1974 publication "A Conservation Model for Archaeology," which characterized archaeological sites as non-renewable resources and stressed the importance of knowing when not to dig. Then came CRM, which comprises most archaeological work in the United States today, and which operates almost entirely in accordance with the mandates of Section 106 of the NHPA and its regulations about minimizing damage to important bits of history.

The thing is, CRM is very rarely a preservation effort. It's more like triage or damage control. The efforts of CRM companies and projects are directed as needed toward sites, structures, or occasionally natural features that are deemed historically or culturally "significant" in terms of the NRHP's four criteria of importance—and then only on public lands, and then only when they're in danger of being damaged or destroyed by some sort of undertaking. The pros come in, do a survey and record what's there, submit recommendations for avoidance or mitigation—usually excavation to preserve the data and repatriate any mortuary components to the Tribes, although mitigation can take various forms—and then the agencies consult with the Tribes and other interested parties before a decision is made to allow development to continue.

Since you can't stop progress, as the old refrain goes, CRM almost never results in halting a development project indefinitely. They'll either route the project around the site, or they'll yank the site from the ground, repatriate the most sensitive patrimony, and curate the rest in a museum or other facility. The report goes on a shelf where it gathers dust. This is why dissolving NHPA wasn't on Project 2025's kill list alongside other protective legislation like the Endangered Species Act. It isn't a barrier to development so much as a speedbump. Although that certainly hasn't stopped people from all across the political spectrum trying to at least weaken it.

Preservation or conservation archaeology grew out of this situation and the frustrations associated with it. The first and most obvious method of dealing with said frustrations was to lean into the fact that federal, state, and municipal regulations only apply to federal, state, and municipal lands. Private land doesn't offer legislative protection for archaeological sites, outside of blanket protections for human remains and mortuary features, but private land also isn't required to generate profits for the American economy the way most public lands are.

This is one of those fun little quirks about American public lands policy that a lot of people don't realize: unless an area is specifically designated as off-limits for development, the whole point of managing public lands is for them to generate revenue. You can lease a thousand acres of BLM land for oil and gas extraction, for example, but you can't lease it just to preserve it. Back in 2007, conservative political humorist P.J. O'Rourke summarized the situation:

> Most members of the US Forest Service joined because they had a mission to grow trees. But, in order to grow trees, they need a richer and more powerful Forest Service. And, because of various laws passed by idiot Congress, the only way for the Forest Service to become richer and more powerful is to cut the trees it grows. It's a little more complicated than that in real life, but that's the gist of it. Public lands are supposed to be used, intelligently and respectfully whenever watchdogs are watching, for the benefit of the public—chiefly its economic benefit."*

Author and conservationist Terry Tempest Williams learned this the hard way in 2016 after she admitted that the twelve hundred acres of BLM land she leased as Tempest Exploration Co. LLC was never going to be drilled. Another friend of mine learned the same lesson a year later when she and her then-boyfriend staked a uranium lease in Bears Ears, to the BLM's genuine amusement.

Private lands, however, have no such edict. This means that a private landowner is free to buy a parcel that contains an archae-

* Reasons like this are why I remain stubbornly sympathetic toward my conservative friends, despite occupying a position of relative polarity on the political prayer wheel. Our system is utterly buggered. The difference is that people of my temperament think we should fix it, while conservatives more often think we should scrap the whole shebang and hand the controls over to corporations and churches—which always sounds to me like responding to an incompetent babysitter by giving up and just handing the baby straight to the kidnappers. But I still see where they're coming from.

ological site just so they can ransack it, but also means a private landowner is free to buy a parcel that contains an archaeological site just to make sure it doesn't get ransacked. I have a good friend who did exactly that about a decade ago when he bought a house that happened to have a Chaco outlier in the backyard.

With that sort of thing in mind, the Archaeological Conservancy was established in 1979 by Mark Michel (who serves as its president and CEO to this day), along with businessman Jay Last and archaeologist Steven LeBlanc, using start-up funds from the Rockefeller Brothers Foundation and the Ford Foundation. Their mission is to buy and preserve archaeological sites, and they're good at it. As of this writing, they manage over five hundred preserves in five designated regions across the United States, including some of the most spectacular and important archaeological sites in the country. The enormous Yellowjacket Pueblo in southwestern Colorado is among them, as are three large Ancestral Pueblo complexes in southeastern Utah. They also manage something like a dozen of the mound sites that got Thomas Jefferson and the early antiquarian archaeologists so hot and bothered.

Older and a lot larger, although not focused on archaeology, is The Nature Conservancy, another nonprofit organization dedicated to acquiring property to protect it. Founded in 1951, they currently have over a million members and boast a total of just under 120 million acres of protected land. Which, naturally enough, means a lot of archaeological sites and objects get protected as well, either by default or by design. One example of this is the Gila River Preserve in New Mexico, focused on preservation of the last of the Southwest's free-flowing rivers. Students from Archaeology Southwest's field school have been investigating the archaeology there for five field seasons, learning about the area, its history, the practical aspects of archaeology, and the importance of public outreach.

Speaking of Archaeology Southwest, they were founded in 1989 by archaeologist Bill Doelle, who—like the Archaeological Conservancy's Mark Michel—remained its president and CEO all the way up until the year I drafted this. Their founding principle, as Bill explained in the Winter 2012 issue of their magazine, is to "optimize what remains for future exploration and discovery." As with early archaeological preservationists like Hewett, it was really about saving archaeological sites so they could be subjected to research later. But they didn't stay that way. Over the past decade, the feisty nonprofit has pivoted hard toward forging partnerships with Indigenous groups and working with them to help protect places they consider important or sacred just because they deserve protection.

They, too, use funds from donors and sales of their magazine to acquire sites and parcels for the purpose of protection, but Archaeology Southwest also advocates for elevated legislative protection of public lands they and their Tribal partners think deserve it. They played an important role in the creation of Bears Ears National Monument and have worked tirelessly for the past several years to try to establish similar protections for the Great Bend of the Gila River in Arizona—not so they could be dug up later, but to make sure they don't get dug up at all.

Other nonprofit organizations have come to follow suit. Friends of Cedar Mesa was founded in 2010 by Mark Meloy, widower of Ellen Meloy—one of my all-time favorite wilderness authors—for the purpose of raising funds in order to provide partnership support for the perennially underfunded federal agencies in southeastern Utah. Volunteering to help build trails, monitor archaeological sites, trim brush, pick up trash, and so on is something innumerable private citizens do every year, but when those efforts are organized by groups with centralized goals and leadership it can be a lot more effective. Just about every wild place in the United States has a Friends Of group offering such services.

By the mid-2010s, under executive director Josh Ewing, Friends of Cedar Mesa also shifted gears toward advocacy for elevated legislative protection. They created their own proposal for a Greater Cedar Mesa National Conservation Area, along with an accompanying issue of *Archaeology Southwest Magazine* guest-edited by none other than Bill Lipe, before abdicating that effort to become the chief conservationist ally of the Bears Ears Inter-Tribal Coalition.

Following the creation of the contentious national monument,

Friends of Cedar Mesa owned up to their new mission by changing their name to the Greater Bears Ears Partnership, and then immediately shortened that to Bears Ears Partnership because board members thought it was easier to say. I've got one of the T-shirts they printed before they dropped the "Greater" from their name, and I wear it to their visitor center on occasion just to be cheeky.

◆ ◆ ◆

The legacy of the Bears Ears Partnership and Indigenous organizations like the Bears Ears Inter-Tribal Coalition also serve as useful springboards for underscoring the importance of including the people whose heritage is under threat in efforts to preserve it. Simply put, "preservation" doesn't mean the same thing to everyone.

Some, like members of Hopi and Zuni communities, see the archaeological sites of their ancestors as living history in the literal sense, complete with spirits and lifespans—and, as such, they prefer that these "footprints" on the landscape be allowed to wither and decay into nothingness the way all living things eventually do. Others, most notably folks that I've met in the Navajo and White Mountain Apache Nations, have a very different outlook: they see these vestiges of Indigenous history on the land as effectively monuments proclaiming WE WERE HERE ALL THIS TIME. They want them preserved for as long as possible, especially if the United States government or its citizens are willing to foot the bill.

This played out in an interesting way in Mesa Verde National Park a few years ago. In October of 2015, the NPS was forced to close visitation of Spruce Tree House after it became clear that bits of the overhanging sandstone—include one "bit" comprising an arch over the entire structure—were on the verge of crushing much of the structure and anyone who happened to be there when it fell. This is a natural result of things like ice wedging in the ceiling of the alcove, and there's evidence to show the Ancestral Pueblo were not unaware of the danger, as they'd apparently wedged sticks into the cracks to monitor how big the cracks were getting. So it's part of the nature of the place, but it does make things like preservation and visitation a bit tricky.

The park consulted with just under thirty Tribes before making any plans to deal with the problem, which is admirable in its own right because consultation often—and infuriatingly—takes place after the fix is in, so to speak. What came back was roughly a 55:45 split between the options of somehow stabilizing the ceiling and letting nature take its course as is its wont. Friend and fellow archaeological conservation tub-thumper Paul Reed heralded the process in an interview with the *Durango Herald*, noting how the debate over preserving or allowing sites to decay has become a major touchstone as Tribes are given more voice in such matters these days. "Which is way overdue," he said. "That process alone is a vast improvement on more than a century of not consulting [with them at all]."

In this case, preservation won out over allowing a natural death—but just barely. The NPS implemented a four-phase approach to stabilizing the gargantuan sandstone arch in early 2022

◆ ◆ ◆

What's missing from this tale, so far, is a conservation archaeology consultation firm. There are for-profit CRM firms that range in size from a single individual with a DBA, like Bruce Phillips and Winston Hurst, all the way up to massive corporations with annual budgets in the hundreds of millions. There is, to my knowledge, no such thing as a nonprofit entity dedicated to heritage management. It's either nonprofit conservation organizations hiring archaeologists—and utilizing volunteers—to help protect sites, or it's for-profit organizations hiring archaeologists to find and record them ahead of destructive activities.

I tried to start one myself for several years: Desert Dog Archaeology. I even paid a small fee to reserve the name in case it ever came to be. Industry demands, however, are too heavily slanted toward profit-driven models to make doing CRM as a nonprofit enterprise a non-starter for most people who aren't millionaires—at least for now.

In any case, just like with outdoor recreation, the world of heritage conservation represents another major opportunity for Indigenous peoples to take a hand in the preservation and management of their material heritage. Conservation in the United States may have started with folks like Teddy Roosevelt and John Muir looking to preserve their favorite stomping grounds—again: pretty uniformly white, male, hetero, and wealthy—but a lot has changed since then, especially in recent years. The case of Spruce Tree House highlights the importance of collaboration at the federal level but, again, cases like that only apply to public lands—and then only when the managing personnel care to take the time. Nonprofits are generally a more effective way to generate a lot more involvement in a lot more places, and they often end up helping federal agencies as well.

Hence many of them changing their titles from Friends to Partners or Partnership, as in the case of Friends of Cedar Mesa morphing into Bears Ears Partnership, as well as that of a nearby group called Grand Staircase-Escalante Partners. Along with Archaeology Southwest and a growing number of other conservation nonprofits in the greater Southwest portion of the US, their stated goal is to collaborate with Tribal partners rather than ask them to check item boxes and/or leave them out of the conservation game altogether. Nobody knows this land and its deep histories better than they do, after all.

Still, despite all this, worrying trends abound. Not long after I began drafting this manuscript in the spring of 2024, I had the great pleasure of visiting the ghost town of Ruby in far-southern Arizona with my friend Jonathan Bailey and a woman I was seeing at the time. Ruby is a privately owned mining town that boomed in about 1877 and un-boomed in the early 1940s. There's an abundance of buildings, an enormous gated-off mine shaft that now serves as a major bat sanctuary, and much else besides. The private owners of the historic town allowed visitors to pay a small fee and then wander around to their hearts' content, making it a fun and visually interesting example of public engagement in heritage management.

That all ended in June of 2024, and in fact we were some of the last public visitors to ever get to see the place—unless it happens to reopen sometime in the future. When I chatted with the current landowner, a leathery and kindly old cowgirl, her stated reason for closing the place was one that I frankly never would have expected: "militias."

Because the ghost town is located very near the border, undocumented migrants will occasionally pass near or even through it, and—surprise, surprise—xenophobic sentiments about just those types of people have been stoked to a fever pitch in recent years. These variables have converged in the form of armed racists prowling the mountainous borderlands like unruly jackals shooting wildly at anything roughly brown in color.

"They killed two people in a canyon not two miles from here last year," someone else from nearby explained to me in exhausted fury. "Cops didn't do nothing, of course. Border patrol don't care. They just lay there and rot until local volunteers went and buried them. Can't be letting people wander around here when there's bullets flying all over the place."

The legacy of Ruby ends there for the moment. A rather poor, if also quite accurate, reflection on the heritage and culture of the United States as a whole.

The road behind us is fun to explore, filled with wondrous and mysterious things for which the interpretation is only half as exciting as the exploration. All the monsters lurking along that road lie dormant and serve best as object lessons for how to be better in the present. The road ahead, on the other hand, includes monsters that are very much alive and well. Facing them down is our biggest challenge if we intend to keep our history—as well as our environment, our democracy, and a lot of our fellow human beings—alive.

CHAPTER 8

THE FUTURE OF THE PAST

So, where does all this stuff lead next? Does it have any practical uses beyond satisfying the curiosity of people with enough free time to muse on those deep histories of the land?

The short answer is: Yes. Sort of. It all depends on how we choose to use it.

Using archaeology to help people understand or reclaim their own history is relatively new to the discipline, but it is arguably the best—or at least the most ethical—use of our skillset. What follows is a short series of topic studies based around that idea. They aren't exactly fun topics to explore, but exploring them is necessary for our overall sociocultural health, and archaeological investigation plays a major role in all of them.

◆ ◆ ◆

To begin with, the history of human bondage in North America is immensely complicated and, if we count incarcerated individuals, spans nearly half a millennium at this point. Doing it any sort of justice in a few paragraphs would be an act of high treason against humanity, so I won't pretend to do that now, but there are a ton of books about the subject.

However, giving the topic of slavery in the Americas just a few paragraphs is exactly what many, if not most American grade school textbooks have done for well over a century. *Hazen's Elementary History of the United States: A Story and a Lesson*, a popular early twentieth-century textbook for young readers that first came out in

1903, recounts how the settlers brought a shipment of Africans to the Americas in 1619 and "found them so helpful in raising tobacco that more were brought in, and slavery became part of our history." That's it. That's all it says until Lincoln singlehandedly frees them all.

A later textbook called *A Child's History of South Carolina*, published in 1916, focuses on how Southern slave owners were reluctant parts of a nonetheless useful economic strategy, claiming that enslaved people "were allowed all the freedom they seemed to want, and were given the privilege of visiting other plantations when they chose to do so. All that was required of them was to be in place when work time came. At the holiday season they were almost as free as their masters." Umm . . . *what?*

Moreover, as the text goes on to relate, most slave owners in South Carolina "were really opposed to slavery and were in favor of a gradual emancipation. Slavery was already in existence, however, through no fault of theirs. They had the slaves and had to manage as best they could the problem of what to do with them." Poor chaps. I can't imagine how hard that must have been for them.

This sort of stuff inspired Black historians and intellectuals to start publishing their own history books in retaliation, including a 1914 book called *The Negro in American History* by John W. Cromwell, which depicts American slavery in all its godawful brutality. However, according to *Vox* journalist Cynthia Greenlee in a literature review on the subject, these books didn't really make much of an impact on the overall American psyche. She quotes graduate student James O. Lewis who laments that in "the greater number of textbooks, slave life is pictured as a not too unpleasant condition; in fact, it was often described as having been rather nice in the sheer beauty of relationship between the slaveowner and the slaves." I even heard some of my own teachers and community elders chanting similar incantations when I was a pup in greater New England.

Much of this criticism of how the history of enslaved peoples in the Americas has been—so to speak—whitewashed culminated in the 1619 Project, a long-term journalistic endeavor effort initiated by Nikole Hannah-Jones and supported by *The New York Times* to attempt to address this sort of thing. Studies supported or collected by the project included a few lit reviews of popular American history textbooks still in use today that offer what is essentially a one-note summary of four hundred years of atrocity. Columbus discovered America, the Native Americans died from diseases or traded their land for beads like imbeciles or lost their lives in skirmishes against the better-armed colonists, then came African slavery, then the slaves were freed by Abraham Lincoln, and then the "real" history of the United States begins—the remaining ninety percent of the text. An estimated nine or ten million human beings from various cultures over hundreds of years summarized entirely as a dot on the timeline between Columbus and Lincoln.

Enter archaeology. Formal archaeological investigations of antebellum slavery commenced in the early 1970s as an ancillary effort of the civil rights movement, tiptoed toward full maturity in the 1980s, but really ramped up heading into the new millennium. Much of it was conducted as an intentional effort to combat the written history that was—and remains—overwhelmingly dominated by literate white scholars for reasons I hope I don't need to explain anymore.

Absent any written records from the millions of enslaved Africans who only spoke broken English or Spanish, and who certainly weren't allowed to do things like keep written records, material history is arguably the best basis from which to construct and frame their history.

The first published effort I can find was by the team of Robert Ascher and Charles H. Fairbanks in a 1971 report titled "Excavation of a Slave Cabin: Georgia, USA" in *Historical Archaeology*. They note, among other things, how a blue bead found within the cabin that "was [likely] carried from Africa to America" was considered in some African traditions to be an "ambassador bead" that was used like a passport between tribal chiefs.

Their approach to the topic is very processual in nature, which makes sense given the time in which they conducted their work, but their research also included supplemental information from Black oral history and documentary evidence. Based on all this, they draw some rather impressive and humanizing conclusions about the lives of these folks, including how enslaved individuals "managed to add considerable protein to their diet" through hunting and gathering to make up for shortfalls in the meager foodstuffs they were provided.

Writing six years later in an edited volume called *Archaeological Perspectives on Ethnicity in America*, John Solomon Otto synthesizes a battery of literary and archaeological evidence to apply another distinctly processual approach to the excavation of sites on the coast of Georgia. Otto also emphasizes the archaeology of foodways as revealed in these studies, because sooner or later archaeology is all about food. He concludes, for example, that the slaves "were more dependent on wild animals to supplement their diet," revealing their humanistic agency in the face of white refusal to provide them with decent meals—the same as Ascher and Fairbanks had found. Skipping ahead a bit, this also explains why so much of what eventually became the ubiquitous dishes of the deep south—and Louisiana in particular—include a substantial measure of native biota, like crawfish and alligator.

From these purely descriptive beginnings, this research focus grew and evolved alongside the rest of American archaeology. Starting in the early 1990s, archaeologists like David W. Babson began arguing for increased studies of racial categories and ethnicity in the antebellum United States as a whole, making one of the earliest stabs at a holistic perspective political scientists would later call "intersectional." He focused in particular on how racism caused the creation of Black community identity, a culture constructed partly from traditions and stories brought over from various parts of Africa and partly from resistance to oppression.

This is why so many scholars today capitalize the "B" when talking about the Black community, but don't bother doing the same with the "W" when talking about folks who look like me. Black culture in the United States is a communal identity—that, yes, takes many different forms—borne out of millions of people over hundreds of years of having their actual cultural identities forcibly erased.

White culture, on the other hand, doesn't exist. Whiteness as a category was invented in the late 1600s to delineate European from non-European Christians to know whose labor it's still okay to exploit, as I covered in a previous chapter. What often gets called "white culture" is mainstream American culture, which is just Anglo-Saxon culture with heavy doses of religion and capitalism mixed in, and emphasizing the *whiteness* of it is . . . not ideal.

Food and music also played immensely important roles in the efforts of enslaved and early emancipated Africans in the Americas as well. Babson points out cases like those of the South Carolina Rice Coast, where an entire plantation system seems to have survived at least partly because white planters utilized "African methods and knowledge" of rice cultivation that simply hadn't occurred to them. Writing a decade after Babson, Maria Franklin makes the case that enslaved peoples used traditional foodways to help form community identity and "position themselves in colonial society" by responding to it with creativity rather than complacency.

As was the cases with Otto and his research, Franklin's chapter in the 2002 edited volume *Race and the Archaeology of Identity* also notes how subsistence became resistance—a lovely little phrase for which I can't take credit; I've heard it numerous times—as enslaved people hunted and gathered the land, often for items to contribute to large communal stews whose pots occur in a lot of archaeological digs. We have this practice to thank for gumbo.

◆ ◆ ◆

Then there's the harrowing case of Malaga Island, where all these and a number of other historic tendrils jumbled themselves into a snarl we are only now starting to unravel. In the 1790s, off the coast of New England, an enslaved man of Senegal-Gambian ancestry named Benjamin Darling saved his owner from a shipwreck in an act of humanitarianism that's hard to fathom given the circumstances.* He was rewarded for this act of heroism with emancipation by that owner, and took a paying job at a local salt mill where he gradually saved up enough money to buy what is now

* This guy was something else. Not content with saving the drowning slaveowner who literally owned him, Darling was badly mauled a few years later when he got into a fight with a bear that was raiding another white neighbor's garden.

called Harbor Island off the coast of Maine.

The year was 1794, the island was then called Horse Island, and the cost was fifteen British pounds—or about $2,500 today. Darling moved there with his wife, a white woman named Sarah Proverbs (more fun with Puritan names), and their family grew and thrived. Their sons Benjamin and Isaac eventually took their own wives from the local mainland communities, raising fourteen children between them.

In related news, miscegenation—or the mixing of the races—was technically illegal at the time. Nobody on the mainland much cared because the Darlings lived on a rocky island off the Maine coast, but this fact would become very relevant later.

By the end of the Civil War, the mostly "mixed-race" descendants of the Darling clan had expanded to nearby Malaga Island, a place that offered easier access to the coast. A multiracial fishing community quickly bloomed. Intermarriage remained illegal, technically speaking, but the residents of nearby Phippsburg still didn't really care—at first. Horse Island was sold to a Maine businessman named Joseph Perry in 1847 by Isaac Darling, prompting consolidation of the rest of the family onto Malaga, where they constructed an entire community complete with multi-story houses and schools.

Technology, meanwhile, continued to grow and evolve back on the mainland. As did racism.

By the end of the Civil War, boats and ships had become much sturdier and more reliable forms of transport, as well as more abundant, especially among the wealthy. At the same time, anti-Black sentiments surged throughout southern and northern states alike, with people of a conservative bent regarding the newly emancipated people as an inhuman plague loosed upon the land and people of a liberal bent regarding them as fully human but nonetheless culturally degenerate.

These elements converged by the terminal 1800s, when the Ku Klux Klan—the first organized terror movement in the United States—established a foothold in Maine and rumors started to spread about the "queer folk" living outside the law on the islands of Casco Bay. That convergence ramped up to a storm when the wealthy people who could afford fancy new boats jumped into the fray. Almost overnight, the many rocky and only marginally habitable islands off the chilly coast looked like prime real estate for vacation homes, if only they weren't inhabited by undesirables.

Thus began a short but fiery propaganda effort to portray the residents of Malaga Island as backwards savages, the pathetic results of race-mixing and its inevitable degeneration of character, and just generally hopeless vagrant scum who lived in driftwood shacks eating dirt. Or something.

Journalists started visiting the island to see this depravity for themselves, coming back with stories of human awfulness that strongly conflicted with their own photographs of a thriving community of sturdy buildings and well-educated kids. Starting in 1892, a pauper relief fund in Phippsburg began helping the residents of Malaga Island during the winter when fishing was less productive—something they'd never needed before and, as far as we know, also didn't ask for—which immediately prompted additional aspersions about their status as welfare parasites.

Things neared critical mass in the early 1900s when local newspapers began extolling the "natural beauty" of Casco Bay, a beauty marred by the "Southern Negro Blood" of its residents. Tourists and missionaries arrived in greater number, spreading the dual-pronged gospels of middle-class elitism and Christian racism. Journalists continued to fan the flames by running bullshit articles about how the residents were lazy, ignorant, immoral alcoholics. They were finally evicted from the island in 1912, thanks to a convoluted snarl of political and land deed shenanigans. All the buildings were destroyed, except the schoolhouse, which was moved to Louds Island in Muscongus Bay. Even their cemeteries were dug up and reburied elsewhere.

To add insult to injury, the government's eviction strategy also included an assessment of the residents' mental conditions, concluding that at least eight residents were "feeble minded." They and their immediate family were promptly trundled off to the recently constructed and very creatively named Home for the Feeble Minded in what is now the town of Pineland.

In 1913, an article appeared in a local newspaper with the title "Cleaning up Malaga Island—No Longer a Reproach to the Good Name of the State." Among other silliness, it played up how "not only have the inhabitants of the island been raised to a standard of living they probably never dreamed of before and all done for them that is possible under the conditions, but the state had saved a nice little bundle of coin as well." The standard of living they probably never dreamed of was abject poverty back on the mainland and, in a few cases, literal incarceration in a primitive nuthouse. The nice little bundle of coin saved by the state was the welfare that, again, the residents hadn't needed in the first place.

And that was that for Malaga Island. It has changed hands numerous times over the years, finally getting acquired by the Maine Coast Heritage Trust in 2001 to protect it from future development.

This move was prompted in large part by archaeologists, who began investigating the island in 1989. Field schools conducted between 2004 and 2008 resulted in identification of around sixty thousand artifacts from just fifty square meters of test and excavation units, and they speak volumes about the people who lived there. "While the state and local media consistently attempted to show that the Malaga Islanders were unable to support themselves and lived like sub-humans, the archaeological record proves otherwise," according to an impressively candid academic piece by Kate McMahon in the Spring/Fall 2013 issue of *Material Culture Review.*

This in turn prompted a series of descendant interviews where the great-great-etc. grandchildren of the original inhabitants were tracked down, an effort that included anthropologists spending many years getting to know local residents and their folklore. A series of documentaries resulted from these efforts, as well as photographic and museum exhibitions. In 2010, the Maine State Legislature passed a resolution in which they expressed "profound regret" for the actions taken in 1912—which I guess was nice of them. The island was added to the National Register of Historic Places in 2023 just a few months before I wrote this.

Despite all the archaeological survey conducted on what is now the Malaga Island Preserve, the location of the original cemetery was never discovered. Nor can I find any documentation of the fates of the Malaga Island residents who were consigned to the Home for the Feeble Minded, one of many historic insane asylums that were really just concentration camps for people of unorthodox consciousness. But the archaeological work and its adjacent efforts have provided the island community's descendants with a tangible history. And history, say it with me, is a living thing. Being part of it is part of being human.

◆ ◆ ◆

Speaking of concentration camps: their history in Western culture is also a lot deeper and more complex than most people realize. American history textbooks often make no mention of them prior to the Nazis, and then fail to differentiate between concentration camps and death camps within the Nazi regime, and then further fail to mention the fact that we've had versions of them here in the United States from the early 1800s right up to the present.

Concentration camps are places where large numbers of people are deliberately imprisoned without being formally convicted of any crimes beforehand. They're places to "concentrate" people who haven't done anything legally actionable but authorities just, you know, want them out of the way. Simple as that.

The earliest known use of concentration camps as we now understand them (an important distinction) occurred during the Second Boer War, a conflict between the British Empire and the two Boer Republics—the South African Republic and the Orange Free State—in southern Africa between 1899 and 1902. The British used several small islands located in Bermuda's Great Sound as natural concentration camps, surrounded as they were by water and all, despite protests by the local government in Bermuda. Thousands of Boers were interned on the islands.

England kept that tradition alive and well during the Irish War of Independence of 1919 to 1920, and again during World War II when refugees who fled from the Nazis—somewhere around seventy-five thousand in total—were detained without trial. Looking even worse, the British Government issued the Balfour Declaration in 1917 during World War I, announcing its support for the establishment of a "national home for the Jewish people" in the Ottoman colony of Palestine. But then after the war, during the period of chopping up and handing out the spoils, the former Ottoman colony was ceded to England as Mandatory Palestine, who immediately backpedaled on their earlier Balfour stance and thwarted the emigration of Jewish refugees to the area. They were instead rerouted to concentration camps in Cyprus and were finally released in February of 1949 with the founding of Israel.

Then there were the Russian labor camps known as *katorga*, which mostly housed Czechoslovak soldiers; and the later Chernokozovo internment camp, used as a means to suppress Chechnya's independence movement. Reports have also circulated since 2017 of concentration camps in the now fully independent and ultra-conservative Chechen Republic, where men suspected of being gay or bisexual are allegedly housed and tortured to this day. Australia uses them for the indefinite detention of asylum seekers, China uses them to house and "re-educate" millions of Muslim Uyghurs, and so on.

They are much more common than most people seem to realize, in other words—alarmingly so. I currently live about an hour from the US-Mexico border where we've had concentration camps up and running since at least the first Trump administration, and the second Trump administration one-upped that by christening our own version of Dachau thanks to a partnership with the dictator of El Salvador. Because empires don't have to build uncomfortable things in their own backyards. Not when there are friendly despots nearby willing to donate their backyards instead.

Still, our own backyard has always hosted plenty of them. Although not quite concentration camps in the formal sense, like those of the Boer Wars, our first large-scale internment of specific ethnic groups within detention centers without trail or conviction were created at the behest of President Martin Van Buren with the Treaty of New Echota in 1838. The treaty called for the rounding-up and corralling of Cherokee families into prison camps before relocating them to places like Oklahoma.

A little under thirty years later, thirty-eight Dakota warriors were hanged—including one that was pardoned beforehand but then hanged anyway—in the largest mass execution in American history by order of Abraham Lincoln for the crime of being taken prisoner in the United States-Dakota Indian War of 1862. This would be considered a war crime today.

The remaining prisoners were sent to prisoner-of-war camps that were established as US military forts, and within the following year they were joined by nearly two thousand Dakota men, women, and children who weren't warriors or involved in the war in any way. That same year, General James Henry Carleton and Colonel Kit Carson rounded up as many Diné families as they could find and herded them into Bosque Redondo in New Mexico, where they remained until a treaty was signed six years later.

Then came World War II and the bombing of Pearl Harbor, which inspired FDR to issue an executive order—EO 9066—calling for removal of all Japanese people and Americans of Japanese ancestry from western coastal regions into concentration camps throughout the West Coast and the Intermountain West. German and Italian citizens in the east were also relocated or interred, but on nothing like the scale of the Japanese internment camps.

Executive Order 9102 came half a year later, forming the War Relocation Authority or WRA, a government agency established to handle and oversee the internment of Japanese Americans during the war, as well as operate the one and only emergency refugee camp for Europeans. Since the primary task of the WRA was to build and maintain rather large concentration camps, a feat that required no small amount of federally funded labor, a lot of workers from the WPA (sister organization to the CCC of the New Deal era) simply jumped from one to the other when the WPA wound down in 1942.

In a weird twist of history, the original director of the WRA—a man named Milton S. Eisenhower, youngest brother of Dwight—was an ardent FDR progressive who despised the idea of mass internment of people whose only crime was their ancestry. He forwarded numerous proposals to curtail the reach of the agency and improve the conditions of its camps, including efforts to limit internees only to adult men and to allow resettlement outside the exclusion zones in hard-hit agricultural areas. To no avail. He headed the agency for just three months, according to historian Roger Daniels in *Prisoners Without Trial: Japanese Americans in World War II*, and his resignation letter states, "when the war is over and we consider calmly this unprecedented migration of 120,000 people, we as Americans are going to regret the unavoidable injustices that we may have done."

Looking back on that quote from the year 2026 . . .

Anyway, opposition to Eisenhower's proposals and to people who just plain didn't want the camps to exist at all came largely in the form of disingenuous rhetoric about protecting Japanese citizens. According to the archives of the World War II Museum in New Orleans, the governors of Montana and Wyoming feared it would spark racial violence. "Our people cannot tell an American-born Japanese from an alien," said Montana Governor Sam C. Ford, according to the Museum's summary report. "When casualty lists start coming in . . . I fear for the safety of any Japanese in this state." We're doing this for your own good, in other words. Better you're imprisoned against your will in a rickety makeshift campground than free to be harassed by rednecks.

Idaho's Attorney General Bert Miller, meanwhile, was a bit more honest about his position. "We want to keep this a white man's country. All Japanese [should] be put in concentration camps for the remainder of the war."

That point about "a white man's country" lampshades some fun realities. While most Americans these days don't seem to know those camps existed at all, even fewer know that many of them were built on Native American reservations, often against the wishes of the Natives themselves. In Arizona, the Leupp Isolation Center was built on the Navajo Nation, the Poston Camp was built on the Colorado River Indian Reservation, and the Gila River camps were built within the Gila River Indian Community. These last four were known collectively as the Rivers Camps in honor of Jim Rivers, the first Akimel O'odham soldier killed in World War I, not because they were built near an actual river.

The Rivers Camps are an especially ugly example of the legacy of these camps on Indigenous reserve lands. The Tribal government initially rejected the WRA's proposal—twice—but narrowly accepted it a third time after the feds promised that, in lieu of monetary payment, the WRA would cultivate 8,500 acres on behalf of the Tribe. Presumably the plan was to use the imprisoned Japanese people as un- or underpaid laborers to do that cultivation, but it's all the same in hindsight because the WRA never bothered to make good on that promise anyway.

In that unfortunate way that history loves to repeat itself, this too is happening again. The Poarch Band of Creek Indians and the Prairie Band of the Potawatomi Nation were both entertaining contracts worth tens of billions to allow Immigration Control Enforcement—the dreaded ICE—to build massive immigrant detention centers on their land in December of 2025. Nothing has been built and no contracts have been signed, as of this writing, but neither contract has been cancelled either. The fact that these Tribal governments are even considering contracts like these have a lot of Indigenous citizens outraged, with Anishinaabe attorney and activist Tara Zhaaabowekwe Houska beautifully summarizing the issue thusly:

> "There are many ways that our nations can financially succeed and survive in this capitalist framework but being in the business of separating Indigenous families should never be one of them. Regardless of political spectrum, it feels like a lot of Native folks are opposed to Native folks locking up Native folks south of the colonial border."

◆ ◆ ◆

As with the hundreds of years of slavery in this country, the topic of Japanese internment camps usually gets maybe a paragraph or two in American history books—if they mention them at all. And none of them that I've found discuss what life was like within those camps to any considerable degree. Therein lies a gap in the human history of our country that begs filling.

Although most of the buildings at these camps were demolished once the people were finally let out of them, archaeological methods aren't so easily thwarted. Archaeological investigation of these camps began in earnest in the early 1990s. As with the African slave communities, archaeological work at these camps has given a sense of identity and agency to the interred residents by documenting the various ways they adapted to—and resisted against—their predicament.

The first such effort took place at Manzanar, a former concentration camp located in the Owens Valley outside Los Angeles. Manzanar was designated a National Historic Site by the NPS in 1992, and a three-volume report came out soon after that, in the words of the *Densho Encyclopedia of Japanese-American History*, "described not only the physical remains of the Japanese-American incarceration [center], but also the archaeological traces of earlier Native American, ranching, and farming occupations of the site."

The investigation also helped dispel a few common misconceptions about life in the camps, including the notion that interred individuals were "coddled" by the government while everyone else was having to deal with wartime rationing and shortages. This is a mid-1900s version of the exasperating "prisoners have it made while the rest of us are struggling" ignorance that gives so many American prisons an excuse to save money by making their living conditions even worse—leading to, among other things, an average mortality rate among prisoners that's about the same as the COVID-19 pandemic at its height.

Life in these camps was anything but cush, which should go without saying. The archaeological investigations further helped to underscore this by finding things like meager subsistence gardens used to buffer shortfalls in the food supply.

While the NPS continues to sponsor and encourage archaeological investigations at the camps under or adjacent to its aegis, academics have also begun investigating the archaeology of Japanese internment camps in recent years. The University of Denver commenced a long-term, community-based archaeology and heritage project at Camp Amache—also known as the Granada Relocation Center in Prowers County, Colorado—in 2005 that included three field schools. A robust handful of articles and masters' theses came out of these efforts, including one on "Confined Cuisine" by Stephanie Skiles and one on "Consumption of Sake at Camp Amache" by Michelle Ann Slaughter, as well as several fascinating studies of ceramics. Starting in 2009, the University of Idaho began their own similar program of studies at Kooskia Internment Camp in north-central Idaho under the direction of principal investigator Stacey Camp. Similar efforts have also occurred in Hawaii.

Among other things, these efforts have helped to give voice, identity, and agency to the many thousands of Japanese and Japanese-American victims of incarceration purely on the grounds of ethnicity. The archaeology shows how the camps' inhabitants found resourceful ways to make their environments more familiar and habitable. Traces of Japanese-style rock alignments, walkways, gardens, and ponds remain to this day, sometimes on the ground surface and sometimes just beneath. In Amache, archaeologists even found evidence that the internees repurposed bits of water pipes as planters, used copper wire to train Chinese elms the way people still do today with bonsai trees, and made the desert soil more fertile by mulching eggshells and other refuse in with it—which, in turn, allowed them to grow vegetables for traditional Japanese foods.

Immense quantities of Japanese ceramics also demonstrate how the internees struggled to maintain traditional cultural identities, since people were only allowed to bring what they could carry when they were harried form their homes and concentrated into the camps. "Take only what you need to survive," as the man said. From this it's fairly self-evident that they considered intricate and often delicate ceramics to be crucial to the survival of their culture, if not their individual survival as people. Nobody was ordering them to stop being Japanese and assimilate to American culture; they just had to stay put. If they remained within the confines and didn't cause too much trouble, they could act just as Japanese as they pleased. So, they did.

The same cannot be said of the millions of Indigenous children ripped away from their own families and confined in what were often far worse conditions at Indian residential schools.

◆ ◆ ◆

In May of 2021, Dr. Sara Beaulieu conducted what's called "remote sensing" at the site of the former Kamloops Indian Residential School in British Columbia using ground-penetrating radar, and concluded that she was able to find at least two hundred underground disruptions that were most likely unmarked graves. Indigenous groups had long suspected this was the case, based primarily on the testimony of survivors from the school who told of kids dying left and right, but no solid proof existed prior to this archaeological investigation. First Nations groups used federal funds they received as COVID-19 relief packages to hire Beaulieu to conduct a technical investigation into these claims.

Upon the discovery, a joint task force was assembled at the behest of Tk'emlúps te Secwépemc, formerly known as the Kamloops Indian Band of the Shuswap Nation Tribal Council, consisting of "various professors as well as technical archaeologists" for the purpose of exhuming, identifying, and repatriating the remains of children from the school, according to Assembly of First Nations regional chief Terry Teegee in an interview with *CBC News* later that same month. To this day, however, it has yet to occur.

Meanwhile, less than a month after this grisly discovery, the remains of 751 people—mainly Indigenous children—were found at the site of the former Marieval Residential School in Saskatchewan. A further 160 undocumented and unmarked graves were confirmed in British Columbia by the Penelakut Tribe in July of 2021. Archaeologists Kisha Supernant and Terry Clark reported at least thirty-five unmarked graves in their own investigations of the Muscowequan Indian Residential School in Saskatchewan by October of that same year, and suggested they were likely to find even more given the nature of archaeological sampling. Indeed, even Dr. Beaulieu reported that the two-hundred-or-so unmarked graves found in her investigation were confined to a sample area covering just under two acres of the total 160-acre residential school site.

In an interview with Anderson Cooper for *CBS News* a couple years later, Supernant relayed to the horrified host how survivor accounts include priests or school officials forcing kids to dig graves for their classmates. "Can you imagine," she asked, "being, like, ten or eleven and digging a grave for your classmate, what that must have been like?"

The hits just kept coming. Inspired by these discoveries, researchers in the United States finally started applying technical skills and methods to investigate long-standing claims by Indigenous groups that thousands of kids had died at our own re-education centers. A federal investigation found evidence of at least fifty-three separate burial sites at various boarding schools in one quick sweep, and reported that this, too, was a tiny sample representing a much larger whole.

This came as part of the Federal Indian Boarding Schools Initiative, ordered in June of 2021 by the country's first-ever Indigenous Secretary of the Interior, Deb Haaland. The history of Native American boarding schools began with the Indian Civilization Act of 1819 and continued with legislation through the 1960s, Haaland said in a statement about the Initiative. "During that time, the purpose of Indian boarding schools was to culturally assimilate Indigenous children by forcibly relocating them from their families and communities to distant residential facilities. The languages, cultures, religions, traditional practices and even the history of Native communities was targeted for destruction."

By May of the following year, roughly five hundred children were discovered at burial sites as part of the wide-ranging investigation, according to a May 2022 report by the Bureau of Indian Affairs. Archaeological excavations at a boarding school in Nebraska were ongoing as recently as 2023, following a lit search that revealed at least eighty-six students had died at a school in Genoa—mostly due to diseases like tuberculosis and typhoid, although at least one of them was blamed on an "accidental" shooting. So far, the researchers have been able to find about half of them, believing the rest of the documented deaths—and who knows how many that weren't documented—are buried in long-forgotten locations someplace on the school grounds.

Of course, the excavation of literally hundreds of the corpses of children by archaeologists may or may not convince everyone of the horrors of colonialism. I've met a full-grown adult—the best friend of an ex-girlfriend, in fact, which helps explain the "ex" part—who believes the Sandy Hook massacre never actually happened. Because people will stubbornly believe absolutely anything if it slots into their preferred worldview. "We were brutal toward them because brutality is all they knew" is a phrase I've heard way too often in reference to the colonial era and its horrendous activities.

The pre-contact peoples of the Americas weren't angels. They were human, warts and all.

But that's rather the point. They weren't *treated* like humans. And that was true right up to the closing of the last Indian boarding school in . . . well, believe it or not, they haven't all closed even now. Riverside Indian School in Oklahoma is still around, although at this point its operations have changed considerably from the "kill the Indian, save the man" ethos of Lieutenant Henry Pratt when he got the ball rolling at the Carlisle School in Pennsylvania.

According to the Heard Museum, at least three other off-reservation Bureau of Indian Affairs boarding schools are still in use, and the National Native American Boarding School Healing Coalition told *Reuters* in 2021 that the number is closer to seventy.

All this sparked an expected explosion of outrage by the Indigenous community and their allies, despite not exactly being new or surprising to anyone who's investigated the topic. The Canadian Government issued a formal apology all the way back in 2008 for its past residential school policies in response to thousands of lawsuits by school survivors. It also set up a $1.9 billion compensation fund and established a Truth and Reconciliation Commission that spent the next six years gathering testimony from survivors across the country. In 2015, the Commission concluded that what had happened was nothing short of "cultural genocide," and had identified more than three thousand children who died from disease, malnutrition, or physical abuse. They also unearthed a government study conducted in 1909 that had found the death rates at these schools were as high as twenty times the national average.

◆ ◆ ◆

All this attention on the unfortunate fates of Indigenous youths forced to live in indoctrination factories also sparked a different kind of backlash—one that's becoming more of a mainstay in modern American culture as social media and political divisiveness have joined forces in increasingly awful ways. In May of 2022, the *New York Post* ran an article by Dana Kennedy titled "'Biggest fake news story in Canada': Kamloops mass grave debunked by experts." The article covered most of what I wrote here about the Kamloops discovery, including the fact that it sparked waves of outrage and vandalism of churches, and recapped how no excavations have yet occurred at the site. It then turns focus toward "a group of about a dozen academics in Canada" who "don't believe the story."

One of them, a professor emeritus in the Department of History at the Université de Montréal named Jaques Rouillard, told the *Post*: "Not one body has been found. After . . . months of recrimination and denunciation, where are the remains of the children buried at the Kamloops Indian Residential School?" Rouillard goes on to claim that he doesn't deny that abuse "may have occurred" at the residential schools, but that he and other academics question the narrative that's floating around without what they consider substantial enough evidence. "They use a lot of words like 'cultural genocide,'" Rouillard told *The Post*. "If that's true, there should be excavations. Everything is kept vague. You can't criticize them. Canadians feel guilty so they keep quiet."

All this because nobody has exhumed any actual bodies at that one location. Yet. Nobody else, apart from the sort of howling morons who believe Sandy Hook was a hoax, or that all anti-fascist protests are paid for by George Soros (still waiting on that paycheck, buddy boy), is casting similar doubt on any of the finds at other locations throughout both countries.

Still, one *Post* article is all it takes for naysayers to grab the baton and run with it. Writing for *Arizona Republic* in December of 2022, in an article titled "Don't get ahead of the facts as the US investigates Native American boarding schools," editorial columnist Phil Boas (no relation to Franz as far as I know) cites the article above as evidence that the media created a "moral panic" that led to lowering of flags, institution of a new holiday to honor missing kids and survivors, and—get ready to clutch those pearls—churches and statues getting vandalized.

Again, the poor fellows. I'm sure nobody in history has ever suffered quite so much.

As with Kennedy's *Post* piece itself, Boas goes on to state how "there has been enough research to know that Indian boarding schools have a dark history," but he insists that history "must be led by objective scholarship" rather than by anyone who happens to have any vocal opinions about the subject. I'll return to the problem of objective scholarship shortly. Boas then tees up the Kamloops case as a cautionary tale, going on to say the following:

> The problem with the story was that there was no evidence of bodies, a group of 12 Canadian academics, including Rouillard, said. "This is the biggest fake news story in Canadian history . . . They have come to believe things for which there is no evidence and it's taken on a life of its own."

This is where he leans heavily on the *New York Post* article. The one that says there's no evidence of bodies because nobody has dug them up yet. That doesn't mean they aren't there, of course—it just means nobody has dug them up yet.

I'll be honest, I don't want the job if or when those excavations do occur, and I can't imagine anyone who's itching to take it. Not among professionals with what I'll guardedly call a sense of humanity, anyway. In the summer of 2023, *CBC News* reported on how "residential school denialists" tried to dig up suspected unmarked grave sites at Kamloops in the middle of the night to "see for themselves" if there are children buried there. Responding to the incident, independent special interlocutor Kimberly Murray remarked how denialism is "the last step in genocide."

No word on whether these scumbags were charged with criminal trespassing, but last I saw Canadian Minister of Justice David Lametti is considering outlawing residential school denialism in the same way criminal and civil measures are used against people who deny or condone the Holocaust. Fingers crossed.

Meanwhile, the utility of archaeology in cases like these does not start and stop with the literal digging of holes in the ground. In many ways the history of archaeology, both here and abroad, can be summarized as an evolution of magnitude. It began with an intense and monocular focus on artifacts, because those could be boxed up and shipped to museums. Over time, however, the focus gradually split toward two disparate levels of magnification: very tiny stuff like atoms and molecules, which can be used for things like dating or sourcing materials, or for recreating past climates and diets; and very large stuff like settlements, communities, and cultural landscapes. Artifacts—and human remains—are in the middle of that spectrum, and a growing chorus of modern archaeologists call for molesting them as little as possible.

To that end, the use of ground-penetrating radar to conduct remote sensing at archaeological sites to determine what, if anything, lies beneath the ground surface is still in its infancy but shows a tremendous amount of promise. The folks from *Time Team America* used a GPR at my field school in Range Creek back in 2008 to bemused applause when it couldn't tell the difference between a pithouse and a burned tree root, but that was almost twenty years ago. It's gotten better since then.

The use of GPR in remote sensing of unmarked graves at Indian residential schools has thus far been invaluable. Limitations in the method mean that a lot of what may appear to be unmarked graves could indeed be something entirely else (see example above), and at this point inarguable certainty could only be obtained by verifying the results through old-fashioned shovel work. But technology tends to improve over time when research and design teams have a reason to make it do so.

We could disturb what are very likely those children's final resting places in a rough and destructive way, in other words—like the fools mentioned already tried to do. Or we could just wait a bit longer while GPR sensors become more refined and effective as non-destructive archaeological tools. I vote for option two.

◆ ◆ ◆

In all these cases, on all these continents, these places were hellish environments. Although not technically concentration camps, the Indian schools were nonetheless places where large groups of people who hadn't been convicted of any crimes were forced to live in cramped and horrendous conditions simply because of their ethnicity. Physical and sexual abuse was rampant, and in the case of Indian residential schools it was also very common for kids to get severely punished just for speaking their own language.

Archaeology can shed light on these and other historical atrocities to impart some measure of humanity to people who are otherwise relegated to a dot on a historical timeline, helping to paint a more accurate portrait of history while—hopefully—helping survivors and descendants deal with the resulting intergenerational trauma. It can also be used to help Indigenous people reconnect with their own history in cases where it was truncated by colonialism. That, in turn, could potentially be of tremendous benefit to us all.

In 2010, University of Utah archaeologist Lisbeth Louderbeck—then a museum curator at the Natural History Museum of Utah; now a professor—noticed what appeared to be potato starch on stone tools from an excavated site near the small town of Escalante. Three years later, with the help of Red Butte Gardens Director of Conservation Bruce Pavlik, the team were able to identify the starch as that of *Solanum jamesii* or the Four Corners potato. They did so by finding live plants growing about a football field away from the site.

It's a tiny tuber that grows wild in the Escalante area and elsewhere on the Colorado Plateau, but this was the first time it was positively identified in an archaeological context—one that stretched back at least eleven thousand years.

Lisbeth and her colleague, along with a growing team of researchers, hadn't by any means discovered the tuber. It was an ancestral food source for numerous Indigenous groups throughout the region, including the Hopi, Diné, Apache, and Southern Paiute Tribes—among others. But she and her team had *rediscovered* it.

The potato grows as abundant little balls of starch about the size of a marble, full of flavor and surprisingly dense with nutrients for such a small thing, but they only fill out their tubers during the abundant rains of the summer monsoon season—which means they only produce food within a narrow window of time each year. Meanwhile, the convergent processes of industrialization, subsidizing of cash crops like white potatoes, efforts by government and church officials to stamp out Indigenous foodways along with every other aspect of Indigenous culture, and the plain fact that Indigenous communities were almost all driven from their ancestral homes caused the Four Corners potato to disappear entirely from their plates.

This is a sad but common occurrence throughout the colonized world. Bannock bread, for example, is a variety of flatbread or quick bread made from flour, baking powder, sugar, lard, and milk, all of which you'll notice are white in color. Keep that in mind. It's regarded as the most universal food item in Indigenous Canadian cooking, and most of the recipes you'll find online even refer to it as Native or Indian bannock. It's a type of frybread associated almost universally with Indigenous cultures within the boundaries of our neighbor country to the north. That should set alarm bells ringing, because almost nothing else is "universal" among the cultures of practically any region of that size, Indigenous or not.

Tech journalist Dan Olson, in a video he produced in 2021 poking fun at the culturally insensitive nature of a lot of cooking videos, notes how it occurs in Native cultures "from the high Arctic to the Pacific coast, over the Great Plains, through the Canadian Shield, to the Maritimes on the East because its ingredients reflect the standard government rations packages that were available after Tribes were forced off their ranging lands and into the reserve system in the late 1800s."

It's true here, too. The so-called Indian frybread found throughout the United States has the exact same base ingredients—flour, sugar, lard, milk—and for the very same reason. And yes, the fact that those ingredients are all white in color is not an accident. The philosophy that "whiteness equals godliness" was a pervasive one for an embarrassingly long time.

Many of today's Indigenous groups no longer practice the traditional foodways of their ancestors because those ties to their past were severed. It's a shame for many reasons but, regarding the Four Corners potato, it's a daunting shame because they can grow under very dry conditions, a thing that cannot be said for white potatoes or any of the other global cash crops—namely rice, soybeans, wheat, and the dominant industrial varieties of corn. According to Diné journalist Alastair Lee Bitsóí reporting on testimony from scientists at the University of Utah and the Indigenous food activists with whom they work, the spud "can stay dormant for years under dry conditions, still offering nutritional benefits like iron and zinc to humans." And climate conditions in North America appear to be tipping toward the very dry, for some reason . . .

Alastair used to work with Utah Diné Bikéyah, the nonprofit nucleus group of the Bears Ears National Monument proposal before the Coalition assumed leadership of the effort. Because of my involvement and support in that endeavor, we got a chance to meet at a large fundraiser in Salt Lake City in 2019 where they served these tiny spuds, along with other Indigenous foods that are actually traditional. They're delicious. A bit more peanut-y than white potatoes.

Rather than publish their findings in some obscure academic journal and move on to the next shiny thing, Lisbeth and her team got together with Indigenous researchers, farmers, and community advocates to attempt to bring the Four Corners potato back into Indigenous gardens throughout the Southwest. The Utah Diné Bikéyah Potato Cultivation Project, within the aegis of their Traditional Foods Program, has largely headed up the non-academic part of the reintroduction effort.

It turns out the Escalante Valley where the find occurred used to be called Potato Valley, according to Lisbeth in an interview she did with Suzi Montgomery and Sheri Quin for *Utah Public Radio*, but "most people don't know that, even though that was kind of their recent history." Likewise, a lot of Indigenous people with whom she spoke had no idea about the Four Corners potato. A few of the elders did, but not in terms of current practice so much as tales of the olden days.

Efforts like these to revitalize ancient foodways are popping up all over the country as part of a growing Indigenous Food Sovereignty movement, which seeks to reconnect modern communities with the crops and practices that worked best in this hemisphere for millennia prior to 1492. Archaeological tools and tricks are especially handy for that sort of work.

◆ ◆ ◆

There's a similar case of a vanished plant in Europe that plays a captivating and, honestly, sort of hilarious counterrhythm to the Four Corners Potato tale. Silphium is an unidentified plant that was used in ancient times as a food seasoning, a medicine, a perfume, and—this is where the trouble starts—for various sexual purposes. It was considered an effective aphrodisiac and contraceptive by the ancient Greeks and Romans, among many others.

Because of this, silphium was a crucial trade item with the North African city of Cyrene where it grew in abundance. So crucial, in fact, that most of their coins bore an image of either the whole plant or its rather uniquely shaped seed pods. The Egyptians and the Knossos Minoans both thought the plant was important enough to warrant its own special hieroglyphs. It is believed to have been in the fennel family, although no samples exist to verify this. It was reportedly delicious, smelled lovely to the point of intoxicating, and could cure or help with dozens of ailments—but its most important uses were sexual. Many of the gold and silver Cyrenean coins that bore a depiction of silphium also bore an image of a seated woman pointing toward her genitals. The message was clear: this stuff lets you have all the sex, and may even help with the process itself, with a minimal risk of pregnancy.

Whatever it was, the plant had seed pods that bore the shape of what we now consider the default symbol for the heart: a double-scalloped ideogram with a V-shaped base, or a "triangle with boobs" as my friend's toddler once described it. A great number of scholars think that's no coincidence.

There are, admittedly, numerous plants with heart-shaped leaves, including philodendron, cyclamen, anthurium or laceleaf, and of course aspen and cottonwood trees. None of those were ever considered such important trade items that they were stamped into coins during antiquity, though. Nor were any of them strongly associated with sexuality in the ancient world—or at least not the ancient European world. There's some debate about this, but a lot of historians think the shape of silphium's seed pod and its importance in sexual health is the very reason we ended up with the now-iconic symbol of a heart that really, when you get right down to it, doesn't look anything like an actual heart. The most likely reason is that it's not supposed to refer to a literal heart at all. It's supposed to reference a plant the founders of Western culture basically considered the gods' way of encouraging sex for pleasure.

With that last point in mind, it took just seven centuries after the plant was first described by Classical scholars growing along the coast of modern-day Libya for it to disappear—a remarkably short time for humans to drive something to extinction without industrial help. "Just one stalk has been found," waled Roman chronicler Pliny the Elder in his first-century *Natural History*, "and it has been given to the Emperor Nero." It's regarded by a number of historians as the first documented case of extinction because of human activities and has been used as a cautionary tale for this reason.

Never mind volumes, this story speaks sagas about human nature.

However, as recently as 2023, publications began to circulate suggesting that a professor and his team in Turkey may have found silphium specimens surviving on Mount Hasan. The plant in question, a giant fennel called *Ferula dudeana*, appears to have anti-inflammatory and possibly even anti-cancer properties, according to a writeup in *National Geographic.* They haven't found much hard evidence to suggest it has either aphrodisiac or contraceptive qualities, so the jury is still out on that—but there are clues that it might indeed retain those properties as well.*

As with the Four Corners potato story, topmost among implications for this is the utility it could offer in the face of things like climate change and mono-cropping. Ethnobotanists like Mark J. Plotkin often lament that medical researchers aren't really looking for new families of antibiotics anymore, since the ones we've got seem to work well most of the time and, anyway, it just makes better fiscal sense to research things like Viagra or antidepressants that people will potentially buy and consume for many years. The irony of the perfect medicine is that it's a medicine you should only have to take once.

The American chestnut blight understandably got people scared about mono-cropping trees for rubber in the early 1900s, prompting Richard Evans Schultes—Plotkin's mentor—to pioneer the modern study of ethnobotany when he went into the jungle searching for alternative rubber-producing plants. He emerged years later with a short list of alternatives, as well as an extensive knowledge of psychedelic drugs that sent everyone's heads spinning for a generation.

Schultes' dogged research and overtly friendly willingness to live and work with Indigenous people caused him to rediscover ololiuqui, an Aztec narcotic made from the seeds of a climbing vine; and, of much greater relevance to Americans, to rediscover another Aztec intoxicant called teonanácatl or "flesh of the gods." We know the latter today as psylocibin or "magic" mushrooms. Ongoing research—when it isn't hampered by draconian drug laws—suggests that psychotropics like these have amazing curative properties for treating things like PTSD and addiction.

These plants, along with silphium and Four Corners potatoes, offer what may be some of the best chances we've got to deal with

* To be clear, extinction is an irreversible condition. Despite what some science-fiction authors, a small number of uninformed journalists, and at least one openly evil and corrupt Secretary of the Interior seem to believe, it is not currently possible to bring dead things from the past back to life and probably never will be. What we can do is muster as many resources as possible to try to preserve any stalwart stragglers found hiding in the shadows after the extinction-causin event has passed.

whatever is coming next. Central to all these and similar cases, however, is the problem of who controls access to, interpretation of, and communication about history and heritage in the post-colonial world.

◆ ◆ ◆

We look at everything through the lenses of our own understanding.

That is not to say I subscribe to the extreme solipsists who think nothing is actually real because it's all the product of our own senses translating vibrations, but whatever. That's putting Descartes before the horse.

Given the plain and obvious fact of a shared physical reality, people nonetheless perceive that reality in terms of an internal built environment, the "built" part having been done primarily by their upbringing and experiences. The best people to investigate and interpret their own material history are therefore the descendent communities of the people who made it. Their history and culture contain teachings, beliefs, practices, and general knowledge and information that outside groups don't possess.

Having recapped a few chapters ago the heinously unethical mtDNA study conducted on skeletal material from Chaco Canyon in 2017, I'm happy to present its counterpoint. In the spring of 2025, mere days before I was finished acting as professional editor for this manuscript's final round of review, a study was published in the prestigious journal *Nature* in which members of Picuris Pueblo in New Mexico teamed up with Western archaeologists on a collaborative study on the very same topic. Input from traditional knowledge keepers and oral histories were combined with laboratory work by University of Copenhagen evolutionary geneticist Eske Willerslev to help "fill gaps in their tribal history using genetic data," according to a summary piece in *Science News*.

With permission and support from the Tribe, the team—which consisted of twenty-one credited authors, including additional researchers from Copenhagen, Texas, Britain, France, and Brazil, as well as Picuris Pueblo—analyzed DNA from sixteen individuals interred at Picuris Pueblo about half a thousand years ago. Thirteen current tribal members also provided blood samples. All this was then combined with genetic data from Chaco Canyon, along with a few other locales, and submitted to analysis. And the results are pretty unambiguous: there's Chaco Canyon ancestry at Picuris Pueblo.

The importance of this study is twofold. First, there's the myth of the Vanishing Indian, which in this case hovers around Chaco Canyon like a fly around feces, floating atop the argument that Chaco's collapse led to a total abandonment of the surrounding region. Because the extant Pueblo cultures are so different from the state-level stratification and other components associated with the Chaco phenomenon, they must have arrived in the region sometime afterward, and their claims of ancestral affiliation are therefore just hot air. It's safe to assume no ethical or rational person ever believed this, and it was always a political expedient for disenfranchising them from the political process, but in any case this study proves that it was always bullshit.

Second, it underscores not only the ethical and moral value but the literal academic value of collaboration with the people whose history you're trying to reconstruct. I've mentioned over and over how the best way to understand the deep history of the Americas is to put down the calculator and prey-choice models (or at least put them in your back pocket for a moment) and talk to the people whose ancestors lived that history.

David Hust Thomas, currently with the American Museum of Natural History and one of our most prolific living archaeologists, remarked that this was "a landmark project" in a research domain dominated by controversy. Northern Arizona University professor Kellam Throgmorton added to the discussion on social media by calling the study a much-needed jab for all the teams doing the same sort of work without any Indigenous involvement.

We have a long way yet to go, we archaeologists. But we've also come a long way already.

◆ ◆ ◆

In a 2024 article, a team of researchers led by the anarcho-archaeologist Black Trowel Collective published an article in *American Anthropologist* called "Archaeology in 2022: Counter-myths for hopeful futures." Underpinning the handful of topics they address is the persistence of four myths that continue to bedevil the field:

1. Archaeology is a neutral and objective exercise;
2. Humans are selfish, competitive, and power-hungry;
3. The current societal order was and is inevitable; and
4. Things will inevitably be better (or worse) in the future.

The second one is the most common fallacy in bottom-up theories of human behavior rooted in mathematical studies of ecology that hold as given ideas like women are always gatherers, men are always hunters, and people in general only care about themselves and maybe their immediate relatives. This is probably the easiest of all to debunk by simply sitting back and looking around. We got here because we're a cooperative species. This is why notions like "ancient women focused entirely on taking care of their own offspring" or "ancient men only hunted in order to show off" are downright laughable. American individualism cast backwards in time as if that could somehow explain the massive communal efforts that led to the modern condition in the first place.

The third and fourth topics are syncretic cartoons. Anyone who thinks history leads invariably toward the present hasn't yet heard how the likes of Henri Poincaré and Niels Bohr showed that determinism isn't even a fixed state in material physics, let alone in something so complicated as billions of human minds bouncing off one another. Anyone who thinks modern science will eventually provide all the answers to problems like climate change or the increasing threats of racist nationalism, or that modern science will eventually reduce all of human civilization to a smoking crater, has been watching too many Hollywood blockbusters. Either of those contingencies is possible, but neither of them is inevitable.

That first one, though . . .

Archaeologists invariably engage in interpretation, to one extent or another. Even a purely descriptive statement like "the ancient structure is four meters by three meters and constructed of two courses of dry-laid unshaped local rhyolite cobbles" is crafted by, and for, an audience who thinks in terms of ancientness, structures, meters, and rhyolite—all four of which are words the original builders definitely never heard. This is an aspect of the postmodern critique of anthropological archaeology, which likes to pretend that it's an entirely scientific and, therefore, totally *objective* practice.

This obsession with objectivity is not inherently unwarranted, given how technical science can't exactly happen if the scientists doing the research have very strong opinions about the outcome. It's just that total objectivity is impossible when you really think about it. Even the decision to conduct a supposedly objective investigation in the first place was a choice that someone made when they could have chosen to do something else. It's even worse in the soft sciences like archaeology because then you've got people investigating people. Both sides of the research dichotomy—the investigator and the investigated—have their own thoughts and opinions and perspectives, and squaring the two while aiming for an accurate depiction told only in the language of one of them can be tricky to say the very least.

Moreover, near-total objectivity when dealing with human things can be downright dangerous. Historians investigating the rise of fascism in Italy and Germany in the early 1900s are often quick to point out how the media—and, in particular, the liberal media—failed to foment any real resistance because they were too busy both-sides-ing the issue. Gotta maintain that journalistic distance, after all. The tradition of framing interactions between clear villains and clear victims as mere disagreements between two groups of varying beliefs is by no means a modern invention.

In his book *Language in Thought and Action*, S.I. Hayakawa even argues that neutral reporting is crucial for the health of a democracy, pitting it squarely against the "propaganda" of the Nazis. This is often a primer for people studying journalism, and there is some sense to it, but that sense starts to waver when coverage is suspiciously even-handed about uneven events. When terrorists from one nation kill a handful of people in a neighboring nation and the response is full-blown genocide, for example, taking the "good people on both sides" approach is nothing short of treacherous. Balanced neutrality in the face of such an unbalanced atrocity softens a blow that really needs to be hard.

This is an example of when the cure's what ails you.

Hunter S. Thompson had something like this in mind when he invented gonzo journalism, generally defined as a style of journalism that is written without any aspirations toward objectivity. It's the reporting of factual details from a nonetheless unabashedly human perspective, no matter how blurry and crazed that perspective might be. I can't bring myself to believe this wouldn't also be immensely beneficial for humanistic research domains like archaeology, where objectivity is both functionally impossible and downright dehumanizing.

Fanatical attempts to chase the dragon of total objectivity have also been utilized for some pretty nefarious ends in their own right. For instance: when discussing the fallacy of biological determinism as a means of assigning value to people based on their inherent distinctions (the technical definition of racism), Stephen Jay Gould laments in his book *The Mismeasure of Man* how such determinists "often invoked the traditional prestige of science as objective knowledge, free from social and political taint." He believes that to be true about as much as I do, and goes on to ponder how "science, since people must do it, is a socially embedded activity . . . Much of its change does not record a closer approach to absolute truth, but the alteration of cultural contexts that influence it so strongly."

In other words, broad cultural trends or specific political aims can influence scientific endeavors as much as they influence everything else that we do—again, even choosing which topic to investigate in the first place is *de facto* a decision biased by the circumstances precipitating it. But most other endeavors don't provide people with the handy flak jacket of claiming those endeavors are totally objective and therefore simply don't care about your feelings.

Much of the criticism of the ridiculous 1994 book *The Bell Curve: Intelligence and Class Structure in American Life*, in which authors Charles A. Murray and Richard Hernstein attempt to breathe new life into eugenics, broke against the rocks of a public that hasn't been properly schooled on scientific objectivity—thereby giving the authors and their supporters ammunition to claim that everyone needs to just accept that the data doesn't care about their feelings. Gould's *Mismeasure*, originally released in 1980, was rereleased in 1996 with additional chapters showing how the problem with Murray and Hernstein's "data" isn't a problem of feelings so much as a problem of being categorically biased and outright incorrect horseshit in the first place.

Scientists on the whole may or may not agree with Gould's critique of the problem of scientific objectivity as individuals, but historians of science know it to be a bedrock truth. Objective reality may indeed be a thing but emotional, opinionated, propagandized animals studying it in pure objectivity simply isn't. Especially when what they're studying is others of their own kind. Imagine a sentient tape measure with strong feelings about inches being tasked with measuring itself.

The dangers inherent in this are legion, but the biggest one is the bulwark it provides against criticism of harmful ideologies. Fascists and other ideologues often take a syncretic approach to their messaging, utilizing aspects of anything from microchemistry to astrology if it helps their message reach more people—hence the Nazis' embrace of both science (such as it was) and pseudoarchaeology. The important part is the conclusion the audience reaches, not the means by which it's packaged to them. To quote journalist Dan Olson again, "one of the main mechanisms of propaganda is to plant the idea of precedence, to alter the audience's own sense of history and the world, and appeal to the seemingly objective authorities of God, History, and Science."

It's the old fallacy of appeal to authority, but in this case the authority is objectivity. Be wary of both.

◆ ◆ ◆

This obsession with objectivity or objective neutrality also leads anthropologists to search for what is, in their totally unbiased opinions, the most "pristine" (read: untouched by civilization) case studies they can find. In a 1992 article for *American Anthropologist*, Richard Lee points out how the anthropological study of hunter-gatherer or forager groups represents anthropologists' obsession with the "search for the primitive," a quote he attests to earlier anthropologist Stanley Diamond. He notes how some people regard this as the thing about anthropology that makes it unique in the human sciences.

His review also mentions how growing numbers of anthropologists find this idea anachronistic, given how primitiveness is a relative and "arbitrary construction of the disembodied 'other' divorced from history and context." Anthropology, Lee contends, has never formally defined itself as either a particularizing historical discipline interested in understanding given cultures, or a generalizing nomothetic search for broad-spectrum answers about the human condition as a whole. Boas and his ilk would lean toward the former. Anthropological archaeologists, rather infuriatingly, tend to lean toward the latter.

On top of all that, just like there are no such things as pristine wilderness in the world, so there are no such things as pristine cultures. The most isolated known group in the world, the people of North Sentinel Island, still contend with the occasional moronic missionary—they dispatched one named John Allen Chau just a few years ago—as well as making sense of planes flying overhead, fish populations declining, and how the climate seems to be going a bit wibbly-wobbly these days. The modern world touches everyone, to one extent or another, so why bother pretending it doesn't?

The Black Trowel gang invokes similar sentiments in their own critique of the field. They note how other scholars, like Professor Donna Hallaway, regard the separation of the past from the present as a "frontier myth" that inhibits people's abilities to build powerful relations that extend across space and time. The past is an undiscovered country, waiting to be explored and plundered, and maybe offering a few lessons for the present. We are unbiased observers from the present looking through pure and unclouded lenses at that far-flung and unknown land with nothing to guide us but our technical prowess—if you ignore all the biases and heavy clouding on the lenses and the voices of people whose oral histories could draw you a pretty good map of the place.

Nobody has any idea what comes next. We're creating future archaeology every day, so whatever does come next will likely include a lot of very confused researchers wondering what a shake weight was used for. But the past is fixed—even if interpretations of it are not—and the best means of interpreting it are through lenses of understanding that are most closely related to it. If total objectivity isn't really possible, and we're trying to construct an accurate narrative about aspects of the human past, it only makes sense to include human voices with the deepest roots in that past no matter how unscientific their perspectives might be.

For reasons like this, growing numbers of individuals and groups are advocating for Indigenous archaeology as an alternative to American archaeology, at least with regard to Indigenous material history. These are the folks with the greatest stores of knowledge about what that material history represents, as well as the greatest stores of living memory about the environmental contexts in which it occurs. Hence the growing chorus of support for Indigenous-led management of public lands, an experiment currently under way at Bears Ears and Baaj Nwaavjo I'tah Kukveni—Ancestral Footprints of the Grand Canyon National Monuments, as well as several smaller cases where Tribes and federal agencies are engaging in co-management of areas and sites throughout the country.

◆ ◆ ◆

Collaborative work in the broader realm of American archaeology also includes a lot of linguistic alteration, arguably for the better in just about all cases. One of Deb Haaland's earliest initiatives after being sworn in as Interior Secretary was to enact legislation (specifically Secretary's Order 3404) creating the Derogatory Geographic Names Task Force that compelled federal agencies to work with Indigenous groups, historians, and archaeologists to seek and replace offensive place names for geographic and archaeological locations.

Further recommendations included revisions to NAGPRA and the NHPA Section 106 consultation process that requires agencies to begin government-to-government consultation on projects likely to affect heritage resources at the start of the process rather than at the end, where it feels more like an afterthought or a final effort to check an annoying box.

Among the revisions to NAGPRA already enacted as of 2024 is closing of the loophole that allowed the Chaco mtDNA and a few other studies of looted materials on the grounds that they were too old to establish legally defined cultural affiliation. Specifically, wording like "preponderance of evidence" was replaced with "clearly" or "reasonably" evidentiary standards; and cultural affiliation as a function of "reasonable connection between human remains or cultural items" was expanded to include traditional cultural knowledge in addition to scientific evidence. Going forward, we can reasonably expect to see fewer photos of looted jewelry on the cover of *American Antiquity.*

Implications of these changes are already being felt in the Indigenous community. While sitting on a recent panel discussion about the sharing of information between institutions and agencies within the state of Arizona, Gila River Indian Community archaeological compliance specialist Larry Benallie, Jr., noted how archaeological consultants are starting to revise their chronologies to show continuity from "prehistoric" to historic and into modernity. "They never used to do that," he remarked. "Archaeologists always drew a clear line between prehistoric and historic. Based on the day they decided history had started."

Nonetheless, Larrie felt compelled to touch on how much work still needs to be done, how words have power, and how the wrong words can have an "adverse effect" [pause for laugher]* on history. How we talk about people, places, and things has a definite impact on how we perceive them, after all. There's a big difference between

* "Finding of adverse effect" is the technical term used in NHPA and NEPA investigations when they conclude that an undertaking may alter, directly or indirectly, any of the characteristics of a heritage resource that make it historically, scientifically, and/or culturally significant.

how we treat "animals" and "varmints" despite them being the very same thing, and there's a comparable difference between how we perceive history through varying linguistic lenses.

Because history is not just a bunch of stuff that happened in the past. History is a living thing. And living things can be mistreated.

◆ ◆ ◆

On that note, the problem of misrepresentation of archaeology in popular culture probably isn't going anywhere, and something tells me the proliferation of social media and large language models isn't going to make the situation any better. Just this morning (i.e., early 2025), the oft-mentioned Jonathan Bailey sent me *yet another* screenshot from a Facebook group festooned with AI-generated images showing all the wonderful ancient marvels one can find in Saguaro National Park—up to, and including, what appear to be enormous Egyptian hieroglyphs carved into what appear to be giant rucked-up carpets of rock with a scattering of both saguaros and ponderosas poking out of them.

These, like such ludicrous and unconscionable claims as the Sandy Hook school shooting being a hoax, are intended to generate interaction. That's it. Whether your engagement is positive or negative doesn't matter, they just want you to engage so you'll also see their ads and hopefully buy their crap. That's how all grifters work. They scream bombastic or scary or exciting or crazy things to get attention in the hopes that this attention brings purchases, or upvotes, or literal votes. It doesn't matter if what they're saying is in any way correct, and in fact the more outlandish it is the more likely people will flock to see the spectacle.

Scams are certainly nothing new. That's true even in an archaeological sense. One of the oldest surviving cuneiform tablets, dating to just shy of four thousand years old, is a letter by a trader named Nanni complaining that a merchant named Ea-nāṣir had falsely represented the quality of his copper ingots.*

About a thousand years later, two Greek sea merchants named Hegestratos and Zenosthemis concocted a plan to enrich them-

* This story is so well-known by now it's become a popular meme on Reddit.

selves by taking out an insurance policy on their ship and cargo. According to the agreement, they were required to repay the loan with interest after successfully selling their merchandise or else the lender would possess their ship. The intrepid grifters decided to just sink the ship in the hopes of keeping the loan and the money from the marketed cargo. Instead, Hegestatos drowned in the process and Zenosthemis was punished by the Athenian courts.

Another millennium or so and an ocean away, in the Aztec empire—or, more accurately, the Mixtec Alliance—cacao seeds were employed as a form of currency. Ten seeds got you a sack of corn flour, fifty got you a jaguar pelt, that sort of thing. Hilariously, if unsurprisingly, both oral histories and archaeological findings document widespread counterfeiting. Pebbles, carved wood and avocado pits, and even dried animal droppings were used by swindlers to bulk up their cacao seed larders. People gonna people.

Modern online and streaming equivalents include engagement farming, or the act of doing whatever it takes to get people to look at your content so it spreads ever further—along with the ads smeared all over it. Archaeology is as much a victim of this as any other domain or discipline.

The way consumers can beat that system is by ignoring it altogether. The way archaeologists can beat that system is by offering equally compelling and entertaining alternatives that also happen to be factual.

Given that government regulation appears unwilling to manifest itself in cases like these, of the two best options listed above I would rather people not ignore archaeology. It's informative, it's exciting, and in a lot of cases it's the primary means of protecting things and places that are culturally important or even sacred. It can be used to shore up gaps in history, to help people reclaim history that was hidden or stolen from them, and it can provide potential answers for how to navigate stochastic political and climatological ballyhoos.

It's important, in other words. Which means it's on us as archaeologists to offer alluring alternatives to the sludge. Entertainment as a preservation tactic, in other words. And we're doing that. Slowly—but we are.

A fantastic documentary about Neanderthal archaeology, narrated by Sir Patrick Stewart, hit screens not long before I finished this manuscript. A controversial one about *Homo naledi* predated it by a couple years, and despite some rather gaping holes in the research and its associated confidence intervals it was still mostly well-received by all but the most uppity of academics. Add to that shows like the Becoming Human series and others in its vein and things are starting to look rather promising.

Perhaps even better was a recent National Geographic series called *Lost Cities* with Albert Lin, where the titular character travels around bringing cutting-edge technology to address data gaps—can't see through the trees, that sort of thing—around some of the most interesting archaeological complexes in the world. What impresses me the most about Dr. Lin, apart from his being an Asian American professor with a prosthetic leg, is the willingness and respect he shows when engaging with local Indigenous knowledge keepers. He even takes part in traditional ceremonies intended to ask the ancestors' permission before approaching their resting places—up to and including consumption of intense narcotics.*

These and a steadily growing number of other examples work because they operate on a principle a lot of those same uppity academics either don't know or don't care about: people don't want data. People want stories. It's literally baked into our evolutionary history. We spent millennia listening to thrilling tales that carried important messages about living life or finding resources—the true function of myth—not staring at reams of befuddling word salad. That part is necessary for the conducting of technical research. The part that's necessary for engaging the public is narrative.

Examples like these all take place outside the United States, unfortunately—and it's easy to see why. The near totality of the deep history of the Americas is Indigenous, while recent history and modernity are both dominated by Western paradigms, and it's the

* That's just generally a good idea, by the way. Not the narcotics bit, unless you're also invited to take part in a traditional ceremony—but the bit about asking permission before approaching an archaeological site. A lot of my Indigenous colleagues are fine with non-Indigenous folks visiting the resting places of their ancestors provided they do so properly. I've included appendices on this topic that I hope readers find helpful.

latter who have all the privilege and resources necessary to create shows and documentaries. That doesn't mean it's impossible to tell a compelling story about integrative or collaborative archaeology that includes Indigenous American input, but it's tricky.

Time Team America tried bringing depictions of actual—if somewhat bombastic—field archaeology that at least included one or two Indigenous perspectives to American audiences in the late 2000s. They even filmed an episode at my field school in Range Creek, and if you watch closely you can see me trying very hard to avoid the camera. But it didn't really land with viewers.

So, for the moment, we're mostly stuck with a polarized range of perspectives in terms of mainstream American depictions of archaeology: impenetrably gated academese on one end, and racist clickbait pseudoscience garbage on the other. The solution to this problem is not somewhere in the middle. The solution isn't on that spectrum at all. The solution is factual storytelling, involving both scientific and traditional knowledge, that's entertaining enough to hold people's interest. It's the last card we've got to play, but it's also the most powerful card in the deck.

◆ ◆ ◆

When all is said and done, the study of the past in the United States has a bit of a troubled past. Rooted as it is in a lot of unpleasant history, American archaeology has some unpleasant roots of its own. But they're also strong roots, comprising intellectual traditions that were oftentimes biased and sometimes outright prejudiced but were, above all, focused on satisfying people's curiosity about the past.

The nature of that history has changed considerably as the field itself—and the mentalities and beliefs of the people working within it—has evolved over time. The practice of American archaeology isn't done evolving, and it remains, above all, focused on satisfying people's curiosity about the past.

The field of medicine has acquainted us with the maxim *primum non nocere* or "first, do no harm." This phrase, anecdotally but not certainly credited to Hippocrates, was expanded upon by nineteenth-century surgeon Thomas Inman as "practice two things in dealings with disease: either help or do not harm the patient." That, too, should apply to the practice of archaeology in a country where the objects of inquiry are most often the material vestiges or literal ancestors of individuals who belong to groups quite different from that of the folks doing the inquiring.

So, do no harm. But also take no shit. Bad actors lurk in all realms like storybook trolls beneath the bridges we walk every day, bridges to work or to family and love or to belief or knowledge or entertainment, and their role is always the same: to send us down the wrong path. Spreading lies about history is a very effective way to sow a garden where lies about the present can grow. The ancient Romans knew this when they created an official history that legitimized some pretty ugly stuff, and that tradition hasn't gone away. Archaeologists are uniquely poised to fight this particular type of evil.

Remember also that public support is the most important element of what we do. Most archaeology in the US isn't happening in universities. It's being done by CRM firms as efforts to comply with legislation like Section 106 of the National Historic Preservation Act, which requires agencies to assess how their projects affect historic and archaeological sites. That's the backbone of American archaeology, not academic grants.

This regulatory framework is why we know about thousands of sites across the country. It's how we find, study, and seek to preserve things like Indigenous sites and cultural landscapes, Black settlements and cemeteries, Japanese and Chinese labor and internment camps, and American homesteads, battlefields, and buildings before the bulldozers get to them.

During 2025, that system was being not-so-quietly gutted.

Federal agencies began cutting NEPA and Section 106 review timelines, slashing or forcing out staff, and scaling back oversight—some by executive order, others through unspoken directives, and still others through good old neglect. Major development undertakings have been delayed, canceled, or pushed through—depending on how compatible they are with current regime policies—with little or no archaeological review. Our preservation infrastructure already has too narrow a focus, applying almost entirely to public lands, and it's being dismantled in real time under the aegis of "anti-DEI" legislation and an illegally created department of efficiency named for a cryptocurrency scam.

This isn't just about losing a bunch of really cool stuff that "belongs in a museum," to quote that guy with a whip and fedora. It's about theft of our collective past—not through neglect, but through deliberate policy.

Defense of America's long human history and the public lands on which most of it resides is one of the biggest battles we face today. Issues like climate change, social justice and equality, and even economic stability are rooted in the past and in the land. Few things fight climate change like robust forests. Few things inform civil policies like an understanding of the historical processes necessitating them. And few things generate more perpetual income with minimal adverse effects like tourism and recreation—especially when paired with respectful and effective management.

Indiana Jones and his onscreen shenanigans may be a flawed representation of real-world archaeological practices, but his Nazi-punching policy is not. That policy is one we need now more than ever, here in the United States of America. Be vigilant. Support the defenders. Protect the sacred and the vulnerable. Explore the past with a light touch and an eye to the future, where a lot of people with close ties to that past still dwell—do not dehumanize them in pursuit of objective truth, because it doesn't exist. There is only human truth.

And that's it. Have fun. Get your boots dirty. Come home with wild stories of historic wonders and a bobcat hanging off your arm. But do so respectfully, obtain permission first, and—whenever and wherever possible—work with or even for the peoples whose heritage you're working to investigate or preserve. Don't stop at just looking and describing. Work together toward reconstructing patches in our collective human drama where holes were cut by historic and modern injustices.

History is counting on us to help keep it alive.

EPILOGUE

In about 1300 BC, the founders of the Nineteenth Dynasty in Egypt set about tearing down all statues and erasing all other documentation of Pharoah Akhenaton and his wife, Nefertiti, rulers of the Eighth Dynasty from about 1350 to 1335 BC. His existence was all but lost to history until the rediscovery of Amarna by British archaeologists in the 1890s. About thirty years later, archaeologists rediscovered the tomb of Akhenaton and Nefertiti's immediate successor, Tutankhamun, whose existence had also been erased from official history by the same Nineteenth Dynasty leaders.

In about 200 BC, the first emperor of the Qin Dynasty—a fellow named Qin Shi Huang—ordered the burning of books and murdering of historical scholars in order to shore up his claim on total domination of the region. Books about the history of the Qin state were fine, but anyone found in possession of *The Book of Songs or Classic of History* was punished with special ferocity.

In the spring of 1933, students in thirty-four university towns across Germany burned an estimated twenty-five thousand books by order and encouragement of Nazi Minister of Propaganda Joseph Goebbels, who kept a growing list of books he considered "alien" or "decadent" for including things like accurate accounts of history. One year later, Josef Stalin began his Great Purge of everyone and everything he deemed a threat to the state. This included tasking people with retouching photographs so they would no longer accurately show the history they'd recorded—starting with Kamenev and Trotsky, and including alteration of the words on protest signs in photos of the October Revolution. This was before Photoshop or

AI tools existed so folks had to doctor them up the hard way.

In 1975, the long-simmering Khmer Rouge movement was taken over by Pol Pot in his rise to power following the Cambodian Civil War, and under his direction began widespread destruction of anything he deemed "corrupting." This included any vestiges of Western culture and influence, aspects of history he found distasteful, historians or other intellectuals that weren't sanctioned by the regime, and much else besides. Pol Pot murdered a couple million people to help achieve these ends, he banned all reading material apart from regime-produced content, principally in the form of a national newspaper that treated history the way Loony Toons cartoonists treated physics.

In 2014, the Islamic State or ISIS commenced wholesale destruction of cultural heritage throughout Iraq, Syria, and Libya. They targeted ancient and medieval artifacts, museums, libraries, religious buildings, and the like—destroying most of it and selling the rest on the international illicit antiquities market. In this regard they were following the path established in part by the Taliban, who bombed the immense statues of Buddha at Bamiyan back in 2001 as part of a massive effort to destroy any un-Islamic imagery and history by decree of supreme leader Mullah Mohammed Omar. This created a handy precedent for the state of Israel to do the same thing to Islamic cultural heritage during their invasion of the Gaza Strip starting in the fall of 2023.

One year later, in the fall of 2024, a majority of American voters elected Donald J. Trump to a non-consecutive second presidential term. He immediately tasked Elon Musk and his illegally created budgetary department with slashing government programs, including what amounted to taking a chainsaw to land management agencies. Trump also announced plans to roll back or altogether dissolve funding for anything even tangentially related to historic preservation, including a proposal to cut the National Historic Preservation Fund down to zero dollars and directing the Department of the Interior to review all educational materials, exhibits, books, posters, signs, and brochures to avoid what the administration calls "ideological bias." This new version of the McCarthy-era witch hunt on Un-American Activities emerged as a March 2025 executive order titled "Restoring Truth and Sanity to American History" in what strikes me as irony so thick you could drive trains over it.

Authoritarians hate real history, and destroying it is always one of their top priorities—right alongside stripping government programs and handing everything over to the private sector. The fascist parties in Germany and Italy both did this as well. This Nazi concept of *reprivatisierung* has been rebranded "reprivatization," and part of its justification, then as now, was that governments are historically inefficient and easily corruptible compared to private enterprise. Emphasis on "historically." That word does a lot of heavy lifting when the actual history of private enterprise is also altered, obscured, or destroyed.

For that very reason they also love supplementary evils like pseudoarchaeology, because it allows them to engage in pleonectic mythmaking to fill the hole where they've yanked the real history out. This is how we got cockamamie nonsense like the Aryan race, ancient aliens, white people having built all the mounds and temples of the ancient Americas before disappearing without a single trace, and . . . of course . . . Atlantis.

In the fall of 2023, for reasons lost to me now, I happened upon a rather startling revelation: according to the Library of Congress and every other source I could consult, there is no copyrighted book titled *American Archaeology*. There's a magazine by that name, which gets a mention at least once in this book, but no actual books. This looming gap was too inviting not to inspire someone like me to leap, and the good folks at Torrey House Press agreed. It would be about the "good, bad, and ugly" of the history and myths and realities of archaeology in the United States—only without that tired old adjective trifecta chained to its ankle.

After the reelected Trump announced—and then began acting upon—his plans to do the same thing as the Nazis, the Stalinists, ISIS, the Taliban, the Israeli Defense Forces, Nineteenth Dynasty Egyptians, Pol Pot, Qin Shi Huang, and basically every other fascist or authoritarian regime in "known" history I received a call from my publisher. Our fun little book about the sometimes grim and sometimes glorious day-to-day realities of American archaeology had quite suddenly assumed a new level of relevance.

The emphasis on history as a living thing was elevated to the forefront, along with the importance of public scholarship, because the former underscores how history is informed by human perspectives as much as it is by the material past and the latter is how we get people to care enough about that to want to defend it. History isn't a living thing in the sense that it eats and breathes, as I am wont to repeat *ad nauseum.* I mean living in the sense that it grows, changes, and evolves over time. It's a domain of narrative about the past that's created by human understanding—which also grows, changes, and evolves over time. It lives in the sense that it carries the breath of life we impart into it.

This is not exactly a novel concept, of course. The concept of history as a living thing is actually baked into the majority of Native American philosophies of which I'm aware. History isn't just the stuff that happened; it's something we create and give life through appreciation and reiteration, often in the forms of stories or songs or monuments but including things like archaeological sites, which people like the Hopi regard as living parts of their culture. What would truly be novel is if mainstream Americans began thinking about history and heritage the same way.

Our past creates our present and our present creates our future, to paraphrase every therapist I've ever met. Destruction of history in the service of present greed or power struggles puts the welfare of the future in increasing doubt. A human world built on a foundation of strong, healthy, living history is a bit like a garden planted in fertile soil, while a human world built on a foundation of lies and propaganda is like a garden planted on asphalt. Roots can't penetrate it. Water evaporates on it. Seeds blow away before they've even sprouted. The only thing left to do at that point is take a jackhammer to the bastard and start all over again.

It would be nice if we didn't have to keep doing that.

ACKNOWLEDGMENTS

The author is eternally indebted to Bill Lipe for his encouragement and mentorship, to Kris Stelter for her editing magic, to Glenn Stelter for knowing way more about Roman history than I do, to Scott Graham and Steve Lekson for reviewing extremely messy early drafts, to Ken Feder for reviewing a much better draft, to Kim Ryan for scrutinizing my history of preservation laws, to Lyle Balenquah and Louis Williams for introducing me to Indigenous wilderness guiding, to Jonathan Bailey and Morgan Sjogren for their constant feedback and companionship, and to Liz Hughes, Shayne Pfenning, Aaron O'Brien, Kate Sarther, Mike Walters, KC Carlson, Jojo Matson, Donna Baker, Kristy Torto, Sarrah Hannon, and Toulouse and Luna for helping to keep the wind in my sails during these turbulent times.

REFERENCES AND FURTHER READING

Sources presented in the order in which they appear in the text. Sources used in more than one chapter are not repeated.

CHAPTER ONE

Shott, M. J. (2005) Two cultures: thought and practice in British and North American archaeology. *World Archaeology*, 37(1), 1–10.

Suchman, Mark C. (2003) The Contract as Social Artifact. *Law and Society Review*, Volume 37, Number 1, 91–142.

Schuyler, R. L. (1971) The history of American archaeology: An examination of procedure. *American Antiquity*, 36(4), 383–409.

Wissler, Clark (1942) The American Indian and the American Philosophical Society. *American Philosophical Society Proceedings* 86:189–204

Strong, Wm. Duncan (1952) The value of archaeology in the training of professional anthropologists. *American Anthropologist* 54:318–321.

Willey, Gordon R. (1968) One hundred years of American archaeology. In *One hundred years of anthropology*, edited by J.0. Brew, pp. 29–53. Harvard University Press, Cambridge

Barnhart, T.A. (2015) *American antiquities: revisiting the origins of American archaeology*. U of Nebraska Press.

Dodson, A. (2012) *Afterglow of empire: Egypt from the fall of the New Kingdom to the Saite Renaissance*. Oxford University Press.

--- (2014) *Amarna sunrise: Egypt from golden age to age of heresy*. Oxford University Press.

Mark, Joshua J. (2017) Khaemweset. Electronic document, <https://www.worldhistory.org/Khaemweset/> accessed January 16, 2024

Lichtheim, M. (Ed.) (2019) *Ancient Egyptian Literature*. University of California Press.

Trigger, B.G. (1989) *A history of Archaeological Thought*. Cambridge University Press.

Gänger, Stefanie, Philip Kohl, and Irina Podgorny (2014) Introduction: Nature in the Making of Archaeology in the Americas. In *Nature and antiquities: the making of archaeology in the Americas*, edited by Kohl, P.L., Podgorny, I., & Gänger, S. University of Arizona Press.

Pocock, J.G.A. (2008) *Barbarism and Religion* (Vol. 4). Cambridge University Press.

Haggard, H. Rider (1885) *King Solomon's Mines*. Digitized by Project Gutenberg.

Locke, John (2022) *Second treatise of government*. DigiCat.

Axtell, James (1982) *The European and the Indian: Essays in the Ethnohistory of Colonial North America*. Oxford University Press, New York

Williams, R. (1997) *A Key into the Language of America*. Applewood Books.

Gaiman, Neil and Terry Pratchett (2011) *Good omens*. Random House.

Mancall, Peter (2021) The 'First Thanksgiving' Story Covers Up the All Too Real Violence in Early America. *Time*, November 24, 2021

Petersen, W. J. (1968) The Joliet-Marquette Expedition. *The Palimpsest*, *49*(10).

Jefferson, Thomas (1998) *Notes on the State of Virginia*. Penguin Publishing.

Aronsson, P., & Elgenius, G. (2014) *National Museums and Nation-building in Europe 1750-2010: Mobilization and legitimacy, continuity and change* (p. 226). Taylor & Francis.

Del Río, A. (1822) *Description of the Ruins of an Ancient City: Discovered Near Palenque, in the Kingdom of Guatemala, in Spanish America*. H. Berthoud, and Suttaby, Evance and Fox.

Headrick, Daniel R. (2000) *When information came of age: Technologies of knowledge in the age of reason and revolution, 1700-1850.* Oxford University Press.

Röhrs H. (1987) The classical idea of the university. In *Tradition and Reform of the University under an International Perspective: An Interdisciplinary Approach*, edited by Hermann Röhrs and Gerhard Hess. Verlag P. Lang, Switzerland.

Kollár, A.F. (1783) *Historiae Ivrisqve Pvblici Regni Vngariae Amoenitates.* Baumeister.

Jensen, O.W. (2004) Earthy Practice: Towards a History of Excavation in Sweden, in the 17th and 18th centuries. *Current Swedish Archaeology*, 61–82.

Gould, Stephen Jay (1996) *The Mismeasure of Man.* WW Norton & company.

Thomas, David Hurst (2001) *Skull wars: Kennewick Man, archaeology, and the battle for Native American identity.* Basic Books.

Parkinson, Robert G. (2021) *Thirteen Clocks: How Race United the Colonies and Made the Declaration of Independence.* University of North Carolina Press, Chapel Hill.

Amsden, Monroe (1928) *Archaeological Reconnaissance in Sonora.* Southwest Museum Papers, Number One.

Chapin, Frederick H. (2001) *The Land of the Cliff-Dwellers* Appalachian Mountain Club, W.B. Clarke and Company, Boston

CHAPTER TWO

McNitt, Frank (1966) *Richard Wetherill: Anasazi.* University of New Mexico Press.

Grant, Edward (1997) HISTORY OF SCIENCE: When Did Modern Science Begin? *The American Scholar*, *66*(1), 105–113.

Magner, L.N. (2003) A history of the life sciences. *Journal of the History of Biology*, *36*(2).

Gould, Stephen Jay (1999) Nonoverlapping Magisteria. *Skeptical Inquirer, July/August 1999.*

Gooch, Jason (2006) The Effects of the Condemnation of 1277. *The*

Hilltop Review, *2*(1), 6.

McGuire, Randall H. (1992) Archeology and the first Americans. *American anthropologist*, *94*(4), 816–836.

Lekson, Stephen H. (2018) *A Study of Southwestern Archaeology*. University of Utah Press.

--- (2009) *A History of the Ancient Southwest*. School for American Research Press.

O'Crouley, Pedro Alonso (1972) *A Description of the Kingdom of New Spain*. Allen Figgis, Dublin.

Eskildsen, K.R. (2019) Christian Jürgensen Thomsen (1788–1865): Comparing Prehistoric Antiquities. *History of Humanities*, *4*(2), 263–267.

Latham, R. (1951) *Lucretius on the Nature of the Universe*. Penguin Books.

Lubbock, John (1865) *Prehistoric Times*. Digitized by Google.

Lummis, Charles F. (1925) *Mesa, Cañon and Pueblo: Our Wonderland of the Southwest, Its Marvels of Nature, Its Pageant of the Earth Building, Its Strange Peoples, Its Centuried Romance*. Century Company.

Feder, Kenneth L. (1990) *Frauds, myths, and mysteries: science and pseudoscience in archaeology* (p. 231). Mountain View, California: Mayfield Publishing Company.

Zaitchik, Alexander (2024) How Pseudo-Archaeology and Phony Alt-History Rose to Popularity in the US *Observatory*, August 29, 2024.

Science Daily (2024) New research challenges hunter-gatherer narrative. *Science Daily*, January 24, 2024.

Lee, Richard Borshay (1979) *The! Kung San: Men, women and work in a foraging society*. Cambridge University Press.

Dahlberg, Frances, ed. (1981) *Woman the gatherer*. Yale University Press.

Aizenman, Nurith (2023) Men are hunters, women are gatherers. That was the assumption. A new study upends it. *NPR*, July 1, 2023.

Dash, Mike (2011) Dahomey's Women Warriors. *Smithsonian Magazine*, September 23, 2011.

Headland, Thomas N. (1991) Four Decades Among the Agta: Trials and Advantages of Long-Term Fieldwork With Philippine Hunter-Gatherers. Presented at the 90th Annual Meeting of the American Anthropological Association, Chicago, IL.

Time (1953) Science: End as a Man. *Time Magazine*, November 30, 1953.

Oakley, Kenneth P. and J.S. Weiner (1955) Piltdown Man. *American Scientist*, Vol. 43, No. 4, pp. 573–583.

Johnson, Daniel (2015) “Hard” Evidence of Ancient American Horses. *BYU Studies Quarterly*, *54*(3), 149–179.

Reséndez, Andrés (2016) *The Other Slavery: The Uncovered Story of Indian Enslavement in America*. Mariner Books.

National American Society, The (1913) *Americana*, Volume 8. Available from the University of Iowa.

Voltaire, Francois (2013) *Candide, or Optimism*. Penguin UK.

Lachtman, Gary (2012) *Madame Blavatsky: The Mother of Modern Spirituality*. Tarcher Perigee.

Purandare, V. (2021) *Hitler and India: the untold story of his hatred for the country & its people*. Westland Non-Fiction.

CHAPTER THREE

Paul, Kevin C. (1988) Private/Property: A Discourse on Gender Inequality in American Law. *Law & Inequality*, *7*, 399.

Junger, Sebastian (2016) *Tribe: On Homecoming and Belonging*. Twelve Books.

Gomez, Michelle (2023) Coastal GasLink fined $346K for erosion, sediment control issues and providing false information. *CBC News*, September 21, 2023

Pieratos, N.A., Manning, S.S., & Tilsen, N. (2021) Land back: A meta narrative to help Indigenous people show up as movement leaders. *Leadership*, *17*(1), 47–61.

Taylor, Alan (2001) *American Colonies: The Settling of North America*. Penguin Books.

Conover, Milton (1923) *The General Land Office: Its History, Activities, and Organization* (No. 13). Johns Hopkins Press.

Gates, Paul W. (1968) *History of public land law development* (Vol. 62).

US Government Printing Office.

Miller, R.J. (2019) The doctrine of discovery. *The Indigenous Peoples' Journal of Law, Culture, & Resistance*, 5, 35–42.

Stegner, Wallace (1992) *Beyond the hundredth meridian: John Wesley Powell and the second opening of the West.* Penguin.

Blackburn, Fred M. (2006) *The Wetherills: Friends of Mesa Verde.* Durango Herald Small Press.

Burrillo, R.E. (2020) *Behind the Bears Ears: Exploring the Cultural and Natural Histories of a Sacred Landscape.* Torrey House Press.

Coates, Ta-Nehisi (2009) Worst Movie of the Decade. *The Atlantic*, December 30, 2009.

Knipmeyer, James H. (2006) *In Search of a Lost Race: The Illustrated American Exploring Expedition of 1892.* Xlibris.

Judd, Neil M. (1968) *Men Met Along the Trail: Adventures in Archaeology.* University of Oklahoma Press.

Dellenbaugh, Frederick S. (1926) *A canyon voyage: the narrative of the second Powell expedition down the Green-Colorado River from Wyoming, and the Explorations on Land, in the years 1871 and 1872.* Yale University Press.

Meltzer, D.J. (1985) North American archaeology and archaeologists, 1879-1934. *American Antiquity, 50*(2), 249–260.

Dahl, Curtis (1961) Mound-Builders, Mormons, and William Cullen Bryant. *New England Quarterly*, 178–190.

Drell, Julia R. (2000) Neanderthals: A history of interpretation. *Oxford Journal of Archaeology, 19*(1), 1–24.

Thoreau, Henry David (2010) *The Maine Woods* (Vol. 22). Princeton University Press.

Gulliford, Andrew (1992) Curation and Repatriation of Sacred and Tribal Objects. *The Public Historian*, Volume 14, Issue 3.

The Maine Woods (Vol. 22). Princeton University Press.

Deloria, Jr., Vine (1988) *Custer died for your sins: An Indian manifesto.* University of Oklahoma Press.

Roberts, David (2010) *In Search of the Old Ones.* Simon and Schuster.

Wissler, C. (1923) *State Archaeological Surveys: Suggestions in Method and Technique.* National Research Council.

Patterson, L.W. (1988) Avocational Archaeology in The United States. *Plains Anthropologist, 33*(121), 377–384.

CHAPTER FOUR

Sheftel, Phoebe Sherman (1979) The Archaeological Institute of America, 1879-1979: A Centennial Review. *American Journal of Archaeology*, *83*(1), 3–17.

Fowler, Don D. (2000) *A Laboratory for Anthropology: Science and Romanticism in the American Southwest, 1846-1930.* University of New Mexico Press.

Sebastian, Lynne, and William D. Lipe, editors (2009) *Archaeology and Cultural Resource Management: Visions for the Future.* School for Advanced Research Press.

Altschul, Jeffrey H. (2005) Significance in American cultural resource management. In *Heritage of Value, Archaeology of Renown: Reshaping Archaeological Assessment and Significance*, edited by Jeffrey H. Altschul, 192–210. University of Florida Press.

Merrill, Marlene D. (Eds.) (2003) *Yellowstone and the Great West: journals, letters, and images from the 1871 Hayden Expedition.* University of Nebraska Press.

Morgan, Rachel (2023) *Sins of the Shovel: Looting, Murder, and the Evolution of American Archaeology.* University of Chicago Press.

Lipe, William D. (2012) Why Did We Do It That Way: The University of Utah Glen Canyon Project in Retrospect. In *Glen Canyon, Legislative Struggles, and Contract Archaeology: Papers in Honor of Carol Condie* (pp. 87–104). Archaeological Society of New Mexico.

Martin, Russell (1999) *A Story that Stands like a Dam: Glen Canyon and the Struggle for the Soul of the West.* University of Utah Press.

Reisner, Marc (1993) *Cadillac desert: The American West and its Disappearing Water.* Penguin.

Woodbury, Richard B. (1990) John Otis Brew, 1906–1988. *American Antiquity*, *55*(3), 452–459.

King, Thomas F. (2013) *Cultural Resource Laws and Practice.* Rowman & Littlefield.

--- (2002) *Thinking about Cultural Resource Management: Essays from the Edge.* Rowman Altamira.

Parker, Patricia L. (1993) Traditional Cultural Properties: What You

Do and How We Think. *CRM*, volume 16, Special Issue.

Romero, Farida Jhabvala (2015) Lake County Cracks Down on Looting of Native American Artifacts. *KQED*, September 21, 2015.

Reid, Nick, and Patrick Nunn (2015) Ancient Aboriginal stories preserve history of a rise in sea level. *The Conversation, 13.*

CHAPTER FIVE

Loewe, Michael (1971) Spices and silk: Aspects of world trade in the first seven centuries of the Christian era. *Journal of the Royal Asiatic Society, 103*(2), 166–179.

Hénaff, M. (1998) *Claude Levi-Strauss and the Making of Structural Anthropology.* University of Minnesota Press.

Hicks, Dan (2013) Four-field anthropology: Charter myths and time warps from St. Louis to Oxford. *Current Anthropology, 54*(6), 753–763.

Boas, Franz (2016) *The Central Eskimo.* Read Books Ltd.

Gillespie, Susan D., and Deborah L. Nichols, eds. (2003) *Archaeology is Anthropology.* American Anthropological Association.

Willey, Gordon R. and Philip Philips (1958) *Method and Theory in American Archaeology.* University of Chicago Press.

Binford, Lewis R. (1962) Archaeology as Anthropology. *American Antiquity, 28*(2), 217–225.

--- (2001) Where do Research Problems come From? *American Antiquity, 66*(4), 669–678.

Fagan, Brian M. (2006) *Archaeology and You.* Prentice Hall.

Carver, Martin Oswald Hugh (2017) *The Sutton Hoo Story: Encounters with early England.* Boydell & Brewer.

Beard, Mary (2016) *SPQR: A History of Ancient Rome.* Liveright.

Arnold, Kyle (2016) *The Divine Madness of Philip K. Dick.* Oxford University Press.

Wilson, E.O. (2000) *Sociobiology: The New Synthesis.* Harvard University Press.

Zahavi, Amotz, and Avishag Zahavi (1999) *The Handicap Principle: A Missing Piece of Darwin's Puzzle.* Oxford University Press.

Hill, Kim (2009) Animal "Culture"? In *The Question of Animal Culture*, edited by Kevin N. Laland and Bennett G. Galef. Harvard University Press, Cambridge.

Cortez, Amanda Daniela, Deborah A. Bolnick, George Nicholas, Jessica Bardill, and Chip Colwell (2021) An ethical crisis in ancient DNA research: Insights from the Chaco Canyon controversy as a case study. *Journal of Social Archaeology, 21*(2), 157–178.

Kennett, Douglas J., Stephen Plog, Richard J. George, Brendan J. Culleton, Adam S. Watson, Pontus Skoglund, Nadin Rohland et al. (2017) "Archaeogenomic evidence reveals prehistoric matrilineal dynasty." *Nature communications* 8, no. 1.

Balter, Michael (2017) Ancient DNA Yields Unprecedented Insights into Mysterious Chaco Civilization. *Scientific American*, February 22, 2017.

Hudetz, Mary (2023) A Scientist Said Her Research Could Help With Repatriation. Instead, It Destroyed Native Remains. The Repatriation Project, *Pro Publica*, July 20, 2023.

CHAPTER SIX

Lipe, William D., and Alexander J. Lindsay Jr., (1974) Proceedings of the 1974 Cultural Resource Management Conference, Denver, Colorado. *Museum of Northern Arizona*, Technical Series No. 14. Flagstaff.

Kaldenberg, Russell L. (2011) Being a US Government Cultural Resource Manager. In *A Companion to Cultural Resource Management*, edited by Thomas F. King, Wiley-Blackwell.

Phillips, David A. (2003) Who's My Daddy? Who's My Mommy? Results of a Poll on the Origins of Private-Sector CRM. *ACRA Edition*, newsletter of the American Cultural Resources Association.

Breternitz, David A. (1993) The Dolores Archaeological Program: In Memoriam. *American Antiquity* 58, no. 1: 118–125.

American Cultural Resources Association (ACRA) (2019) The Cultural Resources Management Industry: Providing Critical Support for our Nation's Infrastructure through Expertise in Historic

Preservation. Electronic document, < https://heritagecoalition.org/wp-content/uploads/2019/08/ACRA-leaflet.pdf> accessed January 16, 2024.

Okoren, Nicolle (2022) The wilderness 'therapy' that teens say feels like abuse: 'You are on guard at all times'. *The Guardian*, November 14, 2022.

Krakauer, Jon (1995) Loving Them to Death: The Story of One Teenager's 'Wilderness Experience'. *Outside* magazine, October 1995.

Zoledziowski, Anya (2022) Paris Hilton Says She Was Sexually Abused in 'Troubled Teen' Industry. *Vice News*, October 12, 2022.

Sjogren, Morgan (2022) *Path of Light: A Walk Through Colliding Legacies of Glen Canyon*. Torrey House Press.

Salvatore, Ricardo Donato (2003) Local versus imperial knowledge: Reflections on Hiram Bingham and the Yale Peruvian expedition. *Nepantla: Views from South* 4, no. 1: 67–80.

Grann, David (2010) *The lost city of Z: A tale of deadly obsession in the Amazon*. Vintage.

Rostain, Stéphen, Antoine Dorison, Geoffroy de Saulieu, Heiko Prümers, Jean-Luc Le Pennec, Fernando Mejía Mejía, Ana Maritza Freire, Jaime R. Pagán-Jiménez, and Philippe Descola (2024) Two thousand years of garden urbanism in the Upper Amazon. *Science, 383*(6679), 183–189.

Handwerk, Brian (2022) Lost Cities of the Amazon Discovered From the Air. *Smithsonian* magazine, May 25, 2022.

Jack, Patrick (2023) Does last Indiana Jones film end 'Indy effect' in archaeology? *Times Higher Education*, July 1, 2023.

JP (2012) 5 College Degrees that Aren't Worth the Cost. *US News*, June 22, 2012.

Willson, Miranda (2023) An archeologist shortage could stifle the climate law. *Politico Energy Wire*, November 11, 2023.

Holly, Donald H. (2015) Talking to the guy on the airplane. *American Antiquity, 80*(3), 615–617.

Feder, Kenneth (2019) *Frauds, Myths, and Mysteries: Science and Pseudoscience in Archaeology*, 8th edition. McGraw-Hill Education, New York

Judge, W. James (1982) Will the Real Archaeology Please Stand up? Comments on the Status of American Archaeology, ca AD 1982. *The George Wright Forum*, Vol. 2, No. 4, pp. 17–34.

CHAPTER SEVEN

Nordhaus, Hannah (2018) What the Bears Ears monument means to a Native American. *National Geographic*, October 18, 2018.

Nelson, Scott Reynolds, and Marc Aronson (2008) *Ain't Nothing But a Man: My Quest to Find the Real John Henry*. National Geographic Books.

Johnston, Lyla June (2018) Reclaiming our Indigenous European Roots. *The MOON Magazine*, December 02, 2018.

Brinkley, Douglas (2022) *Silent Spring Revolution: John F. Kennedy, Rachel Carson, Lyndon Johnson, Richard Nixon, and the Great Environmental Awakening*. Harper.

Ferguson, T.J. (1996) Native Americans and the Practice of Archaeology. *Annual review of Anthropology*, *25*(1), 63–79.

Deloria, Jr., Vine (1992) Indians, Archaeologists, and the Future. *American Antiquity*, *57*(4), 595–598.

Parker, Patricia L. (1991) America's Tribal Cultures—A Renaissance in the 1990s. *CRM*, Volume 14, No. 5.

Chapman, Fred (2019) Medicine Wheel/Medicine Mountain: Celebrated and Controversial Landmark. *Wyoming History*, April 10, 2019.

Birch, Jennifer, Turner W. Hunt, Louis Lesage, Jean-Francois Richard, Linda A. Sioui, and Victor D. Thompson (2022) The role of Radiocarbon Dating in Advancing Indigenous-led Archaeological Research Agendas. *Humanities and Social Sciences Communications*, *9*(1), 1–6.

Prudden, T. Mitchell (1903) *The Prehistoric Ruins of the San Juan Watershed in Utah, Arizona, Colorado and New Mexico*. Digitized by Google.

Archaeology Southwest (2017) *Bears Ears Archaeological Experts Gathering: Assessing and Looking Ahead*. Archaeology Southwest, Tucson.

Lipe, William D., ed. (2014) Tortuous and Fantastic: Cultural and Natural Wonders of Greater Cedar Mesa. *Archaeology Southwest Magazine*, 28(3–4).

Podmore, Zak (2017) Native voices aren't being heard on Bears Ears. *High Country News*, December 21, 2017.

Carbonaro, Giulia (2024) Multiple State Republican Parties Are Going Broke. *Newsweek*, January 8, 2024.

Klee, Miles (2023) Companies That Get 'Woke' Aren't Going Broke—They're More Profitable Than Ever. *Rolling Stone*, April 8, 2023.

Rhodes, Jeanne Eder (2023) Copper Mine or Sacred Land: The Fight for Oak Flat. *National Wildlife Federation*, September 27, 2023.

Lasco, Gideon (2022) Did Margaret Mead Think a Healed Femur Was the Earliest Sign of Civilization? *Sapiens*, June 16, 2022.

Clutton-Brock, Tim H., and Geoffrey A. Parker (1995) Punishment in Animal Societies. *Nature*, *373*(6511), 209–216.

Wiessner, Pauline (1996) Leveling the Hunter: Constraints on the Status Quest in Foraging Societies. *Food and the Status Quest: An Interdisciplinary Perspective*, *1*, 171.

Lee, Richard B. (1979) *The !Kung San: Men, women and work in a foraging society*. Cambridge University Press.

Norton, Holly (2017) The politics and power of American archaeology. *The Guardian*, April 10, 2017.

American Archaeology (2016) The Battle to Protect Bears Ears. *American Archaeology*, Vol.20, No. 3.

Said, Edward W. (1977) Orientalism. *The Georgia Review*, *31*(1), 162–206.

Doelle, Bill (2012) What is Preservation Archaeology? *Archaeology Southwest Magazine*, Volume 26, Number 1.

Lipe, William D. (1974) A Conservation Model for American Archaeology. *Kiva*, *39*(3–4), 213–245.

Leonard, Bryan, Shawn Regan, Christopher Costello, Suzi Kerr, Dominic P. Parker, Andrew J. Plantinga, James Salzman, V. Kerry Smith, and Temple Stoellinger 2021) Allow "nonuse rights" to conserve natural resources. *Science*, *373*(6558), 958–961.

CHAPTER EIGHT

Greenlee, Cynthia (2019) How history textbooks reflect America's refusal to reckon with slavery. *Vox*, August 26, 2019.

Silverstein, Jake (2021) The 1619 Project and the long battle over US history. *The New York Times Magazine*.

Ascher, Robert, and Charles H. Fairbanks (1971) Excavation of a slave cabin: Georgia, USA. *Historical Archaeology*, *5*(1), 3–17.

Schuyler, Robert L., ed. (1980) *Archaeological Perspectives on Ethnicity in America: Afro-American and Asian American Culture History.* Baywood Publishing Company, Inc.

Babson, David W. (1990) The archaeology of racism and ethnicity on southern plantations. *Historical Archaeology*, *24*(4), 20–28.

Orser, Charles E., ed. (2001) *Race and the Archaeology of Identity (Foundations of Archaeological Inquiry).* University of Utah Press.

Barry, William David (1980) The Shameful Story of Malaga Island. *Down East*, November 1980.

Price, H.H., and Gerald E. Talbot (2006) No longer a Reproach: The Story of Malaga Island, by Allen G. Breed; in *Maine's Visible Black History*, edited by H.H. Price and Gerald E. Talbot, pp. 69–75, Tilbury House Publishers, Gardiner.

Orser, Charles E., ed. (2001) *Race and the Archaeology of Identity (Foundations of Archaeological Inquiry).* University of Utah Press.

McMahon, Kate (2013) The Use of Material Culture and Recovering Black Maine. *Material Culture Review* 77/78 (Spring/Fall 2013).

Maine Coast Heritage Trust (2023) Malaga Island: An Overview of its Cultural and Natural History. Electronic document, https://www.mcht.org/story/malaga-island-history/, accessed March 19, 2024.

The National WWII Museum (2024) Japanese American Incarceration. Electronic document, <https://www.nationalww2museum.org/war/articles/japanese-american-incarceration> accessed January 17, 2024.

Rogers, Daniel (2004) *Prisoners Without Trial: Japanese Americans in World War II.* Hill and Wang.

Densho Encyclopedia (2024) About Incarceration. Electronic

document, <https://encyclopedia.densho.org/history/> accessed January 17, 2024.

Cooper, Anderson (2023) Canada's unmarked graves: How residential schools carried out "cultural genocide" against indigenous children. *CBS News*, February 12, 2023.

US Department of the Interior (2022) Federal Indian Boarding School Initiative. Electronic document, <https://www.bia.gov/service/federal-indian-boarding-school-initiative> accessed January 17, 2024.

Wyton, Moira (2023) Residential school denialists tried to dig up suspected unmarked graves in Kamloops, B.C., report finds. *CBC News*, June 16, 2023.

Kennedy, Dana (2022) 'Biggest fake news story in Canada': Kamloops mass grave debunked by academics. *New York Post*, May 27, 2022.

Boas, Phil (2022) Don't get ahead of the facts as the US investigates Native American boarding schools. *Arizona Republic* Opinion section, December 4, 2022.

Louderback, Lisbeth A., and Bruce M. Pavlik (2017) Starch Granule Evidence for the Earliest Potato use in North America. *Proceedings of the National Academy of Sciences*, *114*(29), 7606–7610.

Montgomery, Suzi and Sheri Quinn (2023) Cropping Up: Repatriating the Four Corners potato. *Utah Public Radio*, April 27, 2023.

Grescoe, Taras (2023) This miracle plant was eaten into extinction 2,000 years ago—or was it? *National Geographic*, September 23, 2023.

Schultes, Richard Evans (2001) *Plants of the Gods: Their Sacred, Healing, and Hallucinogenic Powers.* Healing Arts Press, 2nd Edition.

Bower, Bruce (2025) "A Pueblo tribe recruited scientists to reclaim its ancient American history." *Science News*, April 30, 2025

Murray, Charles and Richard J. Hernstein (1994) *The Bell Curve: Intelligence and Class Structure in American Life.* Free Press Paperbacks, New York

Black Trowel Collective, Marian Berihuete-Azorín, Chelsea Blackmore, Lewis Borck, James L. Flexner, Catherine J. Frieman, Corey A. Herrmann, and Rachael Kiddey (2023) Archaeology in 2022: Counter-myths for hopeful futures. *American Anthropologist.*

Lee, Richard B. (1992) Art, Science, or Politics? The Crisis in Hunter-gatherer Studies. *American Anthropologist, 94*(1), 31–54.

Davis, Wade (2008) On Native Ground. *Condé Nast Traveler,* November 11, 2008.

APPENDIX A:

ON TERMINOLOGY

Near the end of the main text, I quote Larrie Benallie, Jr. saying how words can have an "adverse effect" (an obvious but nonetheless clever reference to NEPA) because they shape the ways people approach, treat, or interpret things like material history. George Carlin provided an even more comprehensive quote in 1990: ". . . we do think in language. And so the quality of our thoughts and ideas can only be as good as the quality of our language."

With that in mind, various governmental, institutional, and cultural groups provide guidelines for how to talk about Indigenous material history and cultural components in more sensitive, respectful terminology. Primary sources for this are Utah Diné Bikéyah's Media Sensitivity Training, Arizona State Museum's Respectful Terminology Recommended for Discussion of Human Remains, and the Bureau of Land Management's 8100 Foundations Module.

Note also that language is dynamic rather than static. It evolves over time. Nobody knew what a "blog" was when I was in high school, and nobody knew what "email" was when my father was in high school. And it's the same with intercultural terminology.

Common Term	Recommended Term	Explanation
Abandoned	Depopulated	Abandonment is something you do with a thing or place you don't like anymore.
Analyze	Document	Analysis is impersonal and technical. Analyzing people and their history reducing them to things.
Body	Individual/ ancestor	Also impersonal and technical. People should be treated like people, not objects.
Collect	Gather	Collection implies adding to a personal stash.
Data	Information	Data, too, is impersonal and technical. Information about human beings and their history should be treated as such.
Discover	Encounter	Often used when mortuary features are found unexpectedly, calling it a discovery suggests you've stumbled upon a hidden treasure.
Grave/burial	Funerary/ mortuary feature	Graves and burials refer to specific Western practices.
Grave goods	Funerary objects/ belongings	See above.
Human skeletons	Ancestral remains	See above.

APPENDIX B:

VISITING WITH RESPECT

Visit With Respect (VWR) is an educational initiative developed by the Bears Ears Partnership (formerly Friends of Cedar Mesa) and adopted by the World Monuments Fund, as well as a steadily growing number of other places and organizations. The campaign resulted from decades of watching people flock to southeastern Utah for the specific purpose of finding, visiting, and photographing archaeological sites, a practice more broadly known as "heritage tourism."

In response to this, VWR was developed to encourage responsible visitation and mitigate or minimize destruction to those sites, objects, and locations by weekend warriors. At present, there are nineteen VWR components:

GPS REVEALS TOO MUCH– GPS points often lead uneducated visitors to sensitive sites. When posting online about your trip, remove all references to location.

LEAVE CULTURAL BELONGINGS WHERE THEY ARE– Cultural belongings such as pottery pieces, flakes and stone tools, corn cobs, and textiles left by early Indigenous peoples are still sacred to Tribes and Pueblos. Ancestral items and historic artifacts help researchers learn about the past. It's illegal to remove such items from public lands.

LEAVE FOSSILS AND BONES INDISTURBED– Leave human and

non-human bones, tracks, and other paleontological remains where you find them so future visitors and scientists can learn from them.

PACK OUT YOUR POOP– Human and pet waste threatens fragile ecosystems and drinking water for hikers and wildlife alike. Poop near cultural sites is disrespectful to the Tribes and Pueblos that revere this sacred cultural landscape. When facilities are not available, please pack out your waste.

REFRAIN FROM GRINDING ANCESTRAL SLICKS– Grinding slicks and carved grooves were created by early Indigenous peoples. Respect the ancestors who left them by refraining from touching or using altered surfaces that you may encounter on the landscape.

REMEMBER THAT ANCESTRAL LANDS ARE SACRED– Tribes and Pueblos consider ancestral landscapes a place for ceremony and a place where the ancestors' spirits still reside. The soil, sky, animals, plants, cultural and ancestral sites are all interconnected and hold spiritual significance to Tribal nations.

STAY ON ESTABLISHED TRAILS– Stay on existing trails and routes to protect the living biocrust. Once stepped on, this fragile crust takes years to regrow.

STEER CLEAR OF ANCESTRAL STRUCTURES– Structures are spiritually alive and still hold cultural significance to Tribal peoples. When recreating, visitors should refrain from leaning on walls, no matter how solid they look and avoid touching, standing on, or climbing in structures as they can be easily damaged.

AVOID BUILDING CAIRNS– Building cairns can impact sensitive sites and are a form of vandalism to the natural world. You might not realize it, but some stacked stones may be ancestral shrines. Leave placement of trail directional signs and leveling of cairns to land managers.

CAMP AND EAT AWAY FROM ARCHAEOLOGY– Ancestral sites and structures are where Tribes and Pueblos believe their ancestors' spirits still reside. Camping, fires, and food can damage cultural sites and spoil the view for other visitors. Remember to pack out all your waste, including food scraps and poop.

DOGS AND ARCHAEOLOGY DON'T MIX– To prevent erosion and degradation, dogs are not allowed in or near archeological sites. Always check beforehand if dogs are permitted in an area or region. Remember that many of these sites are culturally significant, so please make sure to leash pets, keep them away from cultural sites, and don't let them dig.

DON'T TOUCH ROCK IMAGERY OR MAKE YOUR OWN– Natural oils on your hands can destroy delicate rock imagery. Vandalism of petroglyphs and pictographs erases stories of early Indigenous peoples and destroys the experience for future visitors.

ENJOY CULTURAL SITES WITHOUT ROPES– This protects delicate ancestral rock imagery and structures from damage caused by falling rocks and looting. The use of climbing gear, like ropes, to access cultural sites is illegal.

GUIDE CHILDREN THROUGH SITES– Sacred cultural sites are not playgrounds. Teach children to respect these places so they can share them with future generations and become better stewards of the land. Keep a close eye on them so they don't get hurt or accidentally damage cultural belongings.

HISTORIC ARTIFACTS AREN'T TRASH– Leave historic artifacts like rusted cans right where they are. They help interpret the past and show who has been there before.

PAY YOUR FEES– It may not seem like much, but your small fee helps support important monitoring, enforcement, and amenities like toilets.

STAY ON DESIGNATED ROADS– Use existing roads that are approved for use by land managers. Driving off-road can damage fragile archaeology and ecosystems.

USE A FIRE PAN– Remember to check when and where fires are allowed. Ground fires leave scars on the landscape and a mess for the next visitor. Bring a fire pan or, at the very least, use existing fire rings. Wait until your ashes are cool to the touch and pack them out.

USE RUBBER-TIPPED POLES (OR JUST USE A STICK)– A rubber tip prevents your metal hiking pole from scratching and scarring subtle rock images on the ground.

VIEW SITES ROM A DISTANCE– Many Indigenous peoples consider this landscape sacred, and numerous Tribal Elders ask visitors to view sites from a distance. This small act honors Tribal beliefs and protects cultural resources from the destructive effects of visitation, like erosion

ABOUT THE AUTHOR

R. E. Burrillo is a researcher, author, conservationist, and cultural preservationist. He holds a master of science in archaeology from the University of Utah and is a research associate with Archaeology Southwest. His writing has appeared in *Kiva, American Antiquity, Archaeology Southwest Magazine, Colorado Plateau Advocate*, and *The Salt Lake Tribune*, along with many regional publications. He is also the author of *Behind the Bears Ears: Exploring the Cultural and Natural Histories of a Sacred Landscape*, which was awarded the *Foreword Reviews* Editor's Choice Prize for Nonfiction; and *The Backwoods of Everywhere: Words from a Wandering Local*, an essay collection published in 2022. He currently lives in Tucson, Arizona.

ABOUT THE COVER ARTIST

Eryon Shondíín Greenburg is a Diné artist from Upper Fruitland, New Mexico and currently resides in Salt Lake City, Utah. She has an Associates degree in Graphic Communications.

Eryon Shondíín has always had a passion for art and started out as a charcoal and pastel artist. Now she uses a combination of traditional art and digital art to create her work, but considers herself a digital illustrator. She draws inspiration from her Diné background and also from her name Shondíín which means sunlight or sunrays. A lot of her work incorporates traditional themes of balance, story, and the Sun. Eryon has collaborated with non-profits such as The Urban Indian Center of Salt Lake and Working Films. Her work has also appeared in the Indian Justice Circle, *Native Tradition is Medicine: Resilience and Native Lifeways during COVID-19* publication. Eryon Shondíín works with Indigenous nonprofits and small businesses to create illustrations, branding and other marketing materials. She hopes to continue working with her community, and to bring an Indigenous perspective to design.

Instagram: @shondiin.art

ABOUT TORREY HOUSE PRESS

Torrey House Press exists at the intersection of the literary arts and environmental advocacy. THP publishes books that elevate diverse perspectives, explore relationships with place, and deepen our connections to the natural world and to each other. THP inspires ideas, conversation, and action on issues that link the American West to the past, present, and future of the ever-changing Earth.

Torrey House Press is a 501(c)(3) nonprofit publisher. Our work is made possible by generous donations from readers like you. Visit www.torreyhouse.org for reading group discussion guides, author interviews, and more.

SPECIAL THANKS

Torrey House Press is supported by Back of Beyond Books, Bright Side Bookshop, The King's English Bookshop, Maria's Bookshop, the Ballantine Family Fund, the Jeffrey S. & Helen H. Cardon Foundation, the Lawrence T. Dee & Janet T. Dee Foundation, the McMullan/O'Connor Family Fund, the Palladium Foundation, the Stewart Family Foundation, the Barker Foundation, Karin Anderson, Kif Augustine & Stirling Adams, Diana Allison, Richard Baker, Karey Barker, Patti Baynham & Owen Baynham, Matt Bean, Klaus Bielefeldt, Joe Breddan, JB Brett & Jeff Grathwohl, Karen Buchi & Kenneth Buchi, Betty Clark & Gary Clark, Rose Chilcoat & Mark Franklin, Linc Cornell & Lois Cornell, Teow Lim Goh, Susan Cushman & Charlie Quimby, Lynn de Freitas & Patrick de Freitas, Pert Eilers, Ed Erwin, Sally Glaser & David Bower, Laurie Hilyer, Phyllis Hockett, Mabelle Hueston & John Hueston, Kirtly Parker Jones, Emily Klass, Rick Klass, Jen Lawton & John Thomas, Kaitlyn Mahoney, Susan Markley, Leigh Meigs & Stephen Meigs, Mark Meloy, Kathleen Metcalf, Donaree Neville & Douglas Neville, Marion S. Robinson, Danny Rosen, Jack Schmidt, Linnea Spears-Lebrun, Jennifer Speers, Molly Swonger, Rachel White, the National Endowment for the Humanities, the National Endowment for the Arts, the Utah Division of Arts & Museums, Utah Humanities, the Salt Lake City Arts Council, and Salt Lake County Zoo, Arts & Parks.

Our thanks to individual donors, members, and the Torrey House Press board of directors for their valued support.

www.ingramcontent.com/pod-product-compliance
Lightning Source LLC
Jackson TN
JSHW020804090326
98765JS00001B/1

* 9 7 9 8 8 9 0 9 2 0 3 2 4 *